Operational Excellence in Your Organization

Organizations are under continued pressure to improve and innovate products and services in order to remain relevant and sustainable. In many cases, some form of "transformation" program is conceived to help achieve this aim. The transformation itself may include the deployment of systems and processes that make the organization more capable of sustaining improvements and driving future change. "Change Agents" often act as coaches, trainers, mentors, and facilitators to embed change. In practice, these Change Agents have to deal with resistance throughout different levels of the organization. These Change Agents must be able to act as flexible, multi-situational problem solvers, and teachers of those problem-solving skills. Only organizations that have developed a strong problem-solving capability can hope to survive for sustained periods of time.

This book describes many of the obstacles that Change Agents must overcome and the knowledge they need to make them credible with both leaders and the workforce they are tasked with navigating through an organizational transformation. Technical subjects such as diagnostic and improvement tools are described as well as pointing the reader in the direction of relevant theory and practical advice from the authors who have collectively more than 45 years of experience in such roles. Subject matter expertise in Lean Operations, Theory of Constraints, Six Sigma, Change Management, Excellence Models, Daily Management, and Problem Solving is used to describe some essential frameworks that can be brought together in a powerful system of improvement to aid organizations, but most importantly to support and encourage the Change Agent wherever they are in their career. At some point, leaders and managers will also be expected to act as Change Agents.

This work brings together simple, universal, accessible, and practical resources to help guide those front-line Change Agents regardless of particular industry or experience.

Operational Excellence in Your Organization

The Change Agent's Handbook for Transformative Initiatives

Revised Edition

Fraser Wilkinson
Hervé Duval

A PRODUCTIVITY PRESS BOOK

First published 2024
by Routledge
605 Third Avenue, New York, NY 10158

and by Routledge
4 Park Square, Milton Park, Abingdon, Oxon, OX14 4RN

Routledge is an imprint of the Taylor & Francis Group, an informa business

ISBN: 978-1-032-77424-4 (hbk)
ISBN: 978-1-032-77423-7 (pbk)
ISBN: 978-1-003-48602-2 (ebk)

DOI: 10.4324/9781003486022

Typeset in Garamond
by MPS Limited, Dehradun

Contents

Foreword

It is a great pleasure for me to write this foreword for Fraser and Hervé's new book.

For many years now it has been realized that success with Lean is not a matter of tools alone; rather, the human dimension is critical. However, today an emphasis on both people and tools is certainly necessary, but no longer sufficient. A significant awareness of rapidly changing digital technology (especially AI) in a VUCA (volatility, uncertainty, complexity, and ambiguity) world is a requirement. Yet another emerging dimension is attention to the environment and sustainability.

There are a large number of texts, and an overwhelming volume of material on the web, that deal separately with all these aspects. (Indeed, I have written several myself.) But this book is unique in the way it gives insights on the practical use of tools, people, and VUCA all working together.

Fraser and Hervé have been in the thick of this challenging environment. This book reflects their experience.

If you read this book from beginning to end, you will very likely discover many useful insights (as I have). However, I think most readers will use this book as a reference, dipping in as and when a situation arises. Doing so will prove a powerful aid. So I believe that this book will become an indispensable companion to other more technical texts on Lean and Six Sigma and in wider operations management. Read the details on the theory in other texts, and then temper your reading with the insight, wisdom, and comments given in this book.

There are numerous outstanding sections in this book. Of particular note for me are the chapters and sections on stakeholder value, diagnostics, antifragile and risk, problem-solving, and change management. All of these sections are accompanied by "Controversy Corners" that had me reflecting on viewpoints that I had not necessarily considered.

The case studies toward the end of this book are also different from the more common "self-promotion" variety. Their frank self-assessments are a pleasure to read.

By the way, it is also refreshing in a book on Lean to not have continual references to Toyota. Although Toyota is the undoubted benchmark on many aspects, there is a whole world out there outside of automotive.

With this book, you are holding a valuable resource in your hand, something that you will return to time and again.

John Bicheno
Emeritus Professor of Lean Enterprise,
University of Buckingham,
February 2024

Acknowledgments

We could not have written this book without the help of many individuals and the organizations they have helped shaped.

We owe a huge debt to a long list of people who helped us to develop our understanding of Excellence during our career. Some of them are colleagues and leaders with whom we rolled out Excellence programs and who inspired us. We are particularly grateful to Marc Baker, Ian Taylor, Kevin Davenport, Leigh Morris, Shaun Thomas, Clare Meek, Philippe Lazare-Lyon, Tom Eussen, Alain Pottier, Jim Naylor, Pierre Schreiner, Terry Goodwin, Pankaj Kumar, Rajesh Bhatt, Avneesh Gupta, Richard Keegan, the Tata family, Jan-Hein de Groen, and Lianne Deeming.

Our friends and colleagues who contributed to this book by providing content or feedback on the manuscript include Shaun Thomas, Clare Meek, and Gareth Duggan. Ernst Hoogenes has kindly agreed to share with us his experience as a leader of a large international company.

John Bicheno's incredibly positive reception of our manuscript gave us the energy to finalize the whole project. His precious feedback helped us make some key decisions.

Our families have had to deal with us during these long years of writing. May, Magali, Quentin, and Laura, thank you for your patience. To Julianne, Conor, Finn, and Iona, thank you for your continued understanding of, and patience with, a passion for the written word.

And finally, thank you to our parents who made us who we are. Their love for books and for sharing knowledge has obviously had an influence on our decision to put pen to paper.

This dedication is a small token of the gratitude we feel toward all these people.

About the Authors

Fraser Wilkinson has been an Operational Excellence professional since 2000 and has worked in a diverse range of industries from aircraft maintenance, coal mining, medical devices, consultancy, and most recently in steel. In his role as a Business Excellence Manager at Tata Steel UK, he has been responsible for defining the Operational Excellence competency levels in the European operations and for delivering common training and development solutions to up-skill the 20,000 employees across the European operations. His focus is largely on the deployment of Daily Management and Practical Problem-Solving. Fraser is a graduate of the Lean Enterprise Research Centre at Cardiff Business School (UK) where he completed the M.Sc. in Lean Operations under Professor John Bicheno in 2003 and is a certified Six Sigma Black Belt from his time at Johnson & Johnson.

Fraser began his career as an aircraft maintenance engineer with the United Kingdom Ministry of Defence where he serviced Phantom F4 and Tornado fast jets for the Royal Air Force. His aerospace career took him all over Europe where he maintained aircraft for Swissair, KLM Royal Dutch Airlines, Lufthansa, Sabena, Cargolux, and Fokker before returning to the United Kingdom to take up a post for British Airways as a maintenance planning engineer in 1993.

He entered full time further education in 1995 and completed a B.Sc. in Energy and Environmental Technology at the University of Glamorgan before being employed by Johnson & Johnson in 1999 to help the roll out of Lean and Six Sigma under the corporate Process Excellence umbrella. Fraser joined Tata Steel in 2006 as a Continuous Improvement Coach where he was also involved in the deployment of Lean, Behavioral Safety, Change Management, and Project Management to deliver significant improvements in business performance.

Hervé Duval has been a Business Excellence professional since 2006. He is currently the Business Excellence Manager of Tata Steel Downstream Europe, a two-billion euros division of Tata Steel that comprises 22 sites in Europe and North America. His knowledge of and interest in Excellence comes both from formal training and practical implementation in a variety of environments, ranging from manufacturing of advanced steel products to commercial and supply chain offices.

Hervé has dual French and Luxembourgish citizenship. He studied material science at the Ecole des Mines de Nancy (France). After experiences in the plastics industry in the Netherlands and France, he joined the steel industry in 1996 in technical customer-facing roles. He subsequently moved to the United Kingdom where he obtained an MBA with distinction at Warwick Business School while leading a customer technical support team. 2005 was the pivotal year during which he returned to France as the first Lean Manager of a 500-employee, 120-year-old plant that was about to embark on its first continuous improvement program. This was a life-changing experiment.

Since 2005, Hervé has been developing, deploying, and using Lean/Operational Excellence tools, techniques, and programs. Having had to combine running the daily business with constantly improving the work in operational positions such as Technical Manager or Operations Manager, he developed a pragmatic approach to Excellence. The takeover of the Corus group by the Tata Group allowed him to complement his Lean/Operational Excellence expertise with knowledge in Business Excellence (the holistic approach developed by the Tata Group). He has subsequently been using this experience in expert positions, leading the Daily Management program of Tata Steel Europe or the overall Business Excellence approach in some of TSE's business units.

Chapter 1

Introduction

Hervé Duval and Fraser Wilkinson

The Premise

Imagine, if you would indulge us, an opportunity to sit down with your younger self: an afternoon of leisure in a quaint town center square somewhere from a treasured memory. The sun is shining, a light breeze rustles the trees, and all is well with the world. You envy your companion his youth and good looks! But put yourself in his shoes; you know how hard the lessons will be, poor fellow. Of course, he has to learn for himself, but some friendly advice is always well received by the youth of today (or yesterday), isn't it? You play the part of wise old mentor, sent by the company to help this newly appointed and romantically named, *agent du changement*. Apart from some badly needed sartorial advice, what do you tell this newly minted business guru?

The subject, of course, is vast. If you thought it was difficult then, it has only got harder, young man. So many different disciplines to master now and so much red tape. Is it any surprise our business leaders struggle to be "excellent" in everything? You start in with this tack, but the look of mild terror soon turns to one of boredom. Maybe, you suggest more gaily, this stuff would be better written down. You can keep it with you then, as a sort of reference book. Much better, says he, and orders more refreshments. Now, about that shirt … .

Why This Book?

Self-reflection is a wonderful practice and a necessary ingredient of all true learning. It is also something that becomes easier with age. So, this book is a

DOI: 10.4324/9781003486022-1

series of self-reflections on many subjects dear to the hearts of the two authors and a setting-out of practical and useful tips for those in the business of change. It is the guide we would like to have had when we started out. We hope it is also a useful companion for those more experienced at the game of change and that you will find it thought provoking, stimulating, and fun.

Who Is This Book for?

In essence, this is a guide for those who find themselves inside an organization tasked with bringing about improvements. Generally, it is written from the perspective of a change agent. We define this term loosely as someone who is charged with helping others to make improvements and not someone who is accountable or responsible for the processes improved. It is a different matter for "operational" people to make improvements than to have an outside agent facilitate those improvements. Similarly, there are subtle differences to your approach when acting from within an organization than you would use if you were an external consultant. If you are a leader with change agents at your disposal, we encourage you to take up the leadership challenges we highlight and be sympathetic to those frontline workers facing the difficult task of changing behavior.

There is a bias toward the manufacturing arena, although service industries require many of the same approaches, and from our experiences, we bring insights from large multinational corporations as well as some smaller-to medium-sized enterprises.

What Is Our Unique Selling Point?

We don't claim great academic rigor or ground-breaking research; rather, we rely on our own experience and empirical evidence of what has worked well for us. There are plenty of business books that give more detail, and we have signposted the ones we have found most useful or insightful. Where we have a level of expertise or sound practitioner knowledge of a subject, we have been more forthright.

This book is also an encouragement for all those who will sample the bitter taste of failure. All that is noble is difficult, and all that is difficult, elicits failure. Failure can also be devastating as well, so we offer some methods, tools, and ways of thinking that will hopefully limit your losses and maximize your gains. Be comforted, however, that with failure, history puts you in exalted company. We offer some of our "best" failures as examples of how not to do it.

Each of us brings our own perspectives to bear, and not everything is black and white after all, so we have introduced our "Controversy Corner" callouts to help us question some of those sacred cows we can get attached to. Everyone has their own preferences and biases, and we encourage you to explore these traits further and in more detail through techniques like Myers-Briggs Type Indicators (MBTI) or Belbin Team Roles. We have a tendency when younger to consider our views to be the only rational ones. Time, and the opportunity to reflect via the kind of techniques mentioned above, will allow you a more balanced and more considerate view of how others might be thinking. This is invaluable when dealing with a wide variety of personalities.

What Can You Expect from This Book?

We offer practical advice to improve and sustain processes. We provide an overall model of how improvement tools and techniques work in synergy to form a whole improvement system. Crucially, you will get an honest view on the life of a frontline change agent with some humor about life in the middle of the sandwich – bridging the boardroom with the engine room and what knowledge, skills, and attributes you will need. Depending on your role, you will inevitably have to develop your sales skills to some extent, and we offer great examples to help you make that pitch.

What Questions Will Be Answered by This Book?

- *How can I add value as a change agent?*
- *How do I get started?*
- *How do I influence the key stakeholders?*
- *How can I gain the trust of the organization?*
- *How can I overcome skepticism about the latest fad?*
- *How do I know what tools and techniques to apply?*
- *How much standardization of improvement methods should we have?*
- *How can I be a multiplier?*

- *How much should I be doing and how much should I be coaching?*
- *How do I know if we are making progress?*
- *How can I tell if what we are doing will be sustained?*
- *How do I improve my own improvement skills?*

These are the sort of questions we have both asked ourselves and our colleagues throughout our careers. We're sure you will have more, and maybe not all are answered conclusively, but the one thing we all deal with is a level of uncertainty. There are too many variables to be able to control all our work situations, but nevertheless, we hope to help you stack the odds more favorably toward success.

What Is the Aim of This Book?

In short, this book aims to help those designated as change agents survive and thrive in a very tricky assignment. As the title suggests, we offer the idea of a handbook: a reference and a source of comfort and inspiration. We offer you the means to help create the problem-solving leaders of tomorrow and how to approach those leaders who can often be part of the problem. So, for the change agent, we offer insight into how both those aims can be furthered. If you are a leader, then we offer no apologies for this. From our experience, we see leadership as being the key to creating an excellent organization where effective and efficient problem-solving is part of the culture. Ideally, all our leaders should be change agents and *vice versa* so the distinction is only applied depending on the current mindset of the individual we are engaging with.

If we are to create problem-solving leaders, then we need to instill a mindset that follows some logical assessment process - a kind of mental algorithm that can kick into action seamlessly when required. Much of the work we do with people is about guiding them through these thought processes. No two situations are exactly alike, so there needs to be a high degree of flexibility and contingent thinking. These kinds of algorithms and machine learning are already being developed through following how several experts deal with a situation and looking at the efficacy of the outputs, particularly for how medical practitioners diagnose and treat conditions as presented. Maybe someone is already working on a problem-solving version that can be applied universally to organizational situations, but until that time, we offer a slightly more human option.

The structure of this book reflects the way we have learned to think about problems and opportunities. We also observe these thought patterns amongst other experienced change agents, academics, and operational excellence practitioners. We don't suggest for a minute that we have a kind of hive mind at work here, and, of course, there are many differences in how individuals will approach a situation. Even given the same methodology and toolsets there will be some differences in the exact journey and maybe in the destination, dependent on what is seen as priority, and how a strategy is interpreted. But it's patterns we are interested in and not robotic adherence to a set of logic gates. The empirical evidence suggests these patterns give a very good probability of success. We can't guarantee success in everything we do, but by following the patterns, we inevitably tip the scales of probability in our favor.

The foundation of these patterns is based on some underlying theories and practices that have proven their worth for many decades in both the physical and the psychological arenas. So, in Chapter 2, we offer a very brief description of some of these foundation frameworks and concepts that we use as references throughout this book. If you are not a student of these, then we recommend some in-depth study of the available literature and online resources.

In Chapter 3, we consider how to select the right problems to work on from a proactive rather than purely reactive stance. It's not good enough to be driven by only reacting to problems as they occur. We also need to create our own performance gaps based on what our strategy and customer expectations tell us. This necessitates being able to diagnose the current condition and be able to make decisions at the tactical level about what to work on and why. We offer a framework to help with a balanced diagnostic of business objectives.

Sometimes we need to react quickly to an emerging situation, be it a full-blown crisis, a major hiccup, or just a drama that needs some rationalization. Chapter 4 offers a method to rapidly assess these kinds of situations, giving the change agent a powerful means of intervention to deal with a situation where a full diagnostic would take too much time. We also discuss how an organization should learn from these situations, build resilience, and even be capable of fully exploiting future instability.

Chapter 5 then deals with the practicalities of how to organize ourselves to be able to improve both performance measures and the culture of the business in order to create a long-lasting improvement. We discuss how to resource a change effort as well as some of the typical deployment vehicles and tools you can use to get the results. Chapter 6 then goes deeper into a continual improvement framework and how to use this to balance the *active* and *passive* improvement efforts in an organization. We also delve into the more technical aspects of how to best categorize problems in order to ensure you select the right methods, tools, and techniques to tackle the Quality, Delivery, and Cost objectives.

If we are to avoid the common pitfall of most improvement efforts, we then need to address the area of sustainability of improvements. In Chapters 7 and 8, we offer two very powerful and well-proven frameworks to ensure we maintain our gains and deliver a stable and capable set of processes that will delight our customers. Finally, in Chapter 9, we take a look at how we can develop the leadership capabilities and attributes needed to bring all of the above together into an overall system of work.

The structure of this book, therefore, reflects the patterns of thought we have observed over many years by many people in the field of operational excellence. It attempts to balance the need for results with longer-term culture change. A set of case studies is provided to underline how we have used many of the thinking patterns and the tools and techniques outlined in this book.

How Can You Use This Book?

At the end of each chapter, we offer you a number of suggested activities (supported by 100 questions) that together form a self-study work-through of this book's main learning points. It is a call to action if you are struggling with how to get started in implementing the ideas we offer. It is easy to pass over these questions but, by forcing yourself to think hard on these questions, it can lead you to all kinds of useful insights and facts regarding your own knowledge and the maturity of the organization you serve.

Summary

I hope by now we have provided ample reasons to use this book for both personal and organizational benefits. We have set out our stall in terms of what this book has to offer the reader, but like anything that is worth doing, the benefits will be in proportion to the effort you put in. The following chapter takes us on a quick journey of the most important background theory and concepts you'll need to get to grips with.

Get started on your Chapter 1 learnings – being clear on what you want to achieve.

I. Define your personal and organizational aspirations.
   a. *What are my top three expectations from reading this book?*
   b. *How will I get help with applying and learning the concepts, methods, and tools?*
   c. *What resources of time, money, and opportunity will I get from my organization?*

Chapter 2

A Bit of Theory

Fraser Wilkinson

> It doesn't matter how beautiful your theory is, it doesn't matter how smart you are. If it doesn't agree with experiment, it's wrong.
>
> **Richard P. Feynman**

Introduction

Whether the topics I discuss in this chapter are really theory or are the collected result of practical application I'll leave for you to decide. Some of them are more properly described as models and as such can only give an approximation of reality. If you are just starting out on your journey of business improvement, they are presented as subjects for back reading and will be useful reference points for the remainder of this book. As a seasoned practitioner, you will probably have some pet theories you return to lovingly when asked to explain a certain way of working, and you may well have rejected others already. In either case, they are all worth examining again under the microscope of practical experimentation. Only by holding up our theories to challenge can we really know how much truth they hold. Try standing up in front of a hostile audience to describe your approach to business improvement with only a pen and flip chart as sword and shield and you will soon come to know how well you can defend your current position. Go on, I promise it will be fun!

DOI: 10.4324/9781003486022-2

Dogmas and Doctrines

I suppose we all cling to some dogma and doctrine in our working lives. Whatever methods and approaches we were first inculcated into will remain beacons even if you have little success with them. Like the music we loved as teenagers, they will always be with us. With all of the management theory written in the last 100 years, it's easy to get overwhelmed when you start out, so we will briefly cover the most recent developments and those that seem to have stood the test of time.

We must educate and train our leaders in an ever-expanding syllabus of technological, social, psychological, legal, emotional, and scientific subjects, and we must require them to fit all of these together into an integrated system of "management" and "leadership." If I sit and reflect on all the skills that a modern manager is required to master, it is quite daunting. I am constantly asked to make things simple - to only cover the essentials and not to scare people with too much theory, and that's fine when trying to get engagement and movement at the start of the journey. But as a change agent, you will need a certain level of credibility, and that will only come through a combination of capability and integrity. You will need to be well grounded in theory and practice before you can simplify in the most meaningful way. There's no way around it, you will have to do some research of your own, but always question why we do things the way we do.

The Traditional Organization and How It Came About

Most of us work in relics of a bygone era. The concept of hierarchical structures and separate functional specializations is a recent concept, however. It was a concept designed to define a strict and direct chain of responsibility and immediately highlight where a "dereliction of duty" had occurred. Peter Scholtes is excellent on this point and is well worth reading (Scholtes, 1998). He points to the genesis and subsequent proliferation of the current organization structures as being a result of the Industrial Revolution and the need to maintain control and responsibility over much larger, more complex, and geographically diverse endeavors than had previously been required during the craft era. Only the military and church had attempted such control previously.

The advent of the railroads in the US was a key turning point in how responsibility would be organized. In 1841, a collision of two Western

Railroad passenger trains instigated a major review and led to a recommendation to instigate what we now think of as the typical hierarchical organizational chart with the leader at the top and layer upon layer of lower-level "management." In this way, a chain of direct responsibility could be defined and with it the means of apportioning blame! This model was also unique in ushering in the ideas of a central office run by "managers" (a new term) with distinct functional divisions and clear lines of communication and reporting. It has become the standard model, but has it run its course?

CONTROVERSY CORNER: ORGANIZATIONAL COMPLEXITY AS A NECESSARY BUT FATAL EVIL

The hierarchical, pyramidal, and functional model of organization is probably coded in our DNA like it is in most social species.

Hierarchy can be observed in other species such as wolves for example. Bees have pushed functional specialization to an extreme point. For humans, layered organizations and specialization have probably existed since human groups started to form beyond a certain size. The larger the group, the higher the need for layers and the higher the benefits of specialization (up to a certain size). Pyramids could not have been built and the first great civilizations of Mesopotamia could not have worked without layered management and specialized functions of civil servants.

However, it must be noted that these benefits will eventually be overshadowed by the cost of complexity. Ultra-specialization leads to an exponentially growing number of interactions. Past a certain point, the cost of these coordination interactions is higher than the benefits. Researchers on complexity estimated that our Neolithic ancestors had ten different roles but have listed more than thirty thousand different roles in modern Western societies. Ultimately, complex societies tend to fall and are replaced with less complex ones. Think of the necessary complexity of the Roman empire that made it too expensive to run and contributed to its fragmentation and replacement by more simple forms of organizations (which in turn grew more complex).

Hervé

The main problem with such a model is that the value-creating chain of events does not run along similar lines. If it did, the head of the company would be very busy indeed with all her customers. Instead, value-creating activity cuts through all specialities and is supported by all the functions. It is at the handover point of departments and functions that the flow of value is most likely to be interrupted. This is one of the key issues that is addressed by the Lean philosophy which is more than simply eliminating waste and doing more things with less people.

You may well understand how your organization has evolved into its current form, and you may have been part of shaping that form, but that doesn't mean it's the right one. Starting out in an organization, you tend to accept that this is the way things are. When you start to analyze problems, however, be on the lookout for issues that are caused directly by the organizational design. There has been much written on moving to a more "value stream orientated" organization, but there are many critics also. In the end, the organization should be best suited to serve the Customer, and that may be a hybrid of functional and value-stream design. Whatever it is, it should be critically questioned on a regular basis.

When you have been in a long-established organization for more than a few years, you will probably have experienced a "restructuring" at some point - usually in the name of efficiency and resulting in a head-count reduction. Although highly undesirable for employees, these restructurings are an inevitable part of corporate life. Some organizations target a yearly clear-out of people they consider to be underperformers. It is a sort of pruning exercise for the removal of "deadwood." This may have its merits in keeping people focused on their own performance, but it can also contribute to an undercurrent of fear and trepidation. From experiences related to the authors by those involved in those organizations, it can lead to a certain amount of self-promotion at the expense of the team effort.

From a change agent's perspective, these types of restructuring exercises can cause a great deal of distraction and can be hard to explain in the context of making efficiency gains. The best we can do is try to understand if there are any guiding principles behind these changes. Even if no heads are lost, re-organization for the sake of re-organization is risky, especially if it is based on personalities and not principles. So, if we can ascertain what problems the re-organization is trying to solve, then it can help us in relating that at the shop floor level.

Even when well-known international consulting groups take on a restructuring, it's not obvious if any organizational design principles have been applied. I suspect a lot of these are based on previous designs and a need to justify a straight head-count reduction rather than an attempt to improve the flow of value in a supply chain. Our advice is not to get too distracted by organizational issues if they are beyond your control or influence.

HERVÉ SAYS: THE MAIN RULE IN ORGANIZATIONAL DESIGN IS THE SUBSIDIARITY PRINCIPLE

I have seen organizations centralizing, then decentralizing, and then centralizing again. Each of these decisions made sense at the time. Decentralization improves ownership and reactivity. But it also creates "baronies" with powerful local MDs, potentially maximizing their own local results at the expense of the overall company results. Whereas centralization improves control and resource allocation, it is often wasteful both in terms of time spent because of bureaucratic control and cost of top-heavy structures. There is no ideal solution. Each organization will choose its own mix of centralization and decentralization. But what is key is that they should embed as much subsidiarity as possible, whatever the structure.

Subsidiarity is "the principle that a central authority should have a subsidiary function, performing only those tasks which cannot be performed at a more local level." In other words, give as much ownership as possible to people lower down in the organization.

Military history illustrates the importance of subsidiarity. From Antiquity till the 18th century, the heroic leader was the typical form of leadership. This was possible because of the relatively small size of armies and limited scope of campaigns. As army sizes grew and scope increased (with many different units operating in wider areas, making coordination difficult), such a centralized approach became an issue. Napoleon's success partly relied on framing the strategy but delegating the tactical execution to able marshals and generals. After the Napoleonic wars, the French forgot the approach and returned to a very centralized command and control style with tactical decisions taken by headquarters distant from the front line (and usually based on outdated information), ultimately leading to the 1940 disaster. By contrast, the Prussians developed in the 19th century the concept of "Auftragstatik." Von Moltke recognized that only the beginning of a military campaign could be planned because of the chaos and uncertainty of war. People who face the enemy and see in real time his reaction have a better grasp of what is really happening and therefore a better chance to make the right decision. Consequently, each unit should be given clear objectives, but should decide how to do it. The German army adopted this subsidiarity principle in the First World War (e.g., with small autonomous assault units called Stosstruppen). The approach was also visible during the Blitzkrieg. Whilst the overall strategy, "the what," was decided in Berlin, the best way to achieve this tactically was primarily decided by the people on the front. In the end, the Germans lost both World Wars because of the massive difference in manpower, access to raw materials, and industrial capacity, but their use of subsidiarity principle allowed them to punch above their weight for a long time.

Equally, the business world has become incredibly complex. Companies that will adopt subsidiarity principles will have an edge over competitors with similar resources: they will make better, faster decisions than their competitors.

The Most Common Frameworks for Improvement

Before we start our brief discussion on some of the more common and widespread improvement frameworks we see today, a word of caution. When we give names to these collections of methods, concepts, and tools, we invite division and offer the opportunity for partisan lines to be drawn. This is becoming less prevalent today, but people can easily fall into one or the other camp depending on which ones they are most invested in. Do not be distracted by this, but embrace them all; they are not in opposition but are complementary, and when blended in a coherent way provide a sound basis for assessing and improving operations. Remember, we are trying to improve the physical reality of our product or service, and the customer does not buy improvement methods, so we need to have some perspective. Be wary of fanatics and missionaries of various frameworks, as they probably miss important lessons from the others. Your task is to see how these ostensibly different frameworks and concepts can all be complementary. The more you learn about them, and practice them the more you will begin to see the underlying principles emerge.

The roots of the four frameworks we discuss below go back many decades and maybe even further. There are others you may discover, but as a starting point, these are the frameworks and concepts we suggest you investigate further.

Total Quality Management

In the early 1980s, American managers woke up to the fact that they had been left behind by the Japanese in terms of product quality. The founders of the modern quality movement, Deming, Shewhart, and Juran, had all been taken seriously by the Japanese after World War 2. American organizations, on the other hand, had been seduced by the marketing man. It was now clear to many that the "quality of management" was more important than the "management of quality." And so Total Quality Management (TQM) was born with the aim of integrating quality principles into all management systems.

Quality planning, quality control, and quality improvement were all required to be managed by everyone in the organization. "Total" refers not only to all processes, but to all people: everyone is responsible for quality, not just the quality control inspectors. Under TQM, the concept of managing the entire organization for quality was intimately related to ongoing financial sustainability, and to that end two important distinctions arose that are very useful to the change agent of today. It was seen that management needed to operate at both a Policy Management and also a Daily Management (DM) level. Policy Management sets the vision, mission, and purpose and instigates the step changes required to be competitive now and in the future, whilst DM deals with the repeatable routines required to keep quality and efficiency high (Figure 2.1).

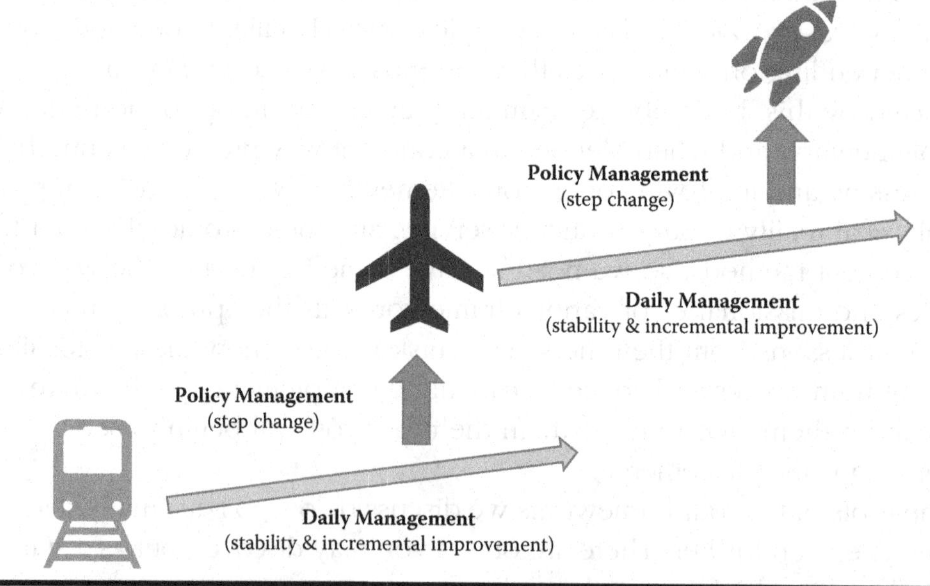

Figure 2.1 The TQM role of Policy Management and Daily Management.

Most of today's quality principles have emerged from the TQM movement, with Six Sigma being the most well-defined framework to capture the tools and techniques developed over many years.

Six Sigma

Six Sigma is a term coined by Motorola around 1989 to describe a method and toolset designed to drive a reduction in the variability of process outputs. The method follows the Define, Measure, Analyse, Improve, and Control (DMAIC) steps, and at each stage a set of process and statistical analysis tools is recommended (see Appendix 3). The principle use of Six Sigma is in analyzing sources of common cause variation. In other words, it seeks to find a quantified relationship between the most important process inputs and the process outputs. By tightly controlling the most important inputs, we can control the output. The aim is to get to a defect level below 3.4 parts per million.

There is some debate amongst those who were part of the quality organization at Motorola that suggests another, much simpler, set of tools developed by Dorian Shainin and elucidated on by Bhote (1991) were actually used to achieve these levels of performance. These tools are also worth investigating. Wanting to keep these tools to themselves, the story goes that Motorola decided to tell the world about another set of tools they were using - the nascent Six Sigma toolset.

The upshot of Motorola publishing the Six Sigma program was that a whole movement and industry sprang up around providing these methods to the wider world. Many of the world's most successful companies adopted Six Sigma programs. Training levels were divided into a series of colored belts that mimicked the martial arts hierarchy. Master Black Belts provided the training and mentoring of Black Belts and Green Belts who were taught statistical analysis tools with varying levels of complexity. Projects with a financial benefit were mandated as part of the training in order that the program paid dividends far in excess of training costs. It was easy to see the attraction.

Problems arose, however, in some instances, as projects were very much directed at local optimization, and the elitist nature of the program flew in the face of TQM principles. The skills taught in Six Sigma are still a very necessary part of a change agent's skill set, and in recent years a more holistic version has arisen that integrates both Six Sigma and Lean Operations. We see an increased focus on problem definition within Six Sigma as a welcome discipline to encourage along with an emphasis on numerical tools and techniques.

Lean Operations

Lean Manufacturing, or more commonly now, Lean Operations, refers to a set of operating principles and thought processes exemplified by the Toyota Production System (TPS). Once America had awoken to the quality revolution happening in Japan, they wanted to know a lot more about what was driving it. As the US automakers were some of the biggest losers in the quality revolution, a Massachusetts Institute of Technology (MIT) study was commissioned in the mid-1980s to benchmark Japanese competitors. What the team found went on to be described in *The Machine that Changed the World* (Jones, Womack, & Roos, 1990) and later *Lean Thinking* (Womack & Jones, 1996). The team found automakers and suppliers operating production processes counter to the principles of mass production that had predominated in the US since the end of World War 2. Economies of scale were less important than economies of inventories. Quality was paramount not just for customer satisfaction, but also to allow Just-in-Time (JIT) to operate effectively.

The guiding light for Toyota was to strive toward single-piece flow of all products and parts and to make only what the customer wanted when the customer wanted it. This is the essence of the Pull vs. Push dichotomy. If you think for a minute what this truly means, then in a Pull situation, a car is ordered in a configuration required by the customer and is delivered in the shortest possible time (1–3 days later) with excellent quality. Only cars that are sold are made. Contrast this with a mass production Push situation where we try to sell everything we make by enticing customers to buy already configured cars from a forecast which is invariably wrong. The upshot of this is that inventory turns increase (a key metric of Lean and often ignored). The difference is profound, and the results have been astonishing, even though no car company has yet come close to realizing this ideal state. Everything that Toyota does is geared to this simple principle, and for over five decades they have been the leaders in manufacturing excellence. It is easy to see why so many organizations want to emulate what they have achieved. Many organizations have tried to copy the TPS, but few have ever come close to realizing the same level of continual improvements. And herein lies a valuable lesson for the change agent. Copying the systems, processes, tools, and techniques of successful companies will only take you so far for so long. The founder of TPS Taichi Ohno was said to have been happy to show competitors around and have them take away the visible methods on show, but what he did not reveal was the underlying principles of flow, or "the river," as he called it.

It must also be noted that the Just-in-Time concept has come under much scrutiny, as supply chains can be severely disrupted by global events. Outsourcing to low-cost locations also contributes to supply chain problems as shipping times add many weeks to delivery schedules. Six weeks at sea can be a long time in fast-moving sectors such as fashion and retail.

The temple analogy (Figure 2.2) is a common depiction of the TPS, but in the early days of the Lean movement, many organizations assumed that, just like building a real temple, you have to build the strong foundations before you put in the pillars, resulting in a lot of 5S (a workplace organization system based on 5 steps commonly defined as Sort, Set-in-Order, Shine, Standardize, and Sustain) and visual management activities that had very little impact on flow. The temple represents the mature state of a Lean organization and not a blueprint for implementation. All of the elements have interrelationships and interdependencies with each other. They are mutually reinforcing and would be more correctly described in an integration diagram with inputs and outputs from each element feeding into and out of each other.

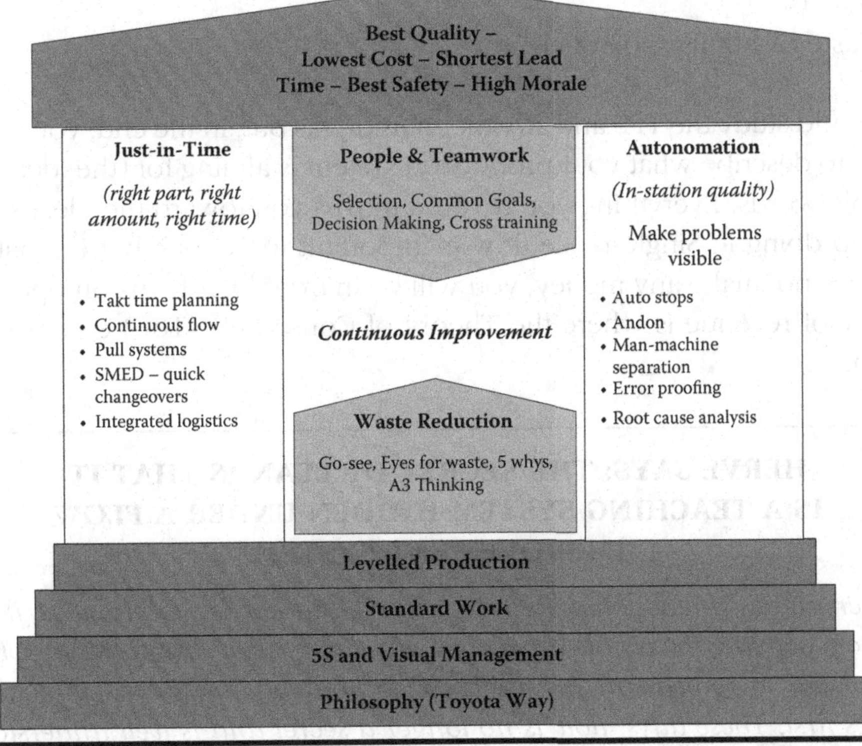

Figure 2.2 The Temple of Lean – modified from Liker's example in The Toyota Way (see Liker & Meier, 2006).

Lean is often only associated with waste reduction and the obvious implications of this approach on reducing workforce numbers. Many organizations have experienced resistance from the workforce when waste reduction is the focus of improvement efforts. But waste reduction is an integral part of improving effectiveness and efficiency along with the flip side of the equation, which is to improve the value proposition. Classic Lean literature lists the 7 Wastes, but some add an 8th. Pure waste is said to be anything that does not add value in the eyes of the customer. Necessary non-value-added activities are those things that must be done for compliance, regulatory, or moral grounds. It's worth familiarizing yourself with the following 8 wastes:

1. Transportation
2. Inventory
3. Motion
4. Waiting
5. Overprocessing
6. Overproduction
7. Defects
8. Waste of human potential

You should study the TPS and all other paradigms but, in the end, you need to be able to describe what your production system is aiming for (the ideal state) in simple words. Everything you do then moves you toward the ideal state or you stop doing it. Single-piece flow is important to Toyota, but if what you flow does not make any money, you will be in trouble. A focus on optimizing the flow of revenue is where the Theory of Constraints (ToC) comes into its own.

HERVÉ SAYS: THE SECRET OF LEAN IS THAT IT IS A TEACHING SYSTEM HIDDEN UNDER A FLOW IMPROVEMENT SYSTEM

Fraser rightly highlighted that the secret hidden by Ohno was flow. Visitors copying the visible aspect of Lean often failed dramatically when they tried to implement Just-in-Time without having solved their flow issues first. These days, flow is no longer a secret and is well understood by even novice Lean students across the world.

However, the real secret is not completely common knowledge: true Lean is a teaching system and not just a system to run operations effectively and efficiently. If Lean was only a "production" system, it could very easily be copied. Lean "program" success rates would be much higher. Yet, most attempts to adopt Lean fail, which shows that there is something else beyond the well-publicized tools and concepts.

Lean is in reality about creating organizational capability to solve problems. The system constantly creates opportunities to learn how to think better. All the Lean tools, if used properly, push in the direction of learning: better understanding of what customers of the process want, better understanding of the nature of problems, better understanding of the details of processes, and better ways of thinking and seeing the world. The real value of a kaizen or a problem-solving exercise is not so much about solving the problem or improving a process. It is more considered as an opportunity for the master to teach the student by helping him to improve things by himself. Even when the master knows a way to solve the problem, true Lean companies consider that there is a higher benefit in letting the student struggle with the problem and eventually find a way through.

I especially recommend the book Managing to Learn (Shook, 2008) *about Toyota's A3 process, as it perfectly illustrates how the master progressively helps the student to self-develop simply by asking questions, which ultimately leads to the student finding a solution after a number of trials. Not only is the problem solved, but the final solution is possibly better than if it had been imposed by the master, and the student has self-developed and will tackle subsequent problems more effectively and efficiently.*

The Theory of Constraints

The physicist and business improvement guru Eli Goldratt coined the Theory of Constraints (ToC) term and published his best-selling book *The Goal* (Goldratt, 1984) to explain to the world at large the importance of seeking the constraining factor in your "system of making money," i.e., your business. As the theory states, every system has a constraint to growth, and this constraint may appear anywhere within the system. If we take a business as an example, it is a system to make money now and in the future: the Goal according to Goldratt. The constraint may be in the market, in the supply chain, in the operations, or even in ambition, but there will be a limiting factor somewhere. What ToC suggests is that the operational constraint must be protected and kept running as much as possible. Since this may be the limiting factor on the entire ability of the business to generate revenue, then throughput at the constraint must also be optimized to give maximum revenue of sales (not work in progress as valued positively by the accountants). So, in ToC, we can improve throughput (in money terms), or we can reduce inventory and operating expenses. These are the only three levers to making more money. The most important thing to bear in mind is that only throughput is theoretically unlimited, whereas inventory and operating expense can only be reduced so far.

The Goal also spread the idea of how many production systems are actually scheduled to fail. If we have dependent events with similar capacity and a degree of variability (as we do in almost all production processes), we need to be aware of a phenomenon that can severely restrict output and is somewhat counterintuitive. Think of the road network and how it operates fairly well for most of the time (barring special causes such as accidents) when utilization is low. However, once the number of cars reaches a critical point, your journey time increases exponentially until gridlock occurs. Most journeys we do could probably bear a 50% increase in cars on the road with a minimal increase in journey time, but once you reach the tipping point, things jam up pretty quickly. In this example, cars are the dependent event; their speed is variable, and the utilization is the number of cars we are trying to "process" through the road. This is explained by the Kingman theory.

The Kingman theory is related to queuing theory, and it is applicable to our production processes as well. Say we have the average capacity at each of our five production units to process 100 items/hour, and we schedule all of them to do this. We know the average rate will never be maintained all of the time, so sometimes we will have shortages and sometimes queues in front of the units. The overall output will invariably be less than 100 items/hr. If we had promised the customer 100 units/hr, then that's not so good. As a rule of thumb, scheduling units above 85% of their average capacity results in an exponential deterioration in throughput. Ideally, we should have extra capacity in reserve to be able to meet 100% customer delivery time. The alternative is to buffer with lots of work-in-progress between the units, but of course this increases our inventory.

The above is a very brief attempt to get across some in-depth concepts set out in ToC, and it's a subject the change agent needs to have a good grasp of in order to be aware that some fundamentals in scheduling and capacity may be causing big issues in the supply chain and no amount of local improvement will alter it. If we increase capacity by reducing downtime, for instance, and we simply up our stated capacity in our scheduling model (SAP-ERP), we will still have a delivery performance issue.

HERVÉ SAYS: TOC ALSO APPLIES TO PROJECT MANAGEMENT

Eli Goldratt successfully applied ToC to project management to create a method called Critical Chain Project Management (CCPM) (Goldratt E. M., 1997). *Goldratt noted that the usual project management approach (based on critical path) leads to a number of inefficiencies that we have all experienced. One of the key issues is that project members tend to be cautious when announcing estimated time required for each task. Once you have announced that you will reach a milestone in 2 weeks, there is little incentive to deliver it significantly faster, even though the tasks might only have a combined duration of 4 hours (the famous "student's syndrome," waiting for the last minute to do the work). Whilst having a buffer is useful as some unpredictable problems will occur, it is statistically extremely unlikely that every single step will face unexpected issues. So rather than building a buffer in each step, CCPM suggests to remove buffers from individual tasks and have an overall project buffer that is smaller than the sum of all individual buffers in classic projects, thus leading to shorter projects. Instead, individual task duration is estimated on a 50% probability basis. Project progress is then monitored by measuring buffer consumption rather than wasting a lot of energy on ensuring that every single task is completed on time.* Figure 2.3 *illustrates how CCPM can reduce planned project duration.*

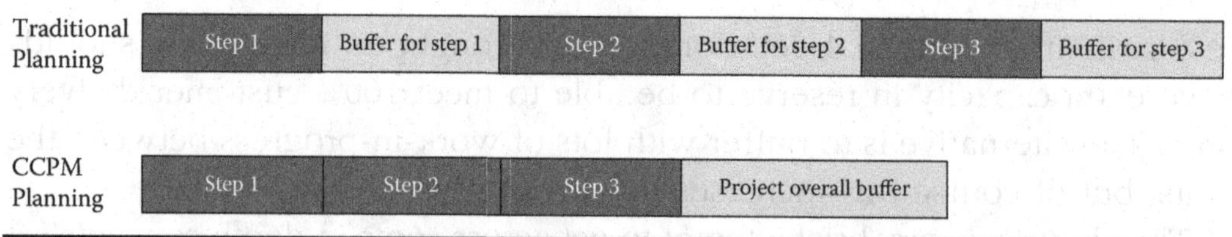

Figure 2.3 Traditional project planning vs. CCPM planning.

A Potted History of Operational Excellence

Operational Excellence is a term that is now much used as a catch-all of the current accepted theories, methods, and toolsets used widely in the industry and beyond. It is a term we will use to describe all of what we consider to be "good" in the field of change management. It also means we avoid appearing to favor any of the camps we described earlier that people sometimes align themselves to.

One of the marvels of the modern age is the ability to create parts and components that are interchangeable with each other with no loss of function. We take this for granted now, but for most of human history this was unthinkable. It has revolutionized manufacturing and is one of the greatest of human achievements. The vestiges of the craft era were still in play when I became an apprentice in 1983. We were taught, briefly, the skill of scraping metal bearing surfaces to match them by hand. This was how it used to be done, and up until the 1970s, most aircraft were put together with a high degree of this "fettling" on the aluminum alloy airframe itself. This was quite effective, but not very efficient and thankfully much less of this occurs now.

The frameworks we have discussed previously were evolutionary, having their basis in much earlier technological, scientific, and cultural changes to how we produced the goods we needed (Figure 2.4). Sadly, much of the history of these improvements is the history of warfare and how to wage ever more technological wars. It's well known that without industrial capability and capacity (and the finances behind it) (Deming, 1982), no modern war has ever been won. Thankfully, the benefits of this improved manufacturing capability are now also put to more constructive use.

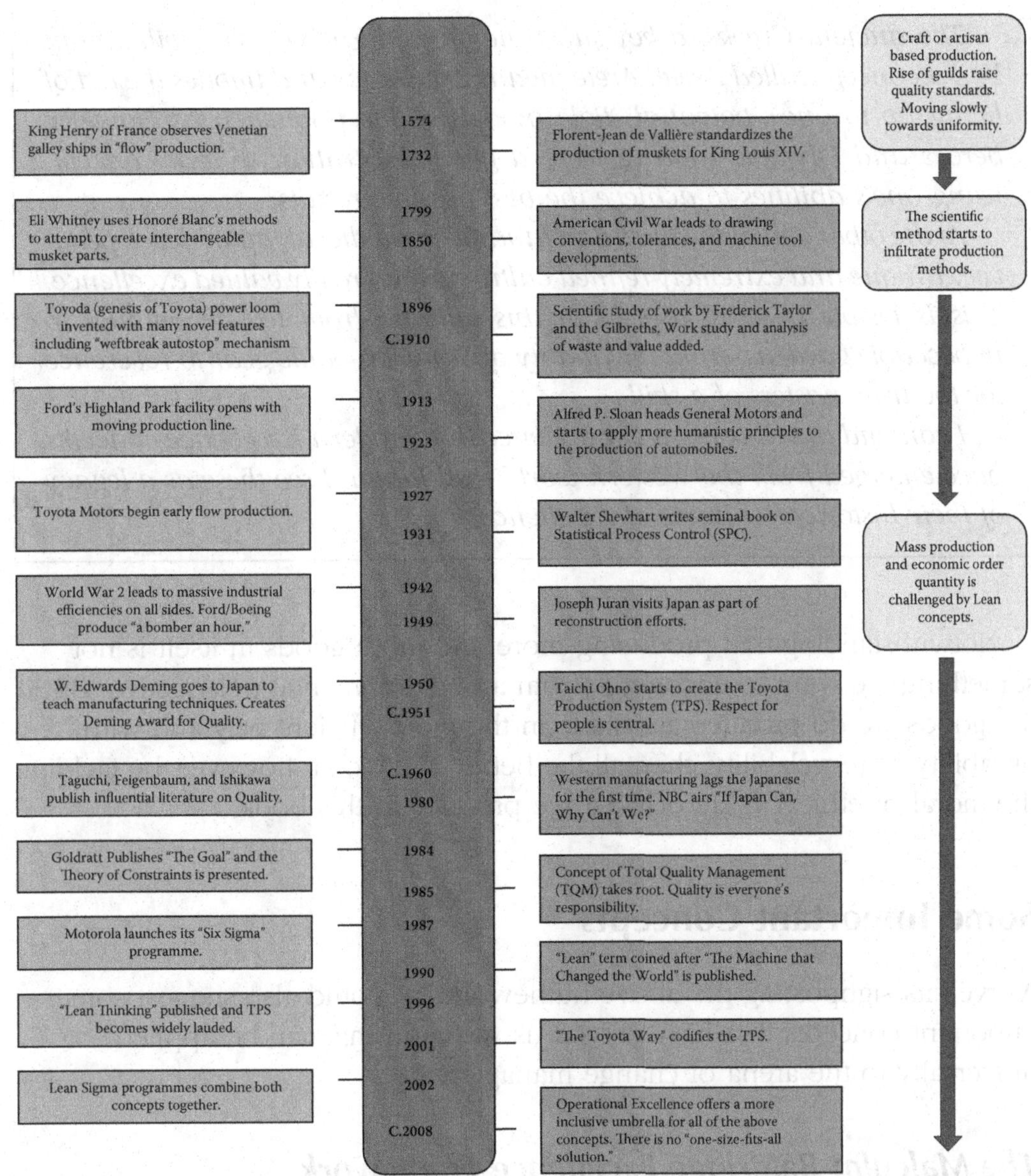

Figure 2.4 A timeline of events in the development of Operational Excellence.

HERVÉ SAYS: EXCELLENCE EXISTED BEFORE EXCELLENCE

In world history, two civilizations developed and valued a concept of excellence based on continuous improvement towards ultimate perfection:

The ancient Greeks, a key substrate of modern Western civilization, had a concept called Arete. Arete means excellence and implies the act of living up to one's potential. Role models of the time such as Homeric heroes and Olympic athletes were a good illustration of that concept, using one's abilities to achieve the best possible results.

At the other end of the Eurasian landmass, medieval Japan developed a very unique and extremely refined culture which really valued excellence. This is visible in most aspects of this culture, from tea ceremonies to impeccable gardens, from the quality of Samurai battle gear to reverence for the true masters of a skill.

I contend that it is not a coincidence that modern Excellence concepts have emerged from the Western world and Japan. I see these as a legacy of their historical cultures of excellence.

Notwithstanding that producing more and more goods in itself is not something we want to encourage from an environmental perspective. But if the goods we do produce are made in the most efficient way and with durability or recyclability, then all the better. We won't, however, be tackling the moral or ethical value of what we produce in this book.

Some Important Concepts

As well as signposting the above frameworks, I would also suggest some important concepts that have served us well and that can be applied universally to the arena of change management.

The Malcolm Baldridge Excellence Framework

The Baldridge Excellence Framework is itself well worth investing some time in understanding. As part of the wakeup call to American industry in the early to mid-1980s, industry leaders and the government conceived a nationally recognized awards scheme and excellence framework that was signed into US law as The Malcolm Baldrige National Quality Improvement Act of 1987. Designed to return a focus on quality and the concepts of organizational excellence, it has since expanded to a worldwide audience, and this has inspired other national frameworks such as the European Foundation for Quality Management model. A scoring element allows the

Baldridge framework to be accessed as a benchmarking tool, and signing up to the awards allows you to utilize the benefits of seeing what the current state of excellence constitutes in your location or sector.

Scoring is divided into Process and Results elements. Processes are scored in relation to their Approach, Deployment, Learning, and Integration (ADLI) and Results in relation to their Levels, Trends, Comparators, and Integration (LeTCI) dimensions. More points are scored the further down the chain you progress, and they reflect the maturity of process management. These concepts really help in understanding how processes can be applied in the most effective way. Just having a good approach won't change anything unless it is well deployed, and if we don't have a learning loop built in, it is less likely to improve. Finally, if it is not integrated with other relevant processes, then it will not be reinforced. When things aren't going so well it's really useful to consider with which of these ADLI elements the problem might lie. When measuring processes, the same applies to the LeTCI dimensions. (The LeTCI dimensions will be explained later in Chapter 3.) The excellence framework always strives for integration as the final stage in process deployment maturity.

Having these elements in mind when confronted with a situation for the first time means the change agent has a quick and logical diagnostic to apply. Where this model is used most effectively is in driving this type of thinking process in the leadership team. I use this model as it is the one I am most familiar with, but having studied the Shingo Business Model, or the Deming prizes, I would say these are also effective models. The Shingo and Deming approaches appear to be more prescriptive than the Baldrige Model, which is a series of questions based around the core subjects of:

- **Leadership:** Examines how senior executives guide the organization and how the organization addresses its responsibilities to the public and practices good citizenship.
- **Strategic planning:** Examines how the organization sets strategic directions and how it determines key action plans.
- **Customer focus:** Examines how the organization determines requirements and expectations of customers and markets; builds relationships with customers; and acquires, satisfies, and retains customers.

- **Measurement, analysis, and knowledge management:** Examines the management, effective use, analysis, and improvement of data and information to support key organization processes and the organization's performance management system.
- **Workforce focus:** Examines how the organization enables its workforce to develop its full potential and how the workforce is aligned with the organization's objectives.
- **Process management:** Examines aspects of how key production/delivery and support processes are designed, managed, and improved.
- **Results:** Examines the organization's performance and improvement in its key business areas: customer satisfaction, financial and marketplace performance, human resources, supplier and partner performance, operational performance, and governance and social responsibility. This category also examines how the organization performs relative to competitors.

For an official application, the answers to the questions are gathered together into a submission document. This is then submitted for an external assessment, and a score is given up to 1,000 points. The benefit of the official route is that you can benchmark against a large and international database of organizations in your sector.

Although an excellence framework is not an operating model like the TPS (Liker & Meier, 2006), it can form the basis of a common language and understanding in a large, diverse, geographically dispersed organization. I have seen it used this way to create a cadre of senior leaders starting at the highest level who have a shared view of the important questions to be asked of any organization. Unlike an operating model, the answers to the questions can be different but equally valuable if they are shown to give the results required. When these senior leaders assess each other's organizations, there is an incredible opportunity to share and learn from outside your own industry and sector.

Iceberg Models

Iceberg models abound in business improvement circles. That's because they reveal a powerful truth about what we see happening and what actually drives the visible world. Behavior is defined as an observable act or the visible iceberg above the surface. What drives behavior is unseen and in the depths and by no means an easy thing to establish, but the iceberg model is an attempt to show general forces at play. When we ask what drives behavior, the model says "our principles" and what drives principles is "beliefs." So, to fundamentally change behavior we have to change beliefs! Beliefs can change, but we are unlikely to be the ones who change other people's beliefs, so the best course of action is to work on principles first. These can at least be codified and agreed upon and taught. We must also recognized the importance of consequences when we try and change behavior. We'll discuss this further in Chapter 5.

Objectives, Goals, Strategies, and Measures and Degree of Hardness

I don't see the Objectives, Goals, Strategies, and Measures (OGSM) concept being widely spoken about in improvement circles, maybe because it is a form of strategy deployment (Hoshin Kanri) and is seen as being superfluous. It seeks to deploy the highest-level Objectives by stair-stepping down a number of levels, with higher-level Strategies becoming lower-level Objectives and higher-level Measures becoming lower-level Goals. What makes this tool different is in how it is deployed, as we shall see (Figure 2.5).

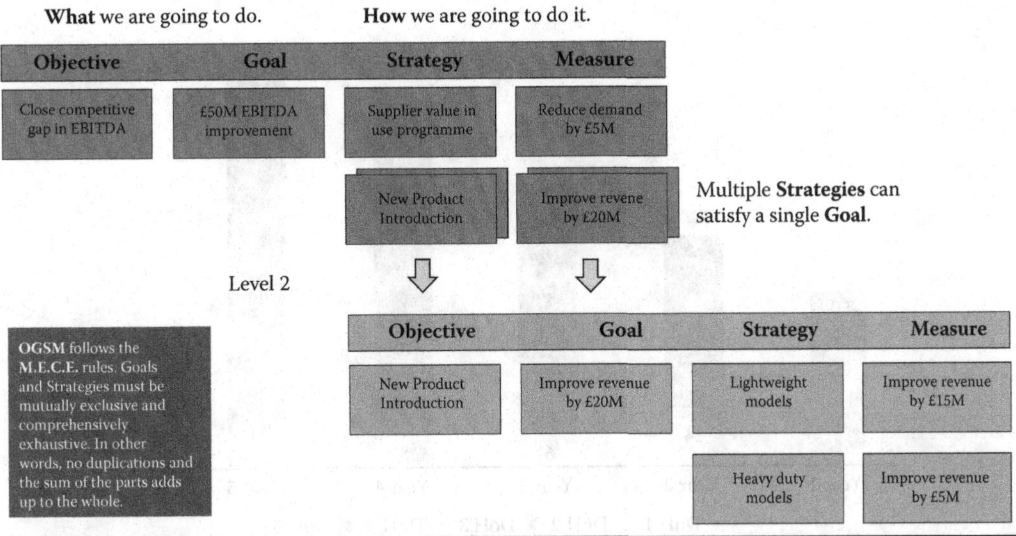

Figure 2.5 OGSM stair-stepping of higher level Objectives into multiple Goals and lower level Objectives.

Degree of Hardness (DoH) does not really translate readily from the German it was originally conceived in. "Hardness" does not relate to difficulty but more to firmness of planning and execution of projects. As it was taught to us, any project goes through 5 degrees of hardness:

- **DoH 1:** Concept or idea
- **DoH 2:** Quantification of benefits
- **DoH 3:** Sign-off of financials/benefits and all interdependencies resolved (Capex, resources, permits, etc.)
- **DoH 4:** Implementation and benefits have begun
- **DoH 5:** All milestones completed and benefits sustainable

This may seem like fairly standard program management theory until you start to add in two powerful elements. The level of project scrutiny and a formal sign-off at DoH 3 and DoH 5 needs to be at a very senior level, including financial controllers. Future program savings are also projected out in a five-year timescale, so each individual strategy must have savings or benefits projected against a baseline (Figure 2.6). When these two elements are coupled together we have a means to show the level of confidence we have in being able to realize future savings. Prudently, we also factor in a 30% drop-off in initial estimates. When you have very tight financial objectives, this tool really comes into its own.

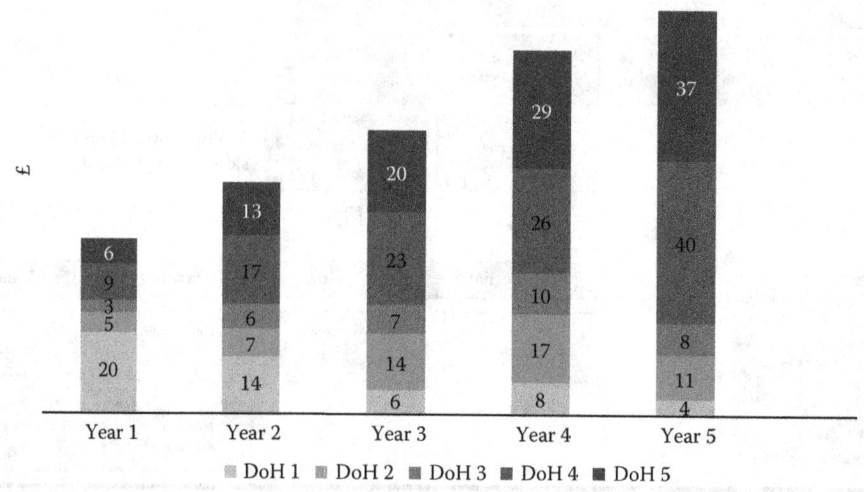

Figure 2.6 OGSM Ramp up of program benefits against baseline Year 0.

WHAT COULD POSSIBLY GO WRONG! THE UPS AND DOWNS

After delivering the majority of the savings in year one, the confidence of the backers was far higher, and OGSM became a key vehicle to show the financial effects of our plans. The downside was that we were making progress in the areas covered by OGSM but were still losing money elsewhere and not seeing all the benefits on the bottom line - hence the need for Daily Management of all key business levers to underpin the Policy Management. We were gaining in some areas and losing in others, which dragged on the overall, bottom-line performance.

Fraser

Variability

Except possibly at the subatomic level, no two things are absolutely identical. This is especially true in manufacturing to a greater or lesser extent depending on your process. We also have variability in human performance. Understanding that there is a natural variability at work in almost everything leads us onto some important insights. Natural or "common cause" variation means that there is a degree of randomness inherent in every process. One day we get great performance and a pat on the back and the next it's terrible and we get the "evil eye," but we don't know why. If something obvious had happened, we could explain it. It would be a "special cause" variation. Both types of variation will need to be worked on, and to understand how to best tackle each, you will need to study inferential statistics (like in Six Sigma) and the theory behind statistical process control (SPC).

Most of the quality gurus major on the need to reduce variability in all our processes, but Deming (Deming, 1982) and Taguchi (Taguchi, 1993) are a good introduction to the subject. Taguchi claims that variability in manufacturing incurs loss for the whole of society, as products are less reliable or less effective. For example, in the 1980s when Ford was having problems with gearbox failures, they discovered the US-made gearboxes were failing far more than the same specification Japanese units. When stripped down and inspected, all the parts were in tolerance in both cases. On closer analysis, more of the US-made parts were much closer to the specification limits. The

US manufacturer was rejecting the tail end of the distribution to be in tolerance, and due to "tolerance stack-up," the gearboxes were failing more often. More disruption to customers, more waste, and more resource usage ensued even though they were in "compliance" with customer specifications.

In a previous organization, we were having quality problems with a very high grade of injection molding plastic. The interaction of the plastic and our reactants was crucial in giving the correct output, and we started to see far greater variation in our testing of the reaction. When we tested the raw stock of plastic before it was injection molded, a strange pattern emerged. Plotting a key variable on a histogram, we saw two triangular shapes at either end of the distribution with nothing in the middle around the mean. On investigation with the supplier, it appeared they had been giving us the tail ends of the distribution because we were a much smaller customer than another and they had all of the product that was missing from our distribution. All the product was within the specification, but for our purposes the effect was amplified, and for the other customer, their use meant it was not so critical. I don't recall that we ever got a more homogenous supply.

Effectiveness vs. Efficiency

Of course, we want to be both effective and efficient, but sometimes the order of these aims is switched, with often negative outcomes. I like to think of effectiveness as being a more customer-focused aim and efficiency more a business priority. When we focus on efficiency, it can distract from delivering the basic requirements of quality and on-time supply, both to paying customers and to internal customers. I often see this in "cost-down" programs where saving a penny in one department leads to spending a pound in another.

Whenever we look at improvements, we need to think in process terms and what the process must deliver to be effective or to deliver effective products. Only when we are sure we are capable of this should we look to make efficiency improvements. Alas, when organizations are in severe financial crisis, they fall into a doom-loop of cost reduction and poor customer satisfaction. It's important to remember the sad truth that for the health of the overall business ecosystem, some organizations need to fail and will fail if the fundamental business model is not sound. No matter how effective and efficient we become, a poor business model will negate all other efforts to thrive.

Maturity Triangles

The maturity triangle concept relates well to many situations in business. The classic use is to describe how the more serious safety performance of an organization is correlated to the many smaller deviations in safety routines and habits we observe. Most people will recognize this as the Heinrich or Bird triangle. At the top of the triangle, we will see very few lost-time accidents or worst still, fatalities. The theory states that the number of these serious incidents is directly related to the number of minor accidents and injuries we see at a lower level. These are in turn influenced by the number of unsafe acts or unsafe conditions we observe. By reducing the number of lower-order deviations, we inevitably reduce the higher-order deviations. The same is also true of quality. Major quality issues such as recalls will be directly related to the number of quality deviations we see in all our processes regardless of whether they directly lead to a defect (Figure 2.7). This is a probability game. The chance of a number of lower-order deviation "lining up" and causing a higher-order deviation is increased in direct proportion. What it tells us is that we can't ignore the small stuff.

The caution here is that most major process safety incidents such as the Piper Alpha fire or the Deep Water Horizon incident would not have been prevented by eliminating all minor injuries such as scraped knuckles or twisted ankles; the root causes of high-severity incidents are mostly of such a different nature even to a single fatality. In the quality arena, the case for a

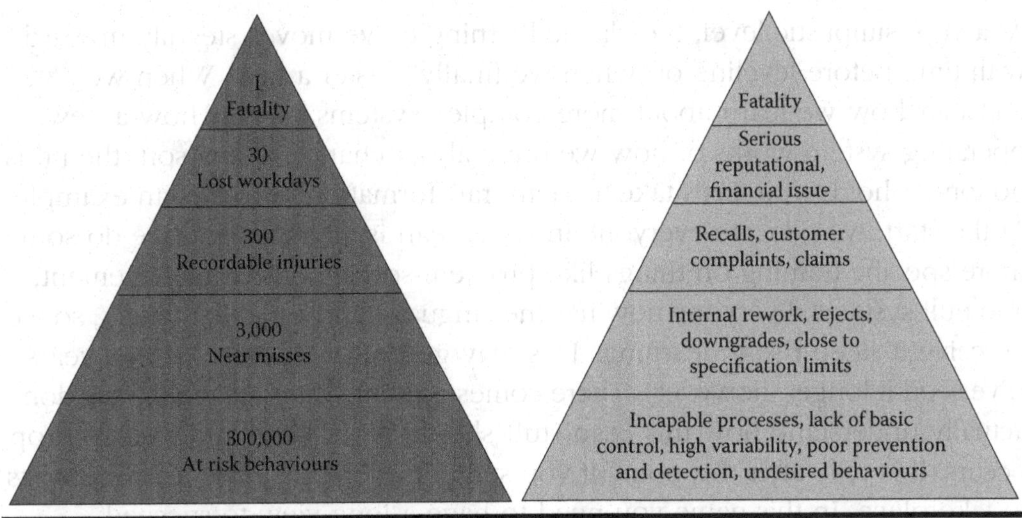

Figure 2.7 The Heinrich Safety triangle (see ConocoPhillips Marine Data, 2003) and the Quality comparison, which is the authors' own.

stronger relationship can be made. There is of course much overlap between the two; poor quality often being the cause of safety issues.

The phenomena we apportion as being inside the conceptual space of the triangle by necessity relate to deviations and failures. As the theory goes, by working to reduce these deviations and failures, we reduce the chance of more serious consequences occurring. This is sound thinking as far as it goes, but we must also consider the conceptual and much bigger space outside the confines of the triangle. If we consider the safety triangle, the lowest level regards unsafe behaviors and all that the definition encompasses. What it does not regard is the number of *safe* behaviors that occur in an equal time frame. If we fail to encourage and reinforce these safe behaviors it is likely that more unsafe behaviors will be observed and counted within the triangle. A similar scenario will occur in the quality dimension. Positive safety behaviors must be a subject of any safety discussions that occur in the workplace. Many organizations are now adopting the same approach to quality as part of leadership Go-see walks. What safety has in its favor is a recourse to a deep emotional drive to avoid the pain and suffering of an accident to yourself and others. The imagination can be employed with powerful effect in this case. This is much harder to evoke with an unhappy customer if the quality issue is not directly related to potential human suffering.

The False Learning Curve

At a very simplistic level, the classic learning curve moves steadily upwards with time before leveling off when we finally master a task. When we consider how we learn about more complex systems such as how a new operating system works or how we bring about change of any sort, then this no longer holds true. Let's take a "Lean transformation" effort as an example. At the start, we educate everyone in what Lean is all about and we do some more specific training on things like problem-solving, visual management, and pull systems. Everyone now has the language and can talk the talk, so we perceive a steep rise in learning. This may go on for as much as five years (I've seen it longer, however). There comes a point when we realize we don't actually understand how this Lean stuff should work at all and a steep drop occurs. It is only after this point, if you still persevere, that true learning starts to take place. In this game you need to have a long view to succeed (Figure 2.8).

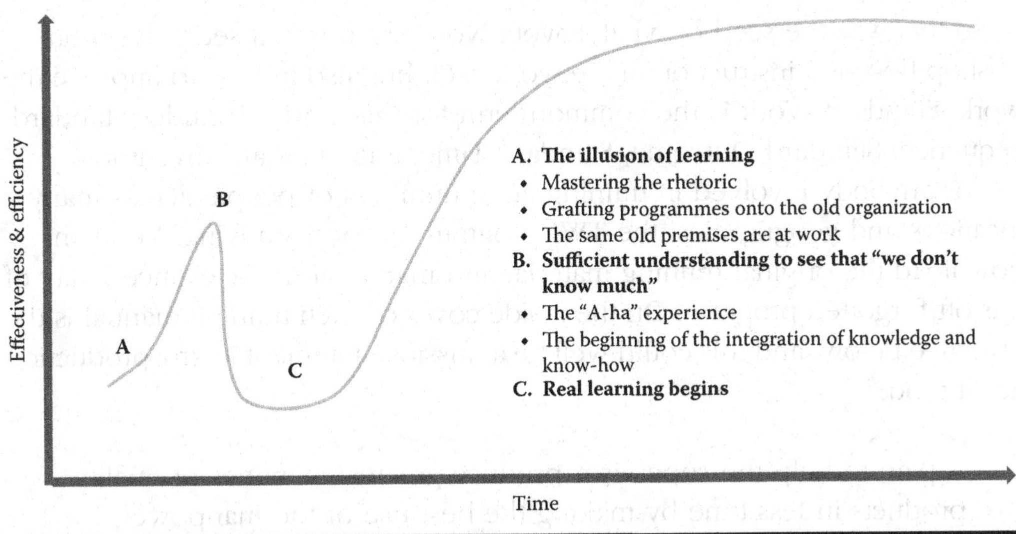
Effectiveness & efficiency
Time
A
B
C
A. The illusion of learning
• Mastering the rhetoric
• Grafting programmes onto the old organization
• The same old premises are at work
B. Sufficient understanding to see that "we don't know much"
• The "A-ha" experience
• The beginning of the integration of knowledge and know-how
C. Real learning begins

Figure 2.8 The stages of the false learning curve (see Scholtes, 1998).

The Power of Standard Work and Training within Industry

Without standards of work to follow and specifications to adhere to, we could not have achieved the interchangeability of parts as described previously. When the US was in need of making a vast array of war equipment during World War 2, they had a major problem. Many of the skilled industrial workers were called up to active service, leaving behind a largely untrained and inexperienced workforce, many of whom had never been in organized work before. Of those with experience, they had probably never before been required to improve work methods so rapidly. Imagine if you were in charge of this workforce and you are tasked with making weapons, vehicles, medical supplies, and communication equipment that would all be relied upon by servicemen and women in the heat of battle. How do you go about training each one in the task required and the supervisors in the human relations needed to ensure production output is continually raised?

The War Manpower Commission developed a solution in the shape of a program of instruction for supervisors in how to create job methods, instruct in job methods, and ensure job relations were in good shape. This was called Training Within Industry (TWI), and it is credited as being a fundamental part of what made the TPS so enduring and successful. The key was to give supervisors the skills needed to set standards and crucially instruct in these standards themselves. There was no option for having a mass of external training resources, so this was the means of multiplying the skills exponentially.

So this was the seed of what Toyota would turn into a secret weapon of shop floor-led instruction in the work itself but also in how to improve the work. Standard Work is the common term for this, and it includes Standard Sequence, Standard Outcome, Standard Time, and Standard Inventory.

For anybody involved in training large numbers of people across many locations and geographies, the TWI program is worth studying. You can download the original training material and marvel at the relevance today of this oft-forgotten program. On the inside cover of each training manual is the objective below, and this could well be a mission statement in any production facility today.

> A plan to help the supervisor produce greater quantities of quality products in less time by making the best use of the manpower, machines, and material that are now available.
>
> Bureau of Training, War Manpower Commission, 1943

The Scientific Method

The scientific method has been the backbone of progress since at least the late 17th century. It is oft quoted in operational management literature, especially in connection with problem-solving methods. The classic definition of the steps involved can be related to the way we think about problems as shown in Table 2.1.

The content of the table may seem to be very theoretical, but as you begin to solve more problems in a structured way, you will start to see what is meant by each stage. What is often missed is the connection between the plans we have to tackle the problem and the concept of the hypothesis. Any change you plan to make in any setting such as a production process or transactional process will only be a hypothesis until such time as you have implemented that change. This could be a setting change on a machine or a new training program. We also tend to miss the importance of target setting before we conduct the change. By reflecting on how close we came to predicting the outcome, we can see how complete our knowledge of the process really is. We can also ask the very important questions about whether we lack a full understanding of the cause-and-effect relationships or whether we didn't conduct the change thoroughly enough and in a controlled manner.

Table 2.1 The scientific method as related to problem-solving

Scientific method	*Related to problem-solving*
1 – Make an Observation. You can't study what you don't know is there.	Observe a deviation.
2 – Ask a Question.	What is the root cause of the deviation?
3 – Do Background Research.	What is the process at work that created the deviation? What is likely to have caused the deviation? What are the facts around that deviation – what? where? when? how many/much?
4 – Form a Hypothesis.	Narrow down potential root causes based on the verified facts. Understand the cause-and-effect relationships.
5 – Predict the Results.	Set a target condition. Predict the magnitude of the cause-and-effect relationships. This tests how thoroughly you have understood the deviation and its causes.
6 – Conduct an Experiment.	Make a controlled change (single factor or multiple factor design of experiment) and run the process again.
7 – Analyse Results and Draw a Conclusion.	Did you get the expected result? If not, was it a failure of approach or deployment?
8 – Report Your Results and Suggest the Next Area of Study.	Standardize the new process and share your learning. What needs to be improved next in the process?

A Balanced Scorecard Approach

In the automotive industry, there has emerged a powerful suite of metrics that are used to ensure that a broad focus of improvement efforts are applied. This is an attempt to avoid too much focus on purely financial metrics at the expense of the overall health of the organization. In its simplest form, it consists of a number of Key Performance Indicators (KPIs) grouped into the categories of Safety, Morale, Quality, Delivery, and Cost (SDQDC). There are variations on these categories, but in broad terms they describe areas that require constant attention if long-term sustainability is to be realized. This concept is one that is not as universally applied as the authors would expect. On several occasions, with both international consultants and individual businesses, the concept has not been recognized. Maybe it's not taught in MBA courses! An additional take on this concept is that the Shingo Institute has noticed that the best-performing organizations in their assessments focus on Key Behavioral Indicators (KBIs) rather than KPIs. Manage the inputs and the outputs will take care of themselves.

Summary

Wherever you are in your change agent career, it never hurts to reflect on what you have learned so far and what you may still need to know. Like any field of learning, it is a never-ending feast. You will start, over time, to form a view on how best to approach different situations and challenges until you have a good and workable model to fall back on. Other change agents will have different reference models, and it would be nice to get a consensus and describe an operating system for the organization. Equally important, however, is to ensure you can describe your approach with conviction. In the next chapter, we discuss a means of selecting how to assess your organization and determine what priorities you need to work on.

Get started on your Chapter 2 learnings – developing my understanding of key concepts.

I. Developing my balanced scorecard (if I do not already have one).
   a. *What did you find easy about this task?*
   b. *What did you find difficult about this task and why?*
   c. *What was your key learning from these difficulties?*
   d. *What can you do to employ and sustain the scorecard?*

II. *Checking the scorecard against the Safety, Quality, Delivery, Cost (SQDC) principles.*
   a. *Are the four basic elements of SQDC present and sufficient?*
   b. *Is there a good balance and emphasis on safety, morale, and wellbeing?*
   c. *Are the KPIs relevant to drive improvement?*
   d. *Do you have a complete set of KPIs to ensure a sustainable organization?*
   e. *Do you have targets for all KPIs and what are these targets based on?*

f. *Do you have benchmarking data or comparators to support the targets?*

g. *What is the review process for the scorecard and is it effective?*

III. *Finding waste and improving the value proposition through application of Lean Thinking and the Theory of Constraints.*

a. *What is the scope of the system, process, or work area I will study?*

b. *What Transport wastes are there?*

c. *What Inventory wastes are there?*

d. *What Motion wastes are there?*

e. *What Waiting wastes are there?*

f. *What Overprocessing wastes are there?*

g. *What Overproduction wastes are there?*

h. *What defect wastes are there?*

i. *What human potential wastes are there?*

j. *What is the system constraint?*

k. *What is the first step to address the system constraint?*

IV. *Committing to self-study to improve my understanding of a key theory(s).*

a. *What theory(s) do I want to study first?*

b. *How am I going to learn more about this?*

Chapter 3

Selecting the Right Problems

Hervé Duval

> There is nothing quite so useless as doing efficiently that which should not be done at all.
>
> **Peter Drucker**

Introduction

In the world of problem-solving, "there is nothing quite so wasteful as fixing the wrong problem." Yet how many times have we seen project teams being formed as a knee-jerk reaction? Some senior leaders might have vaguely heard about a problem with limited understanding of the actual impact of the problem and yet decided to commit resources to an ill-defined task. Unfortunately, this is human nature. Evolution taught us to rapidly react to problematic situations with a "fight or flight" response. We just feel the urge to act.

This phenomenon sometimes has even more perverse causes. The launch of a problem-solving team (or of a committee) is an easy way for someone to be seen to be doing something. It can also be used to deflect blame. We have all witnessed functional leaders asking other functions to create a problem-solving team (or even a committee), even though this problem is minor in the grand scheme of things.

So how do we avoid assigning precious resources to minor problems? We will use problem-solving in the field of human health to illustrate the approach. Health improvement starts with a diagnostic. No doctor prescribes medicine before diagnosing. Personal health improvement programs also

 DOI: 10.4324/9781003486022-3

start with establishing a baseline and identifying our current habits. So why would we start by launching a problem-solving team before a diagnostic is established?

Ok, I get it. Before starting to improve my business I need to do a diagnostic. You convinced me. I'd like my improvement program to start with a full health check-up. How do I do a good diagnostic then?

EXAMPLE: WASTING RESOURCES ON THE WRONG PROBLEMS: COMPLAINING ABOUT OTHERS WILL DIVERT ATTENTION

In one plant, the manufacturing department blamed raw material as the main cause of poor quality performance and requested additional efforts from the Supplier Quality department to solve issues. Pareto analysis later showed that 85% of all rejections had nothing to do with raw materials. Once this fact was shared in the business, manufacturing had no other choice than to improve.

In the same business, some customers commented that complaint resolution was taking too long. The commercial team that had relayed the customer's concern explained that this problem was caused by internal credit note processing procedures that were too complex. The commercial director demanded and obtained the creation of a cross-functional team to speed up the issuing of credit notes. It eventually turned out that the average time to issue the credit note was 11.5 calendar days. Whilst this was indeed too long, this had to be compared with the overall time taken to process a claim (c. 50 days). Nearly 80% of the time taken to issue credit notes from the moment a customer complained was not linked to the issue that the team had been tasked to work on! Once the team started to redefine properly the problem as "complaint processing takes too long," it demonstrated that the two longest steps in the complaint handling process were in fact owned by the commercial function.

On a lighter note, I should mention that the commercial manager who had flagged the problem was one of the main causes of delay in the credit note issuing process, as he was not following the standard vetting procedure.

How to Do a Good Diagnostic

A good diagnostic normally takes place in two steps.

Step 1: Understand the Business

First of all, good doctors will understand the patient's occupation, lifestyle, background, and environment. It is equally vital to understand the business context and strategy if you want to give credible advice. You will therefore need to obtain a general presentation about the business (markets, key customers, customer feedback survey, assets, dimensions, strategy, and financials) before starting the diagnostic.

This objective approach will need to be complemented with more subjective information such as the recent history of the company: Has there been a traumatic restructuring recently? Does the company have experience of improvement programs? Who are the key influencers?

Understanding the operation itself (in general, the plant that you try to diagnose) is the next step. Drawing a simple Value Stream Map at this stage is an important step. A Value Stream Map is the visual depiction on a single piece of paper of the various operational steps and main flows starting with our suppliers and finishing with our customers. The Value Stream Map also shows levels of Work In Progress at each step of the Value Stream, quality levels, typical lead times between steps, and relationships between each step ("supermarkets," "kanban," "pull loops," etc.). Having all this information on one single sheet helps you to describe the current state and will also be a good basis for describing the future state. If you have never seen VSMs before, I suggest you research the approach as this step is very important (Rother 1999).

Finally, you need to find out what is the constraint of the system (see Theory of Constraints in Chapter 2). It is all about maximizing the flow of value. Be careful: the bottleneck is not always a physical step of the process. The bottleneck can sometimes be in sales. If you have not identified this, you might work on increasing plant capacity and yet ending up not selling more at the end of the project. Therefore, I always start with a simple question: "Would you be able to sell more if the plant could produce more?" You might have to check that the answer you are given is based on facts.

If the bottleneck is indeed sales, you will then need to understand which attribute will be key to growing sales. If you are unlucky, the bottleneck is the size of the salesforce and there is not much you will be able to do (other than recommending increasing the size of the salesforce if they can generate a payback). But in most cases, the company does not sell enough either because of price (and therefore cost), quality, or service. In this case, you know which attribute to focus on.

If the bottleneck is not sales but plant capacity, the first question to ask is which process step is the bottleneck.

EXAMPLE: THE MANAGER WHO IMPROVED MANY THINGS WITHOUT IMPROVING THE OVERALL RESULT

Does this story feel familiar?

I was visiting a friend who is a Works Manager during my holidays. After a very nice dinner, the focus of conversation moved to work.

ME: *"How is work?"*
HIM: *"Great, I have been improving the Overall Equipment Effectiveness of most of my process steps"*
ME: *"Super! So how much has your turnover improved by?"*
HIM: *"Well, this is the one issue I have. Despite all these improvements, we still produce the same number of parts every day overall."*
ME: *"Hmm. Do you have a piece of paper? Let us draw your value stream and talk about ToC ..."*

Subsequent discussion led to the understanding that the plant bottleneck was an oven that had received no attention for many years. This is a typical example of unfocused improvements. Local improvements are made, but they do not impact the overall result.

Step 2. Use a "Scientific" Diagnostic Tool: The Stakeholder Value Flow Analysis

Once you have understood the business, diagnostic proper can start. To continue with the medical metaphor, several types of diagnostics exist depending on the patient's need. Do I want to obtain a full picture of my health state (in which case I need a full check-up) or do I want my doctor to fix a specific problem? The following paragraphs will focus on the full check-up. But sometimes the requirements will be more limited.

When doctors diagnose, it might look like a semi-random array of questions. In reality, they have been taught to follow a diagnostic process. Similarly, we need to use a formalized process. I developed my improvement skills in businesses I was familiar with. As I knew by experience what were the key issues (or I thought that I knew), I did not really need a method. But there came a time when I started to receive requests for help from businesses that I was not familiar with. I therefore developed a generic tool that allowed me to carry out a diagnostic even when I did not know the business. I call it the Stakeholder Value Flow Diagnostic (SVFD) as it allows me to look at the needs of various stakeholders, especially owners, customers, and employees. When I subsequently applied it in my business of origin, I realized that I had overlooked several issues, as I had relied on personal knowledge (and prejudice) rather than using a scientific, structured approach.

A diagnostic tool such as the SVFD is about assessing how well value flows from the point of view (POV) of all our stakeholders:

- **Customer POV (Quality, Delivery):** whatever the business you are in, you will not survive long if both your products and service are poor. Customers pay your salaries. A CEO from a famous Japanese automotive company asks the same first question to local management teams during each of his site visits across the globe, even before asking about financials or operational parameters: "are your customers satisfied?"
- **Employees POV (Safety, Morale):** whether you are an idealist or a cynic, attention to safety and employee morale should be paramount. I am the former, so to me, it is obviously important. Nevertheless, if you are the latter, you should remember that poor safety records and low employee morale destroy productivity. Moreover, safety is a difficult topic to crack as it involves mastering the Daily Management cycle (see Chapter 8) as well as human psychology. If you solve safety problems, you will be able to use the same discipline to solve other problems.
- **Shareholder POV (Cost, Finance):** if the business financial results are poor, it obviously cannot be sustained. This is not for the sake of making money, but to make the business sustainable for the benefit of all its stakeholders.

- **Community POV (Environment):** I believe that businesses must respect the communities that support them. I also believe that businesses that do not respect their communities will face challenging times with the rise of activism and social networks. So even if you do not believe in respecting communities, it might still make good business sense to do so.

Step 2.1 Start by Asking the Right Few Questions

A very limited set of questions helps to define the key issues that hamper stakeholder satisfaction. They must be answered with data rather than opinions to make an objective diagnostic. Ideally, express all Key Performance Indicators (KPIs) in terms of losses. Talking about a 5% quality loss is better than speaking of a 95% quality ratio, which does not sound too bad. Using losses also helps understanding better the scale of progress. Moving from 96% to 98% appears to be only a 2% improvement. Talking about reducing losses from 4% to 2% makes you understand that it is about removing half of the losses.

CONTROVERSY CORNER: FOCUSING ON COST REDUCTION CAN BE COUNTERPRODUCTIVE

The SQDCME sequence above is not random. Businesses need first to ensure Safety, then Quality, then Delivery, and then Cost. Unfortunately, many businesses focus on reducing cost when volumes drop. Uncontrolled cost reduction starts the spiral of doom, leading to employee disengagement and more problems, as illustrated by Figure 3.1. *On the contrary, if customers buy less, businesses need to improve product and service quality. These projects improve employee engagement. And cost of poor quality (CoPQ) is usually underestimated. I have worked with lines that reported a quality ratio of 97%. I myself naively considered that Quality was not a priority as 97% was good for the industry they were operating in, and we instead initially decided to focus on manning levels and cost reduction. I subsequently realized that the financial impact of the 3% quality losses was equivalent to half of the site's total salary cost.*

Hervé

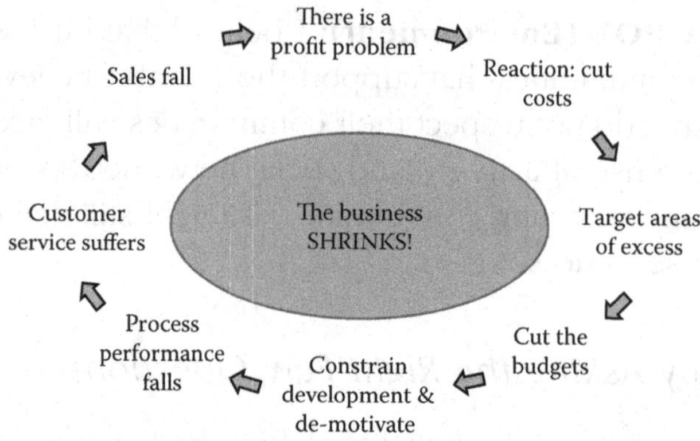

Figure 3.1 The spiral of cost-cutting doom.

> **FRASER SAYS: SQDC HIERARCHY MUST BE TAUGHT**
>
> *The hierarchy of Safety, Quality, Delivery, and Cost (SQDC), the first four elements of SQDCME, is sometimes implicit in organizations or more often is not even discussed openly. I believe it is something that should be explicitly taught to management as a tenet of any Operating System. We should then always try to avoid compromising a higher-level objective for a lower-level one.*

The KPIs described in Table 3.1 are quite commonly used in many industries. I will focus on Operational Equipment Effectiveness (OEE) as OEE is fundamental in a manufacturing environment. If OEE is available, this should be one of the first KPIs you will need to analyze. If OEE is not available, there are good chances that one of your first actions will be to put OEE calculation in place. For the other KPIs, please refer to Appendix 2 for more details on their significance and tips on how to calculate them.

A Focus on Operational Equipment Effectiveness

Operational Equipment Effectiveness (OEE) is a composite measure of how close a piece of equipment is to being problem-free. OEE is a percentage mathematically defined by the product of three elements (also expressed as percentages):

- **Quality ratio:** what percentage of parts produced is prime?
- **Availability ratio:** what percentage of time is the line running?
- **Speed ratio:** (also called Performance ratio) – at what percentage of maximum line speed is the line running when operated?

Table 3.1 Key diagnostic questions

Attribute	*Key diagnostic questions*	*KPIs typically required to answer the diagnostic question*	*Benchmark*
S	Do we provide a safe working environment?	Lost Time Injury Frequency (LTIF) All Known Injury Frequency (AKIF) Number of process safety incidents	National, industry, and/or trade association statistics
Q	Does the customer receive good quality products?	Complaints (incl. warrantee complaints)	How do current results compare with best year/quarter ever? Competitor data obtained from customers
	Do we easily manufacture good products?	Right First Time (RFT), non-prime, scrap, Q ratio in OEE	Unlikely to find relevant external benchmarks (could be a waste of time) How do current results compare with the best year/quarter ever?
D	Do we deliver when we said we will?	Delivery performance/ OTIF (% of orders delivered On Time In Full)	How do current results compare with the best year/quarter ever? Can competitor service performance data be obtained from customers? Are there indications in customer surveys?
	Do we deliver as fast as customers want?	Lead time by product	Competitors, other industries
	Is our value flow slick or is there much buffer?	Stocks (measured in days) – finished goods, intermediate products, and raw materials	Competitors
	How close are we from using maximum theoretical capacity?	Overall Equipment Effectiveness (OEE)	OEE from similar lines (usually internal benchmark) or best OEE ever on this line (e.g., best month, average of best 3 months in the last 12 months)

(*continued*)

Table 3.1 ***(Continued)*** **Key diagnostic questions**

Attribute	*Key diagnostic questions*	*KPIs typically required to answer the diagnostic question*	*Benchmark*
C	What are our key cost drivers?	Cost Pareto	Nearly impossible to obtain relevant external benchmarks
M	Are our employees engaged?	Attrition rate, employee survey results, vitality of suggestion scheme	Industry attrition rates, some external employee surveys will rank your company vs. other companies that they previously surveyed
E	Do we respect the community we live in?	Environmental compliance index, number of community complaints	

OEE is considered by many as the best single indicator to track line problems and target improvements to the overall value chain. Whilst developing OEE is the first piece of advice I give to manufacturing units that do not use it, I am on the other hand very careful when presented with OEE results. I have learnt over the years that OEE can be manipulated in many ways. The most common manipulations I have observed are the following:

- **Quality ratio:** Parts that are reworked are sometimes not considered in the quality losses as they will eventually be good parts. Yet Quality ratio should be measured as Right First Time.
- **Availability ratio:** Some of the idle time does not appear in the calculations (e.g., changeover time, stoppage for lack of orders, ramp-up and ramp-down periods). Yet the basis of Availability ratio should be planned production time (one might remove line stops for lack of order, weekends, and so on).
- **Speed ratio:** I have seen speed ratios higher than 100% because OEEs are calculated against conservative speed tables, or the process has improved but these tables have not been modified. I have even seen

plants where Human Resources management had blocked changes to the speed tables after improvements (leading to speed ratio higher than 100%) because this would have messed up the employee bonus calculations!

Check out the website www.OEE.com for a more in-depth explanation of the OEE concepts and how to use them to improve overall performance. However, please remember that being able to measure OEE does not mean that it will be 100% useful. Keep in mind the Theory of Constraints and the example quoted at the end of step 1 of the diagnosis process. If a piece of equipment is not a bottleneck, improving its OEE will not improve flow in the overall system. Make sure that you closely monitor the OEE of your bottleneck. Measuring the OEE of the rest will bring benefits but probably not of the same order.

CONTROVERSY CORNER: THE FALLACY OF OEE RATIO EQUALITY

OEE has become so popular that it would be blasphemy to criticize it. However, I would like to draw your attention to a perverse effect of OEE. Improving one of the three ratios by 1% mathematically improves OEE by the same amount. Quality, Availability, and Speed are therefore often worked on in parallel, and which one improves does not really matter from a KPI improvement point-of-view. But not all ratios are worth the same. Here are two illustrations:

1. *Improving speed or availability might simply make you stop the lines earlier for lack of orders. That might take out a bit of direct cost but the impact will only be significant if you can turn this freed capacity into productive hours, i.e., you were capacity-constrained and have taken new orders thanks to this improvement. On the other end, improving Quality immediately improves the bottom line.*
2. *Relative financial value of ratios depends highly on average contribution per unit and cost of rejection per unit. In the plant I ran, the average sales price was $1,000 per tonne. Direct costs were $850 per tonne. We were therefore generating $150 of contribution per tonne produced. But rejected material could only be sold at $400 per tonne. The opportunity cost of producing*

a ton of defective material was therefore $600 ($1,000–$400). This simplified calculation demonstrates that for every defective tonne we produced, we had to produce four additional tonnes simply to compensate the opportunity cost. Yet the OEE calculations consider that gaining 1% of quality ratio is equivalent to gaining 1% of speed or availability ratio. On the contrary, in a low-direct cost and high-contribution per unit industry, losing time costs more than producing defective material (as long as the defective material does not reach the final customer).

My recommendation is therefore: use OEE but make sure that you understand how it has been calculated and determine beforehand whether you should prioritize the Quality ratio.

Finally, crafty manufacturing managers focused on keeping their indicators green at any cost can make decisions that hamper the business. I have seen some improving OEE by reducing the number of changeovers (which means longer campaigns and therefore more stocks and poorer service) instead of working on reducing changeover time. I have seen others improving OEE by removing the most difficult products from the schedule (or even from the list of products offered) instead of solving the issues – which leads to poorer service and focus on basic products when the company strategy was to develop differentiated products.

Despite all these traps, it is vital to use OEE to drive progress. However, one must remain vigilant to ensure that business priorities are addressed and do not become victims of KPIs.

Hervé

Step 2.2 Getting Useful Answers

Repeat the same questions in Table 3.1 until you get useful answers. How do you know that the answer you got is going to help you establish the diagnostic? I personally use the LeTCI framework (introduced in Chapter 2 in the Malcolm Baldrige Excellence framework paragraph). I know that I have a satisfactory answer when I have been given the following four elements:

- **Level:** You need numerous answers to your questions. You are trying to deploy a (semi-) scientific approach. "Often" or "Hardly" is not a measure of a level. How could a doctor establish the right diagnostic if the blood pressure monitor displayed "a bit high"? Turning the numbers into a diagnostic that tells a story comes at a later stage.

- **Trend:** Company A has a profit margin of 6%, whereas company B's profit margin is only 5%. Which one has the biggest problem? Looking at the latest company dashboard will give you a good snapshot of this month's performance. However, you want to see the full film and not just a frame. Maybe A was making 10% 3 years ago while B was just breaking even. In most cases, you will need at least 3 years of data to get the full picture (exceptions include fast-changing industries).
- **Comparator:** What can I tell about a business that has a non-quality rate of 2%? Well, not much! The answer will differ quite a bit if the surveyed business is a steel company or a nuclear power plant. Obtaining benchmark data is useful (although not always possible), as performance is difficult to assess in isolation. Running 100 m in 11 s will not get you any medal in the Olympics. On the other hand, it is a very promising result if you are a 15-year-old. Table 3.1 illustrates typical benchmarks that can be obtained.
- **Integration:** I must be sure that I understood why this KPI is important to this business. You might not immediately get the right answer, so you will need to persevere until you obtain the right answer, or it becomes obvious that the business does not have a clear answer (in which case your recommendations should include reinforcing the KPI systems by using the LeTCI approach).
- **Example of useful answers:** "On-Time Delivery is currently 93.1%. It was 92.7% last year and 91.8% the year before. This compares favorably with our competition according to 78% of our customers."
- **Example of less useful answers:** "Our service is good. We deliver on time most of the time." "I think that customer defect rate is approximately 2%. It has been around 2% for quite some time. Sometimes we have good months and sometimes bad ones. Sales think that our quality is not as good as competitor's."

Step 3: Going to the Gemba

Now that you have a feel for what the company is trying to achieve and its overall performance, it is time to go to the Gemba, i.e., the place where the action really happens. For a manufacturing company, it is obviously the shop floor.

An experimented change agent will be able to "read" a plant fast. They will look at several things, sometimes almost unconsciously. In order to shorten that learning curve, the less experienced change agent can use a checklist. You can also build your own checklist. If you choose to do so, consider the following points:

- **Health, Safety, and Wellbeing:** How safe does this plant feel? Are pedestrians and vehicles segregated? Is the workplace clean? Is it unsightly? Are there strong odors? How ergonomic are the working areas? Is there enough light? Can you spot dangerous behaviors? Are there enough fire extinguishers? Are people smiling/happy? Does it feel like watching an ice-hockey game or a ballet performance?
- **Customer centricity:** Is the customer at the center of that plant's culture? Are customer requirements clear? Is there pride in doing a good job for customers? Does this look like a plant committed to quality? Is customer feedback known and visible (complaints, delivery performance, customer concerns)?
- **Visual Management:** Does the plant use visual management and visual factory? Are footpaths and safety exit routes clearly marked? Can I detect through visual management whether there is enough or too much stock of raw materials, WIP, finished products, tools, etc.? Can I see how the plant is performing just through visual management?
- **Layout:** How well is the space used? Is the flow logical?
- **Wastes:** Can you see wastes? Think about Toyota's 7 wastes: Do you see a lot of inventory? Are a lot of rejects visible? Can you see products or raw materials that are beyond the "best before" date?
- **Employee attitude:** What is the atmosphere like? Do workers look comfortable? Do they avoid you? Do they feel empowered? Do they have opportunities to contribute, e.g., through suggestions schemes?
- **Environment:** Does it look like this plant respects the environment and the local community? Can you see leaks? Fumes?
- **Performance management:** Are there clear targets? Can I see how the plant is doing vs. daily/weekly/monthly/year-to-date targets? Do operators know targets?

This rapid assessment on the shop floor will give you a feel for the reality behind the overall results identified in the second step.

CONTROVERSY CORNER: THE ONE-POINT CHECKLIST

If you want to save yourself the trouble of going through a long checklist, you only have to remember one question. The acid test is "would you buy from this plant?"

Asking yourself this question will force you to mentally assess a lot of the dimensions mentioned above. Am I comfortable with their health, safety, environmental, and social practices? Will they care for me as a customer? Is this plant competitive, or is it wasteful?

An alternative acid test is "would I be proud of giving a tour of the plant I am assessing?" During a plant visit in Japan, a local Manager told me "my best salesman is my plant." Ask yourself if that plant would be a good salesman.

Hervé

Step 4: Drilling Down: Complementary Diagnostic

Depending on initial answers and first test results, a doctor would then request additional tests to refine a diagnosis. Similarly, you will want to carry out complementary diagnostics on the most important attributes. For each main attribute identified as a problem area in the first stage of the diagnostic, it will be necessary to carry out a complementary diagnostic. Tools exist for each of the SQDCME attributes. They are listed in Table 3.2.

These complementary diagnostic tools are based on three types of analysis.

1. Systems maturity assessment to understand the harder side of how the organization works. These assessments are common in large organizations and are usually provided by a central expert team.
2. Cultural maturity assessment to understand the softer side of your organization. These are less common than systems maturity assessments, but they are as important, if not more. Businesses might have perfect sets of standards, procedures, and processes and yet will not deliver if the culture is not right.
3. Pareto analysis applied to losses to identify priority topics. Pareto analysis will highlight specific "technical" issues (such as quality issues, safety problems, or environmental weaknesses). This is useful to decide where to direct our efforts. But a solution can only be sustained if the systems and culture are right, so diagnostic should not only be limited to Pareto analysis.

Table 3.2 Complementary diagnostics supporting the SQDCME attributes

Attribute	*Complementary diagnostic*	*Objectives of the complementary diagnostic*
S	Injury analysis Organization Safety maturity (Bradley curve) Safety Systems maturity	To find out what are the main safety issues and how is the safety culture overall
Q	Organization Quality Maturity (Bradley curve) Quality systems maturity Quality losses Pareto analysis	To find out what are the main quality issues and how is the quality culture overall
D	OTIF losses Pareto analysis OEE losses analysis	To find out what causes missed deliveries To find out what causes volume losses
C	Losses Pareto analysis	To find out which cost categories overrun most
M	Segmentation of employee survey/attrition rate to pinpoint key problems	To pinpoint key problems/disengaged employee segments
E	Environmental incident Pareto analysis	To pinpoint environmental risks

Re-arranging the main complementary diagnostics by type, we obtain Table 3.3.

Each of the three types of approach (cultural maturity assessment, systems maturity assessment, and Pareto analysis) will provide you with some indication of the problems that the organization is facing. In fact, the three approaches complement each other very well, especially for safety and quality. Let us review all three in more detail to understand what their benefits and limitations are.

Assessing Cultural Maturity via the Bradley Curve

The Bradley curve is an especially useful way to assess cultural maturity of an organization. It was originally developed by Dupont in the 1990s to assess safety cultural maturity. The main assumption behind the Bradley curve is that organizations go through four levels of cultural maturity as they progress (reactive, dependent, independent, and interdependent). The model assumes a positive correlation between safety maturity and safety results. In other words, the Bradley curve encourages an

Table 3.3 Complementary lower-level analysis

	Cultural maturity assessment	*Systems maturity assessment*	*Data/Pareto analysis*
S	Bradley curve	Safety systems maturity assessment)	Pareto of injuries
Q	Bradley curve adapted to Quality	Quality systems maturity assessment	Pareto of customer complaints, of internal Quality issues
D			Pareto of volume losses, of late deliveries
C			Pareto of cost categories Pareto of cost overruns
M			Attrition rate by employee segment
E		Environmental systems maturity assessment	Pareto of environmental incidents

organization to work on safety culture to improve safety results rather than just on technical measures.

Several tools and techniques exist to move from one level to the next. It is impossible to go straight from reactive to interdependent. The organization must gradually learn and evolve. Table 3.4 lists for each level what is the organizational and individual behavior at that stage, but also what to focus on to progress to the next level.

Of course, like all models, the Bradley curve has limitations. The main issues to be aware of are the following:

- In reality, you will probably find that your organization displays characteristics from several different maturity stages at the same time. This phenomenon is common because some individuals or areas will be more mature than others. Models are always a simplification of more complex phenomena. To define which stage you are currently at, you will have to look at the distribution and select the dominant stage. For example, 20% reactive/60% dependent/20% independent would put your organization in the "dependent" maturity stage. Most of the actions you will need to take will be linked to that stage, but do not forget to tackle the "dependent" symptoms as they will hold your organization back.

Table 3.4 Bradley curve and the behaviors associated with maturity levels

Item	*Reactive*	*Dependent*	*Independent*	*Interdependent*
Who owns safety?	Little management commitment Safety is delegated to Safety Manager	Management is committed	Individuals feel responsible for their own safety	Other's keeper
Motivation	Hardly any motivation for safety	Supervision (fear/ discipline)	Personal value	Care for others Organizational pride
Key tools	No specific tool used	Training, rules, procedures	Near miss reporting	Everyone uses all key tools
Typical symptoms of a maturity level	Numerous accidents Management not enforcing rules	Management is enforcing use of personal protective equipment (PPE) through discipline	Employees wear PPE because they want to. They report near misses affecting them	All employees proactively report all near misses

- Whilst there is definitely an empirical relationship between safety maturity culture and injury rates, do not expect linear performance improvement as you progress along the maturity curve. The curve is based on statistical effects. I have seen sites operating for six consecutive months without an injury, only to face five injuries in the following six months. Whilst the harm-free six months might have been very lucky, the five injuries were equally statistically unlikely. As culture and maturity had not changed overnight, one would have to conclude that high safety maturity increases our chances of harm-free periods but does not make it certain.
- It will not give you a list of things that you can quickly fix (the Pareto analysis is more useful in that case). Instead, it will help you to develop a roadmap for culture change.

CONTROVERSY CORNER: BEWARE OF TARGETS

As focus increases on Lost Time Injuries (LTI), companies tend to do whatever they can to ensure that employees will come back to work, e.g., they will send them a taxi if they cannot walk after the accident and will temporarily offer them a desk-based task. Or they do their best to persuade their employees not to take the injury time they are entitled to. So a decrease in LTI frequency might not necessarily mean a less dangerous workplace. KPI manipulation might be detected by looking in parallel at LTI frequency and Recordable Accident Frequency (RecF). If both decrease in parallel, you can trust that the situation is improving. If LTI frequency improves but RecF does not, it simply means that the company is getting better at managing injured people.

Hervé

Applying the Bradley Curve to Quality

Whilst the Bradley curve was developed and is still primarily used around safety, it can easily be transposed into other areas, in particular around quality (see Figure 3.2). The four stages of quality culture maturity are:

1. **Reactive:** The organization has little care for quality.
2. **Dependent:** The organization has an objective to drive quality, but this

is mostly through control. Hearts and minds are not convinced yet. Employees adapt their behavior when management is checking.

3. **Independent:** Employees individually understand why they need to generate a quality output and try to achieve this outcome, even when management is not looking.
4. **Interdependent:** Employees care for quality, not only for the part that they can control, but are actively involved in helping their colleagues to deliver a quality output.

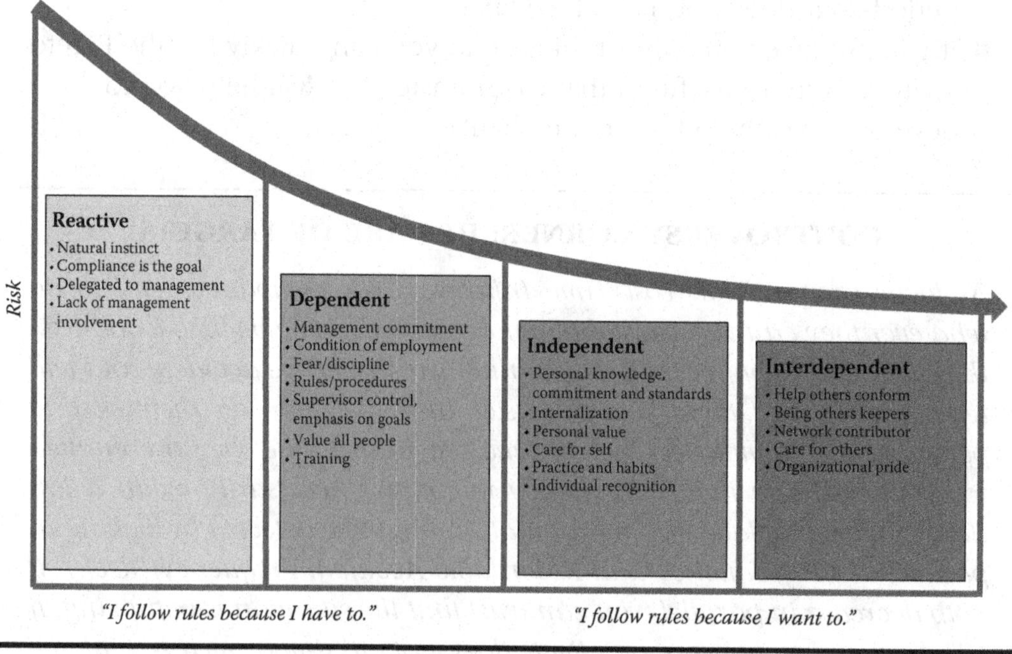

Figure 3.2 The Bradley curve adapted to quality by the author.

Just like for safety, working on the organizational quality culture will help improve quality results (in parallel to the more "technical" specific problem-solving).

Systems Maturity Assessments

Systems maturity assessment is the tool used to determine whether the right approaches and procedures are in place and to what extent they are deployed. They are typically carried out by spending 1–3 days in the location, checking how the operation is doing against a standard assessment questionnaire. In large companies, the assessment questionnaire is usually created by the central function that owns the attribute (e.g., safety or quality) being assessed.

The outcome of systems maturity assessments is usually a list of strengths and opportunities for improvement (OFI), combined with an overall maturity score (used to benchmark with other units of the group). On a practical note, do not underestimate the importance of providing feedback on strengths. Whilst OFIs seem to be more valuable and are usually the focus of most assessors, highlighting strengths is a necessary form of recognition that makes the subsequent discussion on OFIs easier. I once assessed a plant's business systems a week after another team had assessed process safety systems. Even though the plant had a reasonable process safety maturity, their feedback had consisted in 7 strengths and 52 OFIs, which had completely turned off the whole management team. Although the assessors had tried to provide a comprehensive list of opportunities to choose from, the way feedback was given was completely counterproductive. When our team gave its feedback on business systems, consisting of 50% strengths and 50% opportunities, the management team relaxed and engaged in a constructive discussion on how to close the gaps.

Using the Pareto Principle to Select Problems

In essence, the Pareto principle states that 80% of effects are produced by 20% of causes. A corollary is that most losses can be removed by focusing on a limited number of projects targeting the minority of causes.

It is difficult to compare quality, delivery, and costs factors. However, it is possible to rank issues within each of these categories using this principle. If you want to diagnose quality issues, what are the top three quality problems faced by customers? And the top three causes of internal rejection?

Most readers are of course familiar with this tool. However, building a good Pareto analysis might be trickier than you think. The most common pitfalls are the following.

Symptoms, Not Causes

The analysis is often made of symptoms rather than causes (or sometimes the Pareto is a mix of symptoms and causes). This makes it more difficult to select the right problems. For example, you would often hear on the news that the top three causes of death in Europe are cancer, heart diseases, and car accidents. Whilst these are indeed technically causes of death, these are often just consequences of other issues. A better Pareto analysis would be to rank the number of casualties by causes (e.g., alcohol, tobacco, and obesity), although this would be more difficult to do. In a factory scenario, a quality defect Pareto might mention line stop and overcuring in the oven as two bars on the Pareto chart. However, several overcuring defects have been caused by a line stop that caused the product to remain in the oven for too long. Overcuring is a symptom; line stop is a cause of poor quality.

How You Choose to Group Categories

Choice of grouping will alter interpretation of the Pareto. A line stop might be the bigger bar in a Pareto of defect causes. So, it is tempting to focus on line stops. But the same data could also yield to a different Pareto if one counts electrical line stops and mechanical line stops as separate causes of defects. These might then become only the 3rd and 4th bars in the new Pareto chart and are not related. There is no hard rule on how to group, but one must be aware of the phenomenon. In some rare cases, groupings can even be consciously manipulated to lead toward pre-decided conclusions.

EXAMPLE: A FACTORY THAT HAS SIGNIFICANT OPERATOR BEHAVIOR PROBLEMS

A factory that has significant operator behavior problems (causing 70% of defects). The rest of the problems are caused by maintenance (20%) and supplier quality (10%). The same data set could generate two quite different Paretos and therefore two vastly different conclusions:

If the line manager is honest, they would conclude that "Our main problem is operator behavior. Until we fix this, we will not be able to make a step change in quality."

If the line manager wants to deflect blame, they can simply split the behavioral issues into smaller issues (e.g., quality in section 1, section 2, section 3, etc.). The interpretation of the Pareto analysis would then become: "Our main problems are clearly maintenance and supplier quality. Look, they are number one and number two in our

Pareto. Then there is a long tail of small problems (3 to 5% of the total each) that we will take care of once maintenance and supply do their job correctly.

Hervé

The 4W questions derived from Kipling's six honest friends (more on this in Chapter 6) can be used to refine our diagnosis and select a problem to work on. Let us illustrate in Table 3.5 the approach by applying it to a Pareto analysis of safety data. These questions will help us disaggregate the data to help pinpoint discrete causes that can be worked on as a well-defined project.

FRASER SAYS: WHO IS WORKING ON THE TAIL?

Rother makes a great point in his book on Toyota Kata (Rother, Toyota Kata, 2010) *regarding the obsession with only going after the big ticket items in the Pareto analysis. He says we should not ignore the tail of smaller magnitude categories as these may, over time, be accumulating a large proportion of the defects, and they may be fairly easy to fix as part of a shop floor CI program.*

Table 3.5 The 4W questions applied to managing safety

4W question	*Application for diagnosis*
What?	What is the pareto by type of injury (e.g., slip/falls, man/machine interface, etc.)
Where?	In which area/department? Which body regions are injured the most? E.g., 68% of all injuries are hand injuries.
When?	Seasonality, more injuries during night shift?
Who?	Which part of the population is affected the most? Our own workforce, temporary workers, or contractors?

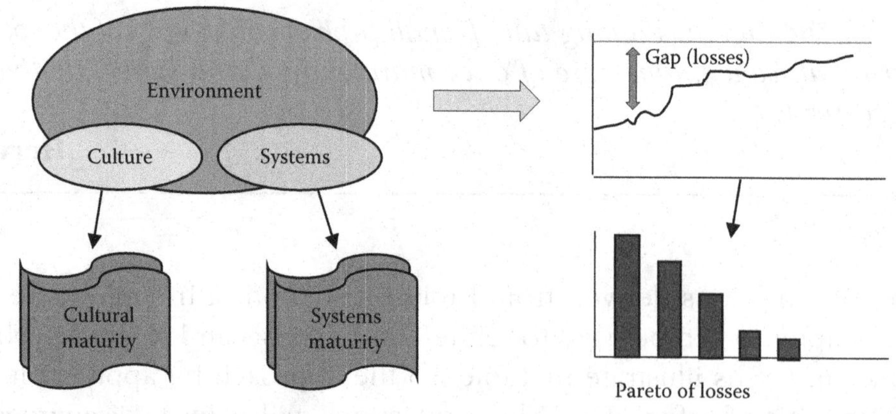

Figure 3.3 How losses (or opportunities) arise from diagnostic of culture and systems aspects.

Output of a Good Diagnostic

Now that you have completed the initial diagnostic and the relevant complementary diagnostics, you will have built a mental picture of the organization you want to improve. In particular, you will have understood the three key elements that drive results: its environment, its cultural maturity, and its system maturity. You will also have gathered data on the key business results, the gap between these results and 100% (aka operational losses), and a Pareto analysis for each gap (Figure 3.3).

The Softer Side of Diagnostic: The Art of Questioning and Storytelling

From what you have read so far in this chapter, you might think that carrying out a diagnostic is quite mechanical. It is true to a certain extent. I developed this approach with the hope that my colleagues with less experience could use this tool to carry out a diagnostic themselves, which would allow me to travel less and multiply our team's impact.

Initially, it did not work. Colleagues were reluctant to use it as it was new. The more progressive ones tried but something was missing from their diagnostic. I then realized that I had provided them with the SQDCME framework but not with the key diagnostic questions. I had not bothered to write the questions because they were obvious to me. In fact, I had forgotten the number of assessments it had taken me to capture and establish these questions as a standard in my mind.

I also realized that providing people with a tool that looks like a grid or a questionnaire naturally leads them to believe that they will get the right answers every time if they ask the same questions.

Unfortunately (or fortunately?), humans are complex. The same question asked to two different people will normally get you two different answers. The softer side of diagnostic is all about understanding at which point you know enough to fill the box in the diagnostic grid. You might have to ask the same question several different ways.

The other point that makes diagnostic not so mechanical is that it can only be established by spending time on the shop floor to get a feel for the culture and confirmation of the story told by your data. If data do not match what you observe, it means that the way the KPIs are measured in this business hides the problem. A 99% quality ratio might hide 7% of rework. A superb safety KPI in a place that looks dangerous might simply mean not all injuries are reported.

But soft skills are not only required to carry out the diagnostic. They are also vital to share the results in a way that will be useful to the assessed organization. The best diagnostic in the world will not improve anything if the decision makers are not engaged and convinced. This is why I strongly advise sharing the diagnostic, and if possible, creating it with key stakeholders such as management teams or cross-functional teams.

Finally, storytelling is an important soft skill. A good diagnostic tells a story. The numbers are used to help you understand the situation and defend your story if challenged, but the numbers are not the story. Telling a good story sells the diagnostic and helps build a consensus on key gaps and priorities. This will be easier and more effective if you focus on the principal issues. Doctors will spend little time prescribing medicine for acne if the patient has at the same time a potentially lethal condition. So why do we jump on the first visible problem? Is your company wasting resources rearranging chairs on the deck of the Titanic rather than launching the lifeboats?

The Role of Leaders in Selecting the Right Problems

What should you do if you are the leader who commissioned the diagnostic? First, you should personally take part in the diagnostic. This will ensure that it is taken seriously, but you will also learn about your business more than by simply being presented with the results.

You should then accept feedback from the diagnostic even (especially) when it hurts. Once you understand and accept the diagnostic, share diagnostic results with your teams and determine how you are going to act on it. Make detailed plans to address the biggest opportunities.

Another key responsibility of leaders is to ensure that your business has the right type of KPIs, so that we focus on the real problems, not just for the diagnostic but also during regular business reviews. If a KPI is not available to answer a diagnostic question, leaders should ensure that it starts to be used in the business. In particular, the following are often missed:

- **Cost of Poor Quality:** CoPQ is invisible in profit and loss accounts (P&L). No one can tell from the P&L whether the company is operationally excellent. Yet CoPQ significantly impacts the bottom line.
- **Contribution to Fixed Cost by Unit of Constrained Attribute:** Is your output limited by machine time? Workforce capacity? Raw materials availability? Whatever the constraint, the key financial indicators should be expressed by unit of constrained attribution e.g., contribution per hour, per man hour or per output unit.

Most of our readers are continuous improvement professionals who are more focused on quality, delivery, and cost than safety, morale, or environment, so this is what we will focus on in the next chapters (even though safety or HR professionals can apply the same CI approach).

CONTROVERSY CORNER: LEAN COUNTERS NOT BEAN COUNTERS

Unfortunately, traditional absorption-based accounting makes it exceedingly difficult to deploy a Lean approach for a number of reasons. Let us illustrate this statement with two important examples:

Traditional accounting leads Management to look at every cost center and individually drive these costs down without understanding links between them. For example, maintenance is seen as a cost, even though reduction of the maintenance budget can often lead to more *breakdowns. Empirical data gathered in one of our plants showed that, past a certain point, every dollar removed from the maintenance budget led to a three-dollar loss because of additional breakdowns. Equally, a Manager who recruits an additional quality engineer would be congratulated for doing $200K better than budget for material consumption. In the same business review, it is likely that he will be subsequently told off because his employment costs went $60K above budget (because of said recruitment).*

Traditional accounting favors push production as production (even of unnecessary additional finished products) absorbs fixed costs. So a factory will tend to keep on producing, consuming cash, even if demand is not there as it (virtually) improves the monthly financial results. Traditional accounting would not recognize that this approach led to spending money on bigger warehouses. A pull-based Lean plant will stop production when demand is not there, thereby avoiding costs from wastes such as excess inventory or obsolescence.

Hervé

We now have a diagnostic, so we know what to work on. You will find in Case Study 4 an example of a completed diagnostic. Even more importantly, the diagnostic phase should have built a consensus on what to work on. So in the next two chapters, we will concentrate on how we can begin to improve these important KPIs.

Summary

It is tempting to start immediately to begin improvement efforts, but the risk is a suboptimal use of resources. You might fall into the trap of pet projects. Therefore, improvements should start with a diagnostic. A good diagnostic is data-based and consists of the following steps:

1. Understand context (i.e., business and operations) by gathering information on the business and carrying out a Value Stream Mapping exercise (ideally combined with Theory of Constraints) on the operations.

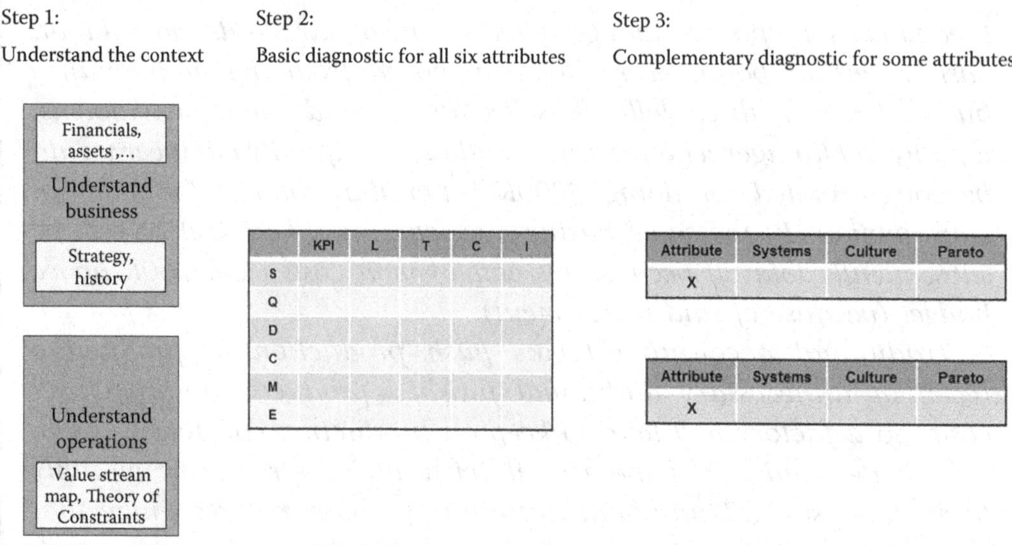

Figure 3.4 Summary of diagnostic approach.

2. Operations can then be diagnosed, ideally using the SFVA (SQDCME/LeTCI) framework. Some operational attributes can be diagnosed in more detail with systems maturity assessments, culture maturity assessments, and pareto analysis.

The outcome of a good diagnostic is a clear understanding of the key problems in the areas selected (SQDCME) backed by indisputable facts. The diagnostic should tell a story. Whilst diagnostic follows a standard approach, it is not mechanical. Spend time on the shop floor to get a feel for local culture and confirmation of the story told by your data. Diagnostic needs to be shared with, and if possible, created with key stakeholders to engage them in the learning process.

Figure 3.4 summarizes this process.

Unfortunately, we do not always have the luxury of having enough time to do a full diagnostic. The next chapter will help us to cope with these situations.

Get started on your Chapter 3 learnings – practicing the diagnostic approach

I. *Collecting facts*
   a. *What are the existing, relevant KPIs?*
   b. *What are the missing KPIs?*
   c. *How can I get data to replace the missing KPIs?*

II. *Analyzing the facts*
   a. *Based on the KPIs and new data, what strengths do I see?*
   b. *Based on the KPIs and new data, what opportunities for improvement do I see?*
III. *Presenting my findings*
   a. *Who am I going to present my findings to and in what format?*
   b. *What did I learn from presenting the findings?*
   c. *What would I do differently next time?*

Chapter 4

Regaining Control of an Emerging Situation (and How to Prevent Emerging Situations)

Fraser Wilkinson

> So what do we do? Anything. Something. So long as we just don't sit there. If we screw it up, start over. Try something else. If we wait until we've satisfied all the uncertainties, it may be too late.
>
> **Lee Iacocca**

Introduction

In Chapter 3, Hervé took us through a structured method to help in selecting a balanced set of measures to be improved. This approach should always be used at the outset of a change or as a regular activity for a business, department, or function. It should be a feed into the annual planning process and target setting. However, as we are aware, most of us are operating in environments where unexpected situations can emerge at any time. Once stable situations can rapidly deteriorate due to single or multiple stressors. A weekend call from the office or shop floor might require our immediate attention despite the best efforts to devolve responsibility down the chain of command. It may be we are blindsided first thing on a bright and breezy

DOI: 10.4324/9781003486022-4

Monday morning. So how do you react to these situations? What mental algorithm comes into play? If you are struggling with an answer, then we would like to offer some effective strategies to help gain control and manage those things within your sphere of control and influence, and how to think about those things beyond your control and influence.

So, this chapter provides guidance on how to approach situations that arise unexpectedly and require immediate responses. It gives a structured way of identifying, separating, and clarifying issues that can be worked on as distinct items following standard approaches, whilst keeping the overall situation in mind.

After experiencing emerging situations and working our way through them we may well get to thinking about whether we could or should have anticipated that situation and made contingency plans in advance. And as a further step, we also look at the idea of creating a more resilient organization and what that may look like.

What Is an Emerging Situation?

For the purpose of this discussion, we should clarify an "emerging situation" as being, at least initially, a negative situation that we have not been confronted with previously or is sufficiently different from a previous situation that we can't simply reenact the same routines. I say the situation is initially negative because, first we tend to see problems as negative, and second, because we rarely think to look for what we can positively leverage from the negative.

Emerging situations are not simply a new problem to tackle. They are those situations that are multifaceted in nature, cut across many parts of an organization, and will require many different approaches to resolve. From a full-blown crisis to an unexpected Monday morning challenge, we can all be faced with this journey into the unknown. Things appear to be out of control or soon will be without a quick intervention. When we don't have the luxury of time to plan and conduct an in-depth diagnostic, we will need to have a structured response at hand.

The Role of the Change Agent

We promote a rational thinking approach to every situation that confronts a change agent, no matter if you work at the boardroom or the engine room.

People will look to the Excellence community in times of stress as a facilitator or support. Many managers and leaders don't have a "go to" formula but will feel the need to take action to be seen to do something. A change agent may have little influence over the approach but can still guide the thinking through careful and sensitive questioning of the premises on which actions are being taken.

Being thrown in at the deep end is often the lot of a change agent, either because you have demonstrated good thinking previously, or maybe to lay down a challenge to the "know-it-all" who always thinks we should be doing things in a better way. These kinds of tests are something a change agent must be able to deal with, for the credibility of the overall Excellence initiative and for the personal credibility you so desperately need to elevate. There is no substitute for this kind of intense, on-the-job learning experience, so don't shy away from them but pre-arm yourself with the kind of routines I'll describe here. If you can observe someone doing this in a real-life situation, all the better. Classroom exercises can only take you so far.

How to Make a Rapid Assessment of the Situation

What is concerning us? Can we break down and clarify these concerns? How urgent or important are they? Can we prioritize these concerns? What standard approaches should we use to analyze and regain control of these concerns?

As with much of operational management, this activity is about risk management above all else. As managers and leaders, we must be able to weigh the risk/reward outcomes in a situation where unknowns are a given. It is a largely subjective exercise and therefore needs input from many diverse opinion and fact holders. Idealism (gather ALL the facts) often has to give way to subjective realism and a consensus view in order to move forward quickly. As with all tools and techniques, they are only as good as the inputs to them, and that means working with a team of stakeholders and knowledge holders as well as some independent voices for balance and perspective. In other words, you need those awkward individuals you may naturally shy away from inviting to these sessions.

This technique can also be applied at any time as the starting point in assessing a situation and is not confined to "rapid" response situations. The basic steps are as follows:

1. List threats and opportunities
   a. What deviations are occurring?

   b. What decisions need to be made?
   c. What plans should be implemented?
   d. What changes are anticipated?
   e. What opportunities exist?
   f. What bothers us about … ?
2. For each of the above separate and clarify concerns
   a. What do we mean by … ?
   b. What exactly is … ?
   c. What else concerns us about … ?
   d. What evidence do we have … ?
   e. What different deviations, decisions, or plans are part of this concern?
3. Consider seriousness, urgency, and growth of the concerns if left unattended (High/Med/Low) and create a priority for attention.
   a. Seriousness – What is the current impact on people, process, and business continuity? Which concern is most serious?
   b. Urgency – What deadlines do we have? When do we need to start? Which concern will be hardest to resolve later?
   c. Growth – What will be the future impact if we do nothing? Which concerns are expanding quickly?
4. Determine the correct method, tool, or technique to apply for each concern. By this stage, you should have a well-developed methodology to apply to each of the following situations:
   a. Problem-solving
   b. Decision analysis
   c. Diagnostics (in-depth analysis, e.g., Value Stream Mapping, Theory of Constraints, Advanced Analytics, Surveys)
   d. Behavioral analysis
   e. Risk assessment
   f. Protect a plan
   g. Idea generation
   h. Resource/skills
5. Determine help needed
6. Allocate actions ownership and deadlines

You can create a simple Excel form to capture this information and to act as a management tool. This is most useful to feedback to a senior team, board of directors, or other group who will be demanding that someone regain control of a situation (Table 4.1).

Table 4.1 Situation appraisal matrix summary

List threats and opportunities	*Separate and clarify concerns*	*Consider current impact, future impact, and time frame*			*Prioritize*	*Determine analysis needed*	*Tool to apply*
What deviations are occurring?	What do we mean by … ?	What is the current impact on people, safety, etc.?	What is the deadline?	What will be the future impact?	High/ medium/low	Is there a deviation? Is cause unknown? Do we need to know cause to take meaningful action?	Problem-solving Diagnostics (in depth analysis e.g., Value Stream Mapping, Theory of Constraints, Advanced Analytics, Surveys) Behavioral analysis Risk assessment Idea generation resource/skills
What decisions need to be made?	What exactly is … ?	Which concern is most serious?	When do we need to start?	Which concern is getting worse quicker?	High/ medium/low	Do we need to make a choice?	Decision Making
What plans should be implemented?	What else concerns us about … ?		Which concern will be hardest to resolve later?		High/ medium/low	Do we have an action or plan to protect (enhance)?	Protect a plan

I have used this method in many situations and it's a great one because it is so universal in application. At the start of an assignment that you are unfamiliar with, it demonstrates a level of control and assurance that all bases have been considered and covered in a logical manner. It brings a sense of order to what can be a fraught time in a leader's work life. As a change agent, anything you can do to help a leader with a difficult situation will improve your credibility. As with all these techniques, however, being sympathetic to the situation and personalities involved is half the battle. That's why you should practice it a few times in a less time-bound and stressful setting. The aim with all these methods we cover in this book is to make them your well-worn routines, and that will permit you to make allowances in the emphasis you put on certain aspects. Knowing the end point will allow you to subtly modify your approach without straying too far from the method. That's what I found as my experience grew. I was more able to see what end point we needed to get to and was thus able to direct the emphasis in certain directions. This is the science and the art of the change agent in a nutshell.

How Do We Become More than Just Resilient?

If we can describe resilience as the ability to withstand or recover quickly from difficulties, then we need to ask if this is enough for organizations to survive in the long run. Resilient organizations may be able to recover their previous status quo position, but what if there were a way to come back even stronger from difficulties. This is the essence of what Nassim Taleb (2013) expounds on in *Antifragile – things that Gain from Disorder*. Taleb brings his experiences from business and trading into the wider world of work and life in a somewhat dense and technical account of dealing successfully with problems of luck, uncertainty, and probability.

In Figure 4.1, we see how the concept of antifragility can be illustrated. What we see is that organizations that are fragile can experience unlimited losses due to unfavorable volatility in all or any aspect of their business. They are unable to fully exploit even the most favorable volatility whilst suffering extreme losses from the least favorable. Robust organizations don't suffer extreme losses, but neither are they able to exploit the most favorable to the maximum. Antifragile organizations are able to minimize downside risk and maximize upside rewards.

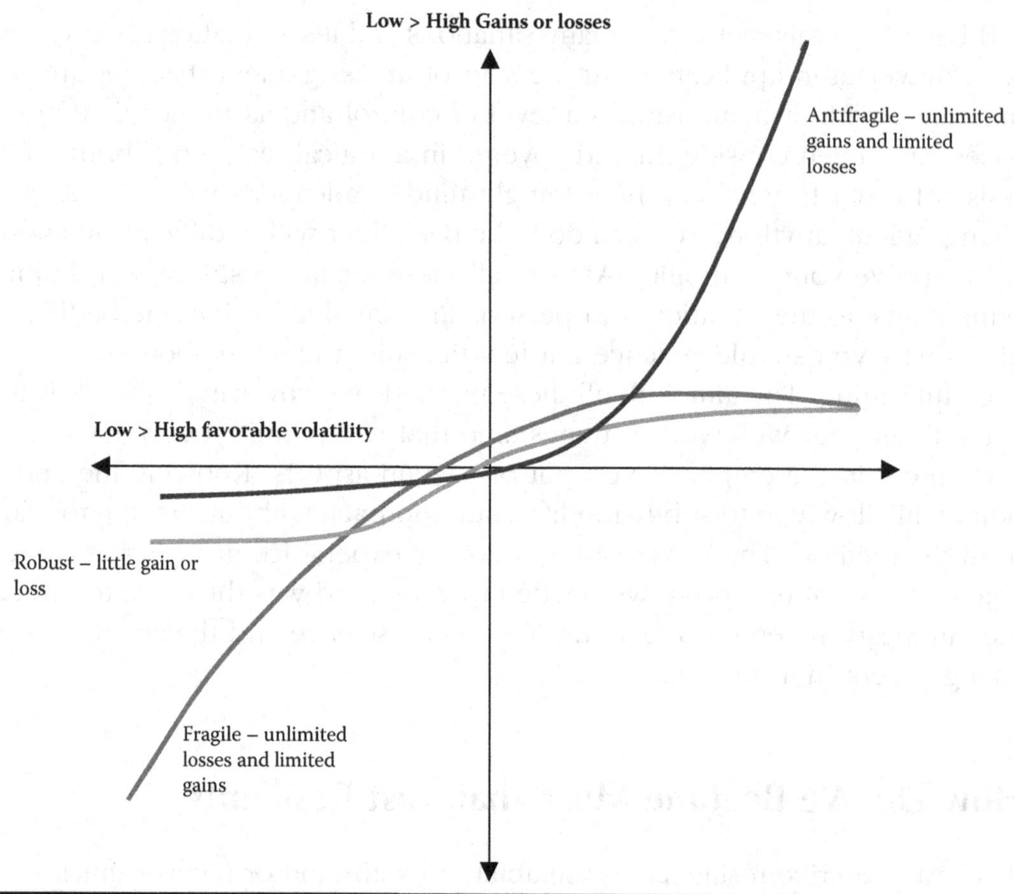

Figure 4.1 The three dimensions of antifragility.

HERVÉ SAYS: LEARNING ORGANIZATIONS BUILD RESILIENCE

Coming back stronger from adversity is the hallmark of a learning organization. Too often we hear of organizations that fail to learn the lessons of history. NASA lost the Space Shuttle Challenger in 1986 mainly due to a culture that failed to act on warnings from senior engineers and a system that incorrectly estimated the risk of failures. Even after that tragic event was investigated and recommendations made, 17 years later Space Shuttle Columbia was lost on reentry. Once again, tragedy could be traced back to a failure of the risk management system.

In contrast, the US Navy nuclear submarine program has an admirable safety record following a change in safety culture instigated by Admiral Rickover. The US Navy has since accumulated over 6200 reactor-years of accident-free experience involving 526 nuclear reactor cores over the course of 240 million kilometers, without a single radiological incident, over a period of more than 50 years. This impressive record resulted in the Navy/NASA Benchmarking Exchange in 2003.

How did the US Navy nuclear program achieve those results? Admiral Rickover was fanatical about people, systems, process, and learning from all sources. Process deviations, even if not resulting in actual deviations, were captured, investigated, and the learnings instigated (Spear, 2009).

Hervé

On a personal note, there are many examples of how we can apply the principles of resilience. In our personal health care, we may look at a medication in light of what the risk-reward may be. If a medication or a supplement is very low risk but with potential huge upside, then we may choose to take it and be happy with any results even if the positive effects are not proven in clinical trials but rather through anecdotal sources only. In the same way, we may think of investing small amounts of capital in high-risk ventures. We have a known and limited downside and a potentially huge upside. Think of early years of Bitcoin and buying them at $1 each. We may place stop-loss limits on stock price volatility so we have a known maximum downside. We should all be asking ourselves what is the worst-of-the-worst situation we could reasonable be in, particularly when we have to make a critical decision. Leaving a safe job, moving house, moving country, and having children all come with a risk-reward profile. But antifragility is more than just resilience as we shall see.

Think of antifragility as a means by which an organization, or indeed an individual, stacks the odds in favor of coming back from a difficulty on a much better, stronger footing than previously. Some of this resilience is seen in nature. Bones grow back stronger after a break, the immune system adapts to threats, and evolution selects the individuals most able to adapt to a volatile environment, not necessarily the fittest or strongest. Humans are the pinnacle of nature's ability to create an adapting organism which as a whole is the most "successful" animal yet seen on earth. As a species, we can be said to be antifragile.

AI and machine learning algorithms benefit from stressors in a way that, over time, means they get fitter and stronger in their chosen specialties to the point where they are more reliable than a human equivalent. Examples abound of AI being utilized in medical diagnostics, stock picking, dating, and geopolitics, to name only a few of the more well-known applications.

So how do organizations capitalize on the concept of antifragility? I am indebted to Dr. Alan Barnard (of The Goldratt Institute) for this advice as my opportunities to apply this model have been limited. Dr. Barnard points out that the crux of everyday antifragility relies on fast and accurate decision making in the face of emerging situations and major organizational strategy changes.

Decision-making analysis can help narrow down options, but we should always consider the risks associated with any chosen option. Using a matrix as shown in Table 4.2 allows decision makers to explore the risk-reward profile for a number of chosen business factors. We are generally proficient in estimating these dimensions of worst and best cases. We can also use this table for scenario planning for upturns and downturns in the market or other external influences. For example, can we add premiums when we have low stock, high demand, and little competition or premiums on faster delivery times. Airline ticket policies are a great example of this type of thinking where dynamic pricing algorithms are designed to maximize revenue.

Table 4.2 Decision risk analysis to exploit antifragility

*State decision option selected:*__________			
	Potential outcomes		
	Worst-of-the-worst	*Likely*	*Best-of-the-best*
Sales			
Variable cost			
Throughput			
Operating expense			
Net profit			
Investment			
R.O.I.			
Productivity			

Building Resilience: What to Do in Advance to Minimize the Number of Crises

There are more traditional routes to building resilience, the most common being risk management process based on risk evaluation and anticipation. Developing and deploying a structured risk management process brings at least three types of benefits:

1. By insisting on prevention, you should naturally be able to reduce the number of crises.
2. Not all crises can be prevented. However, you will be able to reduce the impact of crises (by limiting their duration and/or magnitude). Prior planning will ensure we have some predetermined and well-practiced responses. The quality and thoroughness of these measures are likely to be better than when they are developed while under pressure.
3. A less obvious yet important benefit is the development of teams and people involved in the process. Going through the phases of the risk management process will create a common understanding of the processes we are trying to protect as well as of the wider picture.

So how do we do that? At a micro-level, the Daily Management approach is a form of risk management. The FMEA tool is a risk analysis tool. The OCAPs (Out of Control Action Plans) are predetermined responses to emerging issues. More on that in Chapter 8.

At a macro-level, a risk management process should be developed and sustained:

1. Creating the Risk Register

Start with a brainstorm at Management Team level. What risks can we list? Start with a free discussion but have a prompt list ready to ensure that you have covered all main areas. An example is given later.

Once you have created a list of risks, assign an owner to each risk and ask each owner to score each risk in terms of likelihood and impact. To reduce the subjectivity of these discussions, you should have prepared in advance tables describing what the different likelihood levels and impact scores correspond to. In order to do that, owners should develop a common template scenario(s) leading to this risk, examine existing mitigation measures, and suggest new ones.

You can then represent your risk profile in a matrix by plotting each risk against these two dimensions. The team can then collectively review the scores and look for anomalies. This might lead to the reassessment of some scores.

The risk matrix and the individual risk sheets will collectively form your risk register.

If this information is not too confidential, it is worth communicating the risk profile within your organization to increase engagement and alignment with existing action plans.

On top of that, the organization should develop a Business Continuity Plan (BCP) that lists measures to take to ensure continuity of activities if a business is hit by disaster. BCPs list for example names and contact details of the crisis team, possible remote locations to work from, and so on.

Each individual risk sheets will include a risk mitigation plan. This should not be a separate plan. These actions should be included in the business' existing action plans.

2. Sustaining the Risk Register

Most of these actions will typically be:

- Investments or purchases
- Training, simulations, emergency drill
- Development of alternative sources, suppliers, routes

Action plans should be reviewed as part of regular business reviews. However, it is important to have a regular (quarterly or six-monthly) high-level risk review to:

- Assess if changes in the business' environment mean that likelihood or impact of existing risks has changed
- Review scores of risks for which actions have been completed
- Include emerging new risks in the risk profile

As mentioned earlier, it is useful to have a prompt list to ensure that all types of risk are covered. No two businesses are the same, so risk registers cannot be copied and pasted. However, most businesses will face to a certain degree the following risk categories:

- **Market**
  - Economic cycle. How severely would more difficult market conditions affect us?
- **Competition**
  - Local competition
  - Imports from other regions
  - Breakthrough technology (obsolescence)
- **Operations**
  - Supply chain disruption
  - Operations: What are our critical manufacturing lines? Do we have critical spares in stock (or how rapidly can we source them?)
  - Process safety: How well managed is our process safety if the business relies on industrial processes?
- **People**
  - Retention (macro): How attractive are we?
  - Micro: Are we dependent on some people (especially for small businesses)?

IT – This one can be tricky as many Management Teams will not be very IT-literate and will consider IT as something that needs to be handled by specialists. Unfortunately, these risks cannot be ignored by Senior Management.

- **Obsolescence:** How recent is our infrastructure? Can the business grind to a halt if a system or a server crashes?
- **Cyberthreats:** How protected are we from cybercrimes? How rapidly can we resume business if we are hacked or ransomed?

It is beyond the scope of this book to provide solutions or even pre-made analyses as each of these topics would deserve its own book. Nevertheless, this list should trigger your reflection and invite you to dig deeper into your risk management process.

Summary

Change agents must be able to respond to any situation that arises in the organization. You can only do this if you have practiced the thinking process to quickly assess a situation and bring order to chaos. There is always a way to bring rational thinking to bear on what may at first seem like an impossible situation. After the event is an ideal opportunity to help the organization reflect on how it could have been better prepared to weather the storm and in some cases to exploit the strong winds of change in your favor. When you boil down the essence of good management and leadership, a lot of it is about risk management in all its forms. Taking calculated risks is just a part of growing as an individual, and we have offered a way of thinking about maximizing upside "risk" and minimizing downside risk. You may not win them all, but in the long run, you and your organization can benefit greatly from these ideas.

Get started on your Chapter 4 learnings – regaining control of emerging situations and building resilience

I. *Applying the rapid assessment steps to an emerging situation*
   a. *How can I prepare in advance or practice in a safe setting?*
   b. *What did I learn from applying this in a real situation?*
   c. *What would I do differently next time?*

II. *Checking my organization's risk management processes*
   a. *What formal risk management processes does my organization apply?*
   b. *How well are these processes deployed and used?*
   c. *What actions have been taken to update the risk management process following improvement activity?*

III. *Applying the best-of-best and worst-of-worst model to decision making*
   a. *How can my organization adopt an antifragile mindset?*
   b. *Where can I apply the best-of-best and worst-of-worst model?*
   c. *How can I apply the above two questions to my career development?*

Chapter 5

Deployment Methods

Fraser Wilkinson

> However beautiful the strategy, you should occasionally look at the results.
>
> **Winston Churchill**

Introduction

The area of strategy is one that we hear a lot about in our roles, and it is without doubt a crucial area to get right. Many have been the companies that have withered away due to a poorly thought out or even nonexistent strategy, but getting the strategy right is outside the scope of this book. Let's assume we have a reasonable strategy in place and we are being asked to implement this strategy. Of course, you should always challenge the strategy to test the thinking, but at some point, we are committed to deployment. One of the strategic aims may be to implement a culture of continuous improvement, or Lean or one of the other approaches described in the previous chapters, and there are almost endless ways we can go about implementing these in practice. So carefully choosing your deployment methods is vital and it's not something you can adopt wholesale from other businesses. Every situation is different, and you will need to consider local contingencies such as previous deployment attempts, the capacity and capability of the workforce for change, the business climate, and the maturity of process management, to name but a few.

DOI: 10.4324/9781003486022-5

Deployment for Culture Change or to Get Results

Although not usually an overt topic of discussion, the results vs. culture change debate (Figure 5.1) is a recurring theme I have come across in all programs that aim to deploy new ways of working. How much of our effort and focus should be on getting results and improving the process in the short term, and how much do we put into building the capability and behaviors that will ultimately drive long-term, hard improvements? This is an important consideration for a change agent. You must have a clear view on what is the balance at any point in time and for each situation, or you may be in danger of upsetting the key stakeholders. Many managers simply do not consider culture change and very often production managers are under such pressure that they can only see the hard results as beneficial, since these are what they report on each month. In these cases, you will need to address this with the higher management team. However, when the patients are on life support, you don't lecture them on healthy eating.

Ex-Toyota managers have told me that Toyota concentrates almost wholly on the development of the person rather than the results. I don't doubt this, but that organization is very successful and has a level of process stability that allows that to happen. There is a risk involved in being too focused on either results or culture. Short-term results may give the impression of learning being applied, but without a longer- term building of the culture, efforts can soon degrade.

I think it is important to emphasize the relationship between processes and culture if we are to avoid many of the mistakes of the past. I am defining culture here as the collective behavior and attitude of people in a group. Trying to change the culture of people in the hope that this will improve the processes may be putting the cart before the horse. Good processes make for good attitudes and *vice versa*. If people are continually wrestling with their poor internal processes and these are not designed to serve the customer well, then we should not be surprised to hear of a poor culture developing as a result. I would recommend a reading of John Seddon and the Vanguard experience for a more in-depth understanding of this point (Seddon, 2005).

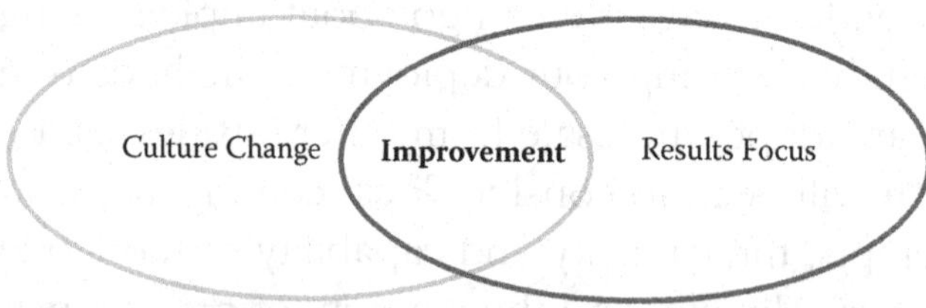

Figure 5.1 Is your improvement effort driven by results or culture change focus?

On a personal note, I have worked in various aircraft maintenance facilities throughout Europe and the happiest, safest, and most productive of these was at the Swissair maintenance base in Zurich, Switzerland. Everything worked! Even as a subcontractor I was treated the same as a permanent staff member, had the same tools and equipment, which were excellent, and all the spares were readily available. Spares and tools are the lifeblood of any maintenance organization and the bugbear of all maintenance technicians the world over. I was looked after and treated with respect. It was a great place to work and was very successful. What I didn't see was how they got to that point and what was their starting point. This is true of many people who have only worked in a continuous improvement environment such as automotive. It is easy to say what should be in place, but an entirely different thing to say what needs to be done to get to that point.

HERVÉ SAYS: THE JOURNEY MATTERS MORE THAN THE END POINT

Fraser is making a very important point here. This is one of the most difficult issues for change agents. Most Lean books explain the ideal state, principles, tools, and culture. But they rarely explain how to reach that level. Equally, visiting excellent companies is great and will open your eyes, but will not tell you how to do it. The plants I visited in Japan were wonderful, but their practices were so ahead of ours that it was difficult to draw conclusions on how to reach this level. Knowing where you want to go to is a good start, but when the destination is the moon, the journey can be daunting and one might not even know where to start.

What matters more is the journey. All these ideal practices cannot be just observed and studied, they have to be understood through practice and struggle. The TPS was not something that was designed. It is the codification of the state that Toyota reached through experimentation over many years.

As a change agent, you will sometimes need to roll up your sleeves and get stuck in with facilitating and applying the tools to get the results. Other times it will be a case of teach-a-little, do-a-little. In all cases though, there should be an element of "I will, if you will." Over time, one of the key ways of judging if you are making sustainable progress is the fact that you will be called less and less to step in and do the lion's share of the facilitation, and there will be more and more capability in the operational organization to do these activities themselves. In my experience, most automotive assemblers and many first-tier suppliers don't have a large pool of central experts but instead rely on their operational management to drive the deployment methods and the use of tools and techniques. This should also be your aim as these are the people closest to the value-added processes and can have direct and longitudinal observation of the production facilities.

Of course, the only way to build this capability in the line is to develop it through application and practice (70%), self-development (20%), and formal training (10%). This is the so-called 70:20:10 model of learning and development (Figure 5.2). The model reflects the need for action-based learning in the workplace. Organizations that want sustained improvement in how they improve will be building into the personal development plans those competencies, skills, knowledge, and behaviors required at each level and for each role that will drive continuous improvement. General Electric (GE) is a great example of this. In one of their major aero engine facilities, and

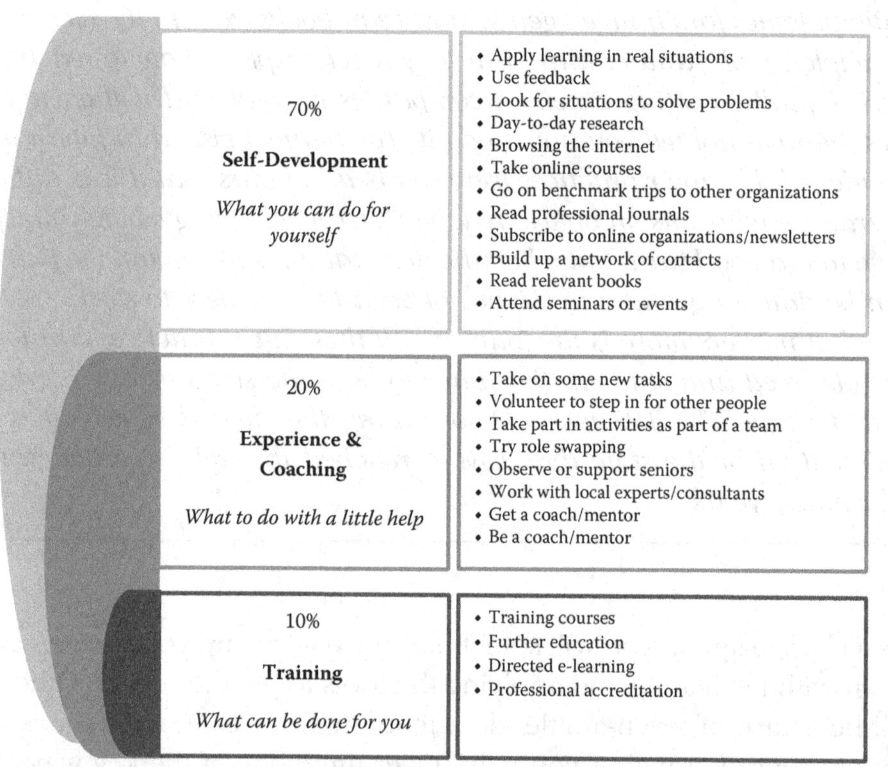

Figure 5.2 The 70:20:10 model of learning and development.

elsewhere, everyone at a certain grade of management is trained in Lean Six Sigma to Green Belt level. Each year a small number of high-potential employees are selected to be further trained to Black Belt level. They work within a central improvement function for two years to fully learn the skills before taking up a higher-level post. Not only do they apply Six Sigma, but also the GE Workout methods which is a focused 3–5 day cross-functional improvement activity and may include suppliers and customers. In this way, the senior managers are all fully able to coach and mentor their teams in the standard methods, and they will also have the experience to back it up.

How GE achieved this level of maturity in the deployment of both Six Sigma and the GE Work-Out method is well worth investigating (Ulrich, Kerr, & Ashkenas, 2002). It was not without difficulty, and there was a lot of resistance to adopting these new methods. Both methods were introduced and deployed in the first instance by consultants working very closely with the senior team, and there was a very clear vision of what the company needed to achieve in relation to a culture change.

Change Management Theory

As a change agent, it is incumbent on us to try to understand some basics of change management and behavioral modification theory even though the workings of the human mind are indeed something I don't claim to know too much about, and even though I own and sometimes even use one myself.

I would introduce here the *caveat* that all behavioral models are subject to change, modification, and revision, and some of the older ones based on the responses of rats and pigeons may have made dubious inferences. The basic question we need to answer is how to change the culture of an organization. I think anyone who has worked at several organizations will understand what is meant by culture. Culture is the collective behaviors and attitudes prevalent in an organization. Even on a single military base, there will be an overall cultural tone, but this will change subtly between individual units, so what makes the difference?

The change models that make the most sense to me through observation of real-world situations and an examination of my own behavior are those that emphasize the need to pull on many levers simultaneously. Failure to exert enough force on any of the levers can result in setbacks very quickly, but the biggest factor of all is the everyday processes we expect our people to operate and the level of leadership required in improving these processes.

There are two models I'd like to share as a brief introduction, but much more in-depth investigation of these is recommended. The first is the McKinsey change model (Figure 5.3) Figure 5.4 and the second is the What?/How? Connection (Figure 5.4) (Leake & Kendall, 2005).

McKinsey Change Model and the What?/How? Connection

McKinsey Management Consultants brought this model to my attention during some high-level interventions. It is only part of a much broader approach that often starts with an Organizational Health Index (OHI) survey. The output of this survey is used to plan new future states in organizational attitudes and improve the overall employee experience of working in an organization. Many consulting firms used the "hard" and "soft" analysis approach. Assess both the process and people before embarking on change.

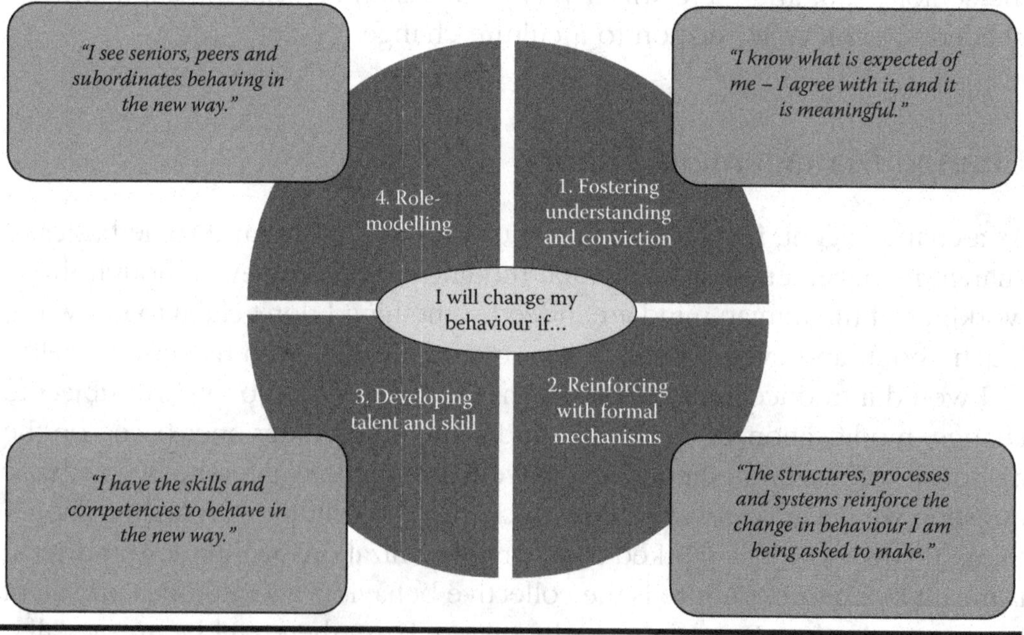

Figure 5.3 The McKinsey change model.

At the center of the model, we start with you and me, the individual. I will change my behavior if certain criteria are met. Take some time to consider how you changed your behavior at work and what were the influencing factors. You will probably recognize the presence of the four sectors in the model at play. Clearly, people can change their behaviors in certain environments, and indeed, we often observe that behaviors at work can be different to those in other settings such as sports events and social events.

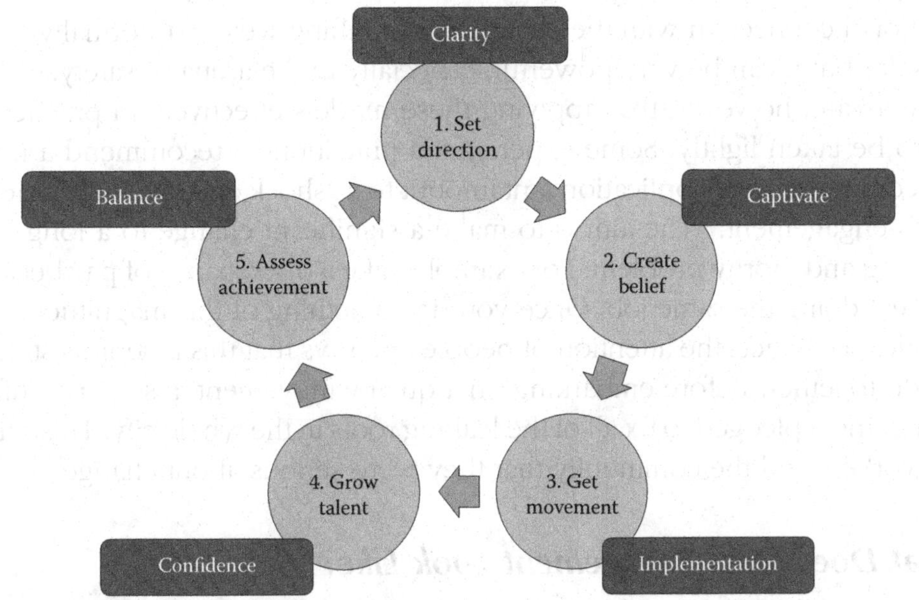

Figure 5.4 The What?/How? Connection (With permission from © Clive Leake Whow Leadership).

When making a change that requires a change in behavior, we must consider pulling on all the levers we can.

The What?/How? Connection model has five dimensions to consider, but the usefulness in all these models is thinking about how we are covering the very real requirements suggested. Use it to reflect on where change may have not been successful or at the start of a change to try and ensure you have in place the elements to improve the success rate. Again, there is no magic wand to apply in change management to guarantee success; all we can realistically do is try to stack the odds in our favor. The second step of this model about creating belief relies heavily on getting people engaged in the change. Many people talk about engagement sessions and on-boarding sessions where we shall tell people about the change and what we expect, but maybe we need to think a bit deeper on what gets true engagement. Most people are on a scale of fully engaged to not-engaged. Some have even flipped over to being *dis*engaged entirely from the change and actively shun all association with the change.

The second element of "Create belief" uses an engagement triangle to explain the dimensions we need to cover to captivate the audience and get engagement. This is the Think, Feel, and Act triangle. So, any change needs to be logical (think), something I can own and be part of (feel), and it is supported by my boss and my boss's boss doing this thing as well (act). Making an emotional connection with the change is something we don't normally consider but it can be very powerful, especially in the arena of safety.

Be aware, however, that applying these models effectively in practice is not to be taken lightly. Some experienced practitioners recommend a rapid and comprehensive application tantamount to a "shock and awe" approach or "mass engagement." The aim is to make a significant change to a long standing and thorny problem. For example, take a discrepancy of pay between workers doing the same job. Once you do something of this magnitude and significance, it gets the attention of people and says that this is serious stuff we can do together. Before embarking on a quality movement, a steel manufacturer in India pledged to fix all of the leaking roofs in the whole city. This said to the workers and the community that they were serious about change.

What Does Mass Engagement Look Like?

Mass engagement means everyone in the organization is involved in defining what the future state looks like and is then expected to contribute to the changes envisioned. Rapid mass engagement means that initial activities such as workshops are held in the shortest possible timescale to cover the majority of people, often within days or at most weeks. This means that there is a common feeling of engagement for all and not just a few chosen change agents, and that what is worked on is what is important to the majority of workers and management to the overall betterment of the organization.

Some of these mass engagements have been quite radical in scope, application, and output. An associate of the early UK Lean movement, Frank Devine of Accelerated Improvements (Devine, 2010), has developed a rapid mass engagement model that has been applied in many challenging situations, and the results have been extraordinary. Frank understands the Lean methods, tools, and techniques, but these are not what he uses to engage people. Starting at the very top of the organization, he works with the senior leaders to gauge if he thinks they are really up for the challenge, even to the point of realizing that some of them may not survive the exercise in their current positions. The rules of engagement are set, and what is in or out of scope agreed upon. Sometimes these include pay and conditions, working hours, joint decision making at all levels, bonuses, hiring and firing decisions, contracts, performance management, and any of the usual sources of management/worker conflicts that are often at the root of why a culture may be defined as "toxic." However, most traditional engagement efforts shy away from such controversial areas and concentrate on behaviors alone. If you don't tackle these difficult subjects, reasons Frank, then you won't really change the culture. Culture eats consultants for breakfast as well as strategy.

The subjects mentioned above are areas that can reshape what people believe about the organization and reflect what the true values are within the organization. It's easy for a top management team to work with a consultant and dream up vision, mission, and strategy statements, but if these are not aligned with the reality that follows, then we have cognitive dissonance. For workers the words don't ring true and the belief that the us-and-them mentality prevails. It would better to be honest about what the organization is and is not. Some very successful organizations still have terrible management/worker relationships and the most honest ones don't hide that fact.

It is a brave management team that embarks on the type of mass engagement that may wrest many of the levers of power out of their hands, but the energy, excitement, and danger are intoxicating to hear about, never mind be involved in. If you have been around change programs for any length of time, you would recognize that potential for culture change is enormous. However, more likely is a mass engagement aimed at the workforce by management who see very little to change in themselves. They stand up and make grand pronouncements before handing over to the "change team" to make it happen. You would be very lucky to get involved in the first scenario, but there are degrees in-between that can also give an enormous sense of achievement to the change agent.

One such effort aimed to change the safety culture in a large, heavy industry that had tragically suffered a number of fatalities over several years. Fatalities in these types of industries were once thought of as inevitable due to the nature of the work involved. The MD of the site was brought in from a more enlightened safety culture, and when tragedy struck under his tenure, he decided he must do something radically different than the corporate change program was suggesting. What followed was a multiyear effort to engage many thousands of workers, managers, trade union representatives, contractors, contract company owners, and suppliers in a quest to make "zero accidents" an ongoing goal. Some people still disagree as to whether this is ever possible to achieve, but just like "zero-defects," it must become a belief. If we don't believe it's possible, then at what point do we stop trying? One death every five years, ten years?

By every measure of safety, the change program was a huge success. The organization neared best-in-class levels and has stayed in touching distance ever since. There was a fundamental change in how people approached safety at all levels. There follows a brief description of the key events that unfolded over those 4–5 years.

The top 100 managers were brought together at an event offsite in a prestigious location. The event was set up to be poorly run for the first half-day. The escalators didn't work, drinks were late, there was a mess in the foyer, and other small irritants were set up. Did the managers see these things wrong? Of course they did, and in the sessions that followed, they were shown pictures of their own work areas that were poorly maintained. They had accepted it in one setting but not another. In the second half of the day, everything worked perfectly. This was all about reflecting on their own shortcomings and why they had allowed the behaviors to prevail that led to these conditions.

CONTROVERSY CORNER: HAS LEAN LOST ITS WAY?

The Lean movement that sprung up after the publication of The Machine that Changed the World *(Womack & Jones, 1996) has acted like a gravitational tractor for all sorts of new and old management theories. As its density increased, its attraction become greater and more of the improvement world was pulled into its orbit, eventually becoming a singularity about which all other programs and philosophies merged. Okay, this may be a bit dramatic, but this phenomenon was witnessed first-hand as everything that was "good" was suddenly a part of the Lean subject matter and anything discredited was shunned by the academics at the core of the movement. Even the 5 Lean Principles seem to have disappeared from much of the subject matter.*

Reminder ….

1. *Define value from the eye of the customer*
2. *Align the value stream*
3. *Create flow*
4. *Create pull*
5. *Seek perfection of the above*

Fraser

A dedicated team was set up to manage the change program and it was housed in a newly refurbished part of the main building to create the feeling of transition. Modern office conditions with the latest equipment and working environments were designed to show what was possible. Other work areas followed suit, including the welfare facilities and locker rooms for the workers that had deteriorated through underinvestment but also through a general decline in standards of behavior from obscene graffiti and vandalism to much worse.

Engagement days for every work area were used to discuss the current conditions and undesirable behaviors. These were often very fiery occasions with much for both workers and management to complain about each other. There was a very obvious divide in the two groups at that time. Senior Trades Union representatives were very much on board with the change efforts, so they had a big part to play in managing this conflict. After all, how could they oppose an improvement in safety culture? Out of these days came small improvement projects and volunteers to run them with much success.

The Works Rule Book was revised with representatives from all levels and disciplines. Everybody was asked to physically sign up to these new rules and with a small exception, everybody did. If you didn't sign, you were asked to explain to the MD why not.

The directors were all given "bicycle projects" by the MD. These were very significant changes to be managed and this was a test of their leadership. The idea being that if you fell off the bicycle, that was okay as long as you got back on and tried again. Some never even attempted to ride and delegated responsibility.

A level of intolerance was set for undesirable behavior and how to tackle it. This became known as the "Man United" model based on the premise that Alex Ferguson the manager of Manchester United Football Club would not allow poor behavior for too long in his team. After being advised of the behavior in question and given the time and resources to change, if the behavior continued, the player would no longer be on the team. Examples were made of those who refused to change and examples were made of companies that were also found wanting with contracts canceled.

A newspaper was printed every 2 weeks that showed the good and the bad of what was happening on the site. The paper won many awards for internal communications, and it was always focused more on the people than the plant.

Dedicated safety teams were established, and every person was cycled through the teams for 2 weeks and given some basic continuous improvement training as well as safety engagement training. Again, improvement projects were expected of everyone.

Support for outreach work in the community was funded and this included a full-time dedicated drugs and alcohol team that also worked on the site for those workers and families in need of help.

These activities continued for many years and in totality had the desired effect of permanently changing the attitudes of everyone with regard to safety. So what was the next stage of the journey? Did the program have a second stage? The answer unfortunately was "no." The opportunity to move onto a wider operational excellence approach was missed. That's not to say operational performance was not part of the original program, but the same approach, the same levers that were pulled for safety, were left untouched. Think about how easy it would be to replace safety with quality in the above approaches. Both aims are not entirely comparable as there is an emotional element to safety that is hard to reproduce with quality, but the foundations were there.

As change agents, we must always be thinking in terms of legacy. What will remain when we or the management team move on. How much is really embedded in the DNA of the organization? Does your organization even have what's meant by DNA, or is it open to the many mutating forces at play in the world of work?

CONTROVERSY CORNER: ARE YOU A CRUTCH OR A MULTIPLIER?

In order to achieve mass engagement, change agents need to inculcate a huge number of people. Given that there will be, at most, one change agent for every one hundred employees, your only chance to succeed is to create disciples. Trying to do everything by yourself is a recipe for disaster. You will never have the time necessary to have the deep interactions required with this multitude. Unfortunately, we quite like to do things ourselves because it is satisfying to see immediate results. Imagine, for example, that you run a process improvement event yourself because you are the local expert. You will probably improve the process, which is great. But people will not have learnt to run a process improvement event. So next time an event is required, you will be asked to do it again. You will have become a crutch for the organization. You could have instead chosen to coach a less experimented person running that event and building up their expertise. You would then have multiplied

> *the organizational capability. So bear in mind this simple question every time you plan an activity: If I do it this way, am I a crutch or am I a multiplier?*
>
> **Hervé**

What Drives Behavior?

Before we discuss this question we also need to establish what constitutes "right" behavior and "wrong" behavior. These can be very specific descriptors regarding a standard work instruction to ensure product quality, for instance, but it can also be a much more generic behavior such as morals, cultural norms, or values that are expected to be upheld. For example, when confronted with a problem, what do we expect people to do? What behavior should we expect to observe? If we are not clear on these, then how can we set expectations?

If culture is mostly a collection of behaviors, then we need to have a framework to help modify behavior. Much has been written on this subject in the context of organizational change, but I think it is useful to think about a time when we have changed our own behavior and what prompted that. Much of our behavior is habitual; we keep doing what we do until something makes us reassess what we do. When we attempt novel behavior, we also assess the outcome to see if we should keep doing the same thing. What most behavioral research majors on is the fact that consequences drive our behavior. Sometimes we see the consequences and it's obvious what we should do, but other times we need someone to tell us what the unseen consequences are. This is where feedback is so important. To change our own behaviors we need to be able to honestly self-reflect on situations and also be open to receiving feedback. The best and most effective feedback is a positive reinforcement of a desired behavior. Of course there is a place for negative feedback, but on balance praise is far more effective. One of the best and most accessible books on this subject is *Other People's Habits* by Aubrey C. Daniels (2001). Hervé also has a view on this in his section on Sustainability.

Organizing for Deployment

So, now we know that we ultimately want to change both the culture and the results, then we need to decide how we are going to organize ourselves to achieve this. In this section, we discuss some of the factors to be considered.

Assess the Current Situation

Your situation might be at a single site or a large multi-site, multinational operation and, related to the above, is the question of standardizing the change efforts. Do you want to have a single approach at all sites or do you allow leeway to design the deployment themselves? In short, I'd favor a standard end point (e.g., an Operational Excellence Model) but with a lot of room to deploy in different ways. I am less and less in favor of "programs" as time goes on, especially when previous "programs" have not been as successful as expected. Making big announcements and plans for a new version can feel like a hollow rebranding exercise, and people will be deterred by these constant and ineffective methods. It could be time to just start on what you want to achieve with the right leaders and begin to make the changes at the appropriate level.

Another consideration when dealing with a community of people such as an organizational unit is the degree of affinity people can feel within a group whose size is over a certain number. There is empirical evidence from the military and the army in particular that the basic unit of a Company, Battery, or Troop is between 130 and 150 people and that this number produces the best *esprit de corps*. At this level, we have a chance of knowing each individual on a personal level over time and have a good chance of developing a distinct culture within a unit of this size.

The question of how much standardization of methods we should aim for will arise at some point, and you will need to have a common view on this as change agents. I would always have a standard available but allow for variations that accomplish the same end. In that way, you don't have conflict with existing standards especially in a large multi-site situation where standards are likely to have grown up and diversified already. Move toward the new standards at a suitable point in time. For new standards, these should always be required to be used from the start.

If you are at the start of a journey of change, you will quickly need to establish the current level of maturity in the business to accept new methods and ways of working. You may want to undertake an organizational health check to be able to gauge the current state, but this should still be backed up by getting as much exposure to the employees as possible. Spending time at the production areas is essential even if you don't have a particular problem to work on, as people are far more willing to open up in their familiar environment than in an interview or a classroom. You will soon get a feeling for what deployment methods will work best. Try to spend the majority of time with both the most senior and the most junior levels in the organization rather than the middle management groups, as I think you are more likely to detect the difference between the espoused theory of how the business works and the reality of how the business works. This is what Nassim Taleb (2013) might call the barbell or bimodal principle. Taleb can be a difficult read, and his thinking is not always readily applicable to the life of a change agent, but the barbell principle, in essence, states that the greatest returns can be found at the extremes of any position, as, of course, can the greatest risks.

The level of process stability is also a key consideration in choosing deployment methods and vehicles. In highly regulated industries, processes will be highly documented and tightly managed for compliance. There may be an air of control, but this can mask ineffectiveness in the supply chain, scheduling, and inventory control. A good diagnostic approach should uncover these (see Chapter 3). In less regulated industries, there may be little or no documented working practices. It may be that deployment of tools and techniques needs to wait and a focus on basic standards and behaviors is required first.

Use of Internal Resources, Buy-ins, or Consultants

EXAMPLE: "WE ARE NOT DOING LEAN HERE!"

One of our colleagues was interviewing the Managing Director of one of our very large business unit as part of his studies in Lean Operations. The corporate change office had issued a set of guidebooks developed in conjunction with a leading Lean Consultancy, and as a change group we wondered why this executive was not espousing the Lean philosophy. Our colleague was told in no uncertain terms, "We are not doing lean here!" Having recently come from an outside organization, this director could see that the culture was so far from the norms of the day that Lean would have no chance of sticking, so we were all tasked to work on challenging unacceptable conditions and behaviors for the next several years!

There are many ways you can organize for deployment, but experience gives some pointers as to what may work best in the longer term, assuming your organization has committed to pursuing a culture change agenda. Most organizations opt for a central pool of resource to drive the changes forward. This can be a Lean Promotion Office or a Program Management Office, but their duties are likely to be the same. These offices usually have the role of:

1. Providing the expertise in all aspects of change management.
2. Developing the frameworks to deploy.
3. Managing the deployment plans with hard and soft targets.
4. Defining the standard tools and techniques.
5. Training and development of capability.
6. Knowledge sharing and best practice tours both internally and externally.
7. Coordinating maturity assessments and reviewing progress.

Sometimes the organization has people within that can step into these roles, maybe because of past experience with other organizations or because they fulfill similar roles in the current set-up such as Quality Assurance (QA). It's worth mentioning here that in many organizations, the Quality Assurance groups are also responsible for Continuous Improvement in line with the most recent requirements of the ISO9001 standards. It's vital to include QA in the change program as the new management standards also drive toward overall business improvement and not simply compliance to a standard. Of course, other functions also need to have a representation and will be key to long-term success. Human Resources (HR) systems can be utilized to drive the right knowledge and behaviors. Finance must understand the consequences of improving flow and reducing WIP, and they will need to sign off on the financial savings claimed by the improvement efforts.

When the expertise is not available internally you have a couple of choices. You can go out to the job market and look to recruit experienced staff to help set up the internal organization, or you can hire consultants. Depending on the size of your organization, it may be a combination of all three approaches, but the caution is with not involving the current key influencers in setting up these offices and setting the agenda for change. Key stakeholders are always the people who have the accountability for the production and support processes. These will be the production manager and team leader levels without whom very little will change. In an ideal world, these people will be involved from the start and at every step along the way. In fact, these people must be the drivers of the change effort with the central office as a support function. All too often the support office is seen as another painful distraction to getting product out of the door.

Most experienced change agents agree that you can't change the culture if the central organization continues to be the only driving force. Part of the plan must be to deploy the expertise to the frontline organization. Small steering committees made up of frontline employees can be used to set the direction of travel, aided by a number of support staff.

EXAMPLE: WHO SHOULD OWN "OPERATIONAL EXCELLENCE"?

One of our major sites has used the production managers group to own the Operational Excellence program. After all, who owns "operations"? This group was first taken through a workshop on the TPS 14 Principles (for Liker & Meier, 2006) and asked to develop a gap analysis against their own operations. This then formed the basis of a maturity score, and each one was asked to cross-assess another production area. Each one was also given responsibility for a particular element of the Operational Excellence program. The support office acted as the facilitator, but now the program is owned by the key influencers. In another site we had far less success by simply introducing that same, predetermined program to a different set of production managers. Without having gone through the learning and self-reflection, the second group found it harder to associate their particular problems with the "solutions" provided. It takes longer but it is worth the extra time up-front to engage those key influencers. As they say, "if they build it they will protect it."

External consultants can be extremely useful, even when they don't actually bring any skills that you don't already have within the change office. I am resigned to the fact that, however much you know, the business usually listens more to an external voice delivering the same message. It could be argued that this is simply a lack of influence on the part of the internal change agents, and I accept that may sometimes be the case. However, consultants usually cost a considerable amount of money if they are good, and the business has a much more focused interest in listening to advice they've paid handsomely for. Consultants are also likely to have been brought in by the senior team and as such they have a vested interest to make whatever they propose work.

The top consultancies such as Boston Consulting Group, McKinsey, Accenture, etc., are also likely to have established direct reporting lines to the C-suite executives, and once this is known they command a certain level of compliance to deploy their methods. These groups also have access to a phenomenal resource base of general and industry-specific experts and associated data for the purpose of benchmarking. Generally, the caliber of these consultants is also extremely high, as they get to choose the top talent from around the world. If you are, let's say, closer to the end of your career than the beginning of it, many of these consultants will appear to be very young, and it is tempting to dismiss what they do because of this. You can be sure, however, that they are being mentored by more experienced consultants. They can also be very driven, ruthless, and sometimes quite rude, but that's how they get things done. After all, they can leave the business and are only there to achieve a specific goal, which they will attempt to do at all costs. I'm not saying all engagements follow this pattern, but be prepared for it. Once you understand their motives, it's easier to work with them and observe how they operate and learn from what they do. I would even try to get some feedback from them if they've seen your work up close, but be prepared for a very honest and hard-hitting assessment.

Whatever consultants you use, try and get as much from them as possible in terms of approach, methods, and tools. Observe how they operate as a team and be energized by them. Being an internal change agent, you can fall into a pattern all too easily and "go native" if you're not careful, and external resources can help refocus you. Our coaching expert always pointed out that if you don't have the big PEE (Passion, Energy and Enthusiasm), then stay in the office until you do.

WHAT COULD POSSIBLY GO WRONG! THE CLIENT DIAGNOSTIC

As part of a Continuous Improvement Coach training program, many of us were given the opportunity to undergo a coaching program with a trained psychologist. When you are asked to be a coach, then it's very difficult to measure and show how successful you are since it's your client who is supposed to make the changes and not you. To help establish what our clients might value and determine who we would be developing and in what techniques, I created a very comprehensive diagnostic tool to use with our clients. When I tried to deploy this to the older and wiser heads in our team, it was met with a stony silence. Great idea, but it won't work here, I was told. I'd failed to consider the level of maturity we were dealing with to be able to deploy this tool successfully. I know in other business it would have been seen as a very pragmatic way of documenting our coaching efforts.

Fraser

In most cases, the best option is generally a hybrid solution with a non-negotiable, wide deployment of the basic principles across the company and a more aggressive approach in a few key pilot areas.

The exact balance will depend on companies' situations and culture. For example, the ones struggling for survival will need to go for a fast, resolute action on a few selected items that will generate rapid benefits and will not have the luxury to create a polished company-wide program.

EXAMPLE: PLAYING THE NUMBERS GAME

A relatively recent experience has led me to conclude that a mass engagement approach has a very good chance of successful change. If we take an operational unit of between 150–300 people and take them through a well-defined process over 12–14 weeks with intensive coaching of leaders starting with the senior group but then concentrating on operation levels, a significant change in both culture and performance can be achieved. We have seen this delivered by consultants. The key here is that everyone is experiencing the same change, so there is no pilot group as such and no excuse not to do it. This takes around 10–12 full time coaches. There is nothing in the approach we haven't tried previously, but the deployment method was novel.

Whatever the choice, it is important that it is made consciously and not by default, but also that the wide vs. deep selected balance is explained. Good communication will increase motivation of the pilot areas, but also will avoid that the other areas consider the program optional (Table 5.1).

Table 5.1 The pros and cons of different organizational options for change

Organization for change	*Pros*	*Cons*
Internal resource	Lowest initial cost. Known by the organization. Understands the history/culture. Opportunity for succession/ development.	Too close to the main players. Lacks a critical perspective. May be part of the problem. May lack knowledge and experience of change.
Buy-ins	Can select suitable person. Speeds up implementation. New perspective. No baggage.	Headcount cost. May be seen as a threat.
Consultants	Independent. Experience and knowledge. Ear of the C-suite. Back up and resources. Pace of change. Opportunity to learn from them.	Cost. Resistance from organization. Reversion when they leave. Skills and knowledge leave with them.

HERVÉ SAYS: THE MOST DIFFICULT DEPLOYMENT CONUNDRUM: WIDE OR DEEP?

One question that always surfaces at the deployment stage is "are we going wide or are we going deep," i.e., are we going to communicate and deploy in the whole company or are we going to target a limited number of areas to start with?

	Wide	*Deep*
Pros	*Creates the conditions for change across the company* *Makes it easier to improve transversal processes* *Better formalization of trainings, tools and methods*	*Speed* *Provides a shining example that will be used to generate interest in other parts of the company* *Limited use of resources*
What to watch out for	*Pace* *Time before achieving first tangible results (an issue when financial improvements are rapidly needed)* *Resource intensity, most employees will sit on the fence for some time*	*Choice of pilot requires motivated leaders of opinion and reasonable chances of success* *Widening gap between pilot and non-pilot areas*

HERVÉ SAYS: DO WE REALLY NEED A PROGRAM?

I have seen so many corporate programs in the last 25 years. Most of them have failed. None of them failed in a dramatic way, but they just all withered until companies moved to the next program. And these quiet failures were never officially acknowledged. The lack of obituary prevents PDCA thinking (i.e., asking why the program failed), leading these companies to repeat the same failures over and over again.

The typical life cycle of change programs or cost saving programs looks like this:

1. *The CEO/someone very senior read an article/attended a conference/got briefed by consultants about the latest management trend.*
2. *A new program is announced, led by a program manager, managed by a transformation office, and supported by consultants. The programs usually also have a very impressive name (the business equivalent of "Operation Desert Storm").*
3. *After an initial sheep dipping (sorry I meant to write "first wave of mandatory trainings"), some quick wins are obtained in a few areas, seemingly vindicating the initiation of the program.*
4. *After 12 to 24 months, the program clearly stalls. Most people can feel it, but it is not fully visible in the dashboard as it is in no one's interest to bring the bad news.*
5. *After a while, the dashboard is no longer reviewed, so even paying lip service is no longer necessary.*
6. *Ultimately, a new management fad gets preference or a new leader arrives and the cycle restarts.*

This simply reminds me of people starting a diet. They temporarily lose weight but eventually gain it back and move to the next popular program. Like in the diet example, these corporate programs will only be oscillations until the fundamental causes of these gaps are addressed.

This might sound very cynical, but these comments are backed not only by personal experience, but also by research. Ironically, this field is well-researched by the very consulting companies that support this type of transformation. McKinsey, one of the largest of these companies, reported in two separate surveys success rates of 20% and 26%. I am not sure that executives are fully conscious of the odds at the start of these programs.

However, one should not conclude too hastily that programs are a complete waste of time and resources. After all, some of these programs succeed. Formal programs allow the mobilization of resources and send the message that Senior Leadership is serious about change. This is a necessary but not sufficient condition for success. The McKinsey surveys highlight a number of characteristics that improve the odds. These will be discussed in Chapter 9.

Role of a Sensei

No matter the level of ability and knowledge, we can all benefit from a good coach. Coaching is a skill in itself and developing this skill is not to be taken lightly. A 1-day coaching course is not going to cut the mustard. The role of Sensei is slightly different in as much as the Sensei is also an expert in the subject matter. The role of the Sensei (or one who teaches) is classically seen as that of the enigmatic elder who appears when needed and poses a few carefully chosen questions to stimulate the deep thinking required of the student.

When we talk of a Sensei today, we generally think of those who have some direct connection with the Japanese practices of TQM or Lean and more specifically with the iconic early work of Taichi Ohno and his cohorts. For most of us, we are unlikely to have access to someone from this direct line, but that should not deter us from seeking out someone who can perform the role of arch-questioner. These Sensei are, after all, only following in the footsteps of the great philosophers such as Socrates whose aim was to help others "give birth to their own ideas." Ideally, though, it is the CEO who really needs a Sensei. Are you ready to perform that role?

Methodologies, Deployment Vehicles, and Tools and Techniques

It is important to establish what is meant by Deployment Vehicles, Methodologies, and Tools and Techniques, since these terms are often used interchangeably. If we start with a methodology such as Six Sigma or the DMAIC process itself, then that method of problem-solving can be deployed through a number of different vehicles. It can be in the traditional Six Sigma project format with a project team meeting over a 3-month period to solve

Table 5.2 Distinguishing Methodology, Deployment Vehicles, and Tools and Techniques

Methodology	*Deployment Vehicle*	*Tools and Techniques*
A series of interconnected steps to go through in sequence or iterations thereof	*The way we organize to perform the steps described in the methodology*	*The detailed analysis or improvement activity that is used at each stage of the method*
DMAIC/Six Sigma	Kaizen Blitz	Pareto
Hoshin Kanri	SWAT/Tiger Team	Value Stream Map
Lean Principles	Project Team	5 Whys
A3 Thinking	Small Group Activity	Ishikawa diagram

a problem, or you could just as easily use the DMAIC steps in a rapid, focused improvement "event" over a number of days. At each of the DMAIC steps, you may use a number of different tools and techniques such as a Pareto chart. So you see the Pareto chart is just a lower-level tool and in itself will not guide the overall improvement effort. All these interventions, however, will need to be guided by the requirement to study the processes in question, starting with demand and customer requirements. In PDCA, or as it was originally called, Plan, Do, Study, Act (PDSA), the place to start is Study and not Plan (Table 5.2).

Typical Deployment Vehicles

This section will describe some of the main deployment vehicles I've used and seen used to varying degrees. All of them are almost universally applied in the field of continuous improvement. Once again, you need to consider many factors before choosing the particular vehicle.

Kaizen Blitz, GE Work-Out (Ulrich, Kerr, & Ashkenas, 2002)

The key with these approaches is the speed of implementation of improvements. In a well-defined time period, usually 3–5 days, a team of people come together for an intensive improvement effort with the intention of making as many positive changes as possible. These events can be either passive or active in defining the focus of the work, depending on the individuals involved and being sensitive to the situation at the workplace. By passive, I mean that the team themselves decide what they want to work on improving. This is sometimes necessary to gain the trust of the team and grow confidence if there are underlying issues that might need addressing first. For example, if you want to make some hard progress in output or cost reduction but the workplace itself is not well designed, is poorly laid out, or is seen as being in any way detrimental to a healthy, safe, and pleasant environment, then these hygiene factors will get in the way of progress. On the other hand, in more mature organizations, the efforts can be directed by a focus on Quality, Delivery, and Cost targets derived from a diagnostic approach.

These events require considerable planning and need experienced facilitators to teach people the process and the tools and to keep on track to finish with a positive outcome. A diagnostic phase between 6 and 8 weeks out from the event can help determine the focus of the event and allow time to gather the data required to help analyze and direct improvement efforts. I've run these events in Six Sigma organizations where we followed the DMAIC steps, but you could also use PDCA or the A3 Thinking steps or in GE the steps are defined as:

1. Plan the Work-Out.
2. Conduct the Work-Out Event.
   a. Work-Out introduction.
   b. Small-group idea generation.
   c. Whole-group idea assessment – the "Gallery of Ideas."
   d. Small group recommendation development.
   e. Final-decision session – the "Town Meeting."
3. Implement the Work-Out ideas.

Interestingly, the GE method calls for the Sponsor of the event to make an on-the-spot, public yes/no decision on the ideas presented. I suppose this helps to make decisions that have a good chance of success, but it also forces managers in front of employees! I have also seen this same type of idea generation used by McKinsey in a transformation program where "waves" of idea generation and selection are launched on a ten-week cycle. More so than Six Sigma, Work-out is often quoted as being the major reason for GE's success following the massive downsizing in the 1980s because it allowed people to tackle bureaucracy and eliminate the frustrating and non-value-adding activities that appear to clog the arteries of any organization that doesn't take regular, heart-rate-raising exercise.

Small Group Activities or Quality Circles

These activities have their origin in the TQM movement and they are based on a simple premise that those closest to the work are those best able to see how the work can be improved. However, unless they have the mechanisms and support, they are unlikely to be able to put these ideas into practice. Usually, these activities are led by the Team Leader level and use very simple tools such as the Seven Quality Tools (see Appendix 8) to help analyze problems. A regular meeting is established, and concerns or ideas can be worked on by the team. Even a 15-minute end of shift, stand up meeting with a flip chart can constitute Small Group activity. I have successfully run these at a white board in a biological formulation facility after the end of shift clean-down activities, and we worked on improving documentation, cleanliness, productivity, and safety items. My mistake as a young change agent was to not formally include the coaching of the Team Leader who much later admitted feeling threatened by an "outsider" engaging with his team. I had thought that by role modeling he would see how easy it was and pick it up himself.

Specialist Weapons and Tactics Teams, Tiger Teams, or Rapid Response Teams

By definition, a Specialist Weapons and Tactics (SWAT) team has resources that are not usually found in the mainstream workforce, and they are available to respond to a crisis at short notice. These resources can be equipment, expertise, methods, analysis tools, or any other non-normal response. If we think of the medical analogy, most frontline health problems can be tackled by the General Practitioner and Health Workers, but for those occasions where trauma is involved, we need paramedics to respond and accident and emergency units and even life support services to kick into action. Acute quality or delivery problems may need the same approach but, just like the emergency services, we need to have a well-rehearsed protocol to put into action to be most effective. Some organizations have a standing SWAT Team like volunteer lifeboat crews who are trained and experienced in established methods (like A3 or DMAIC) but can also work effectively together to quickly establish root causes and organize corrective and preventative actions. SWAT Teams may also be full time and move from one chronic condition to another.

KATA Coaching Techniques (Rother, 2010)

I have to admit to not having much formal experience of the Kata approach, but I have applied the principles in cell design and layout exercises. In essence, we can't always grasp how to get to a desired situation, so we come up against our threshold of knowledge. The way forward is unknown, so what we need to do is iterate our way forward one step at a time, testing at each step if we are moving in the right direction. But the key is to first realize that we don't have the answer. Sometimes our brain fills in the gaps unconsciously and we proceed as if we do know the final solution. This is all tied into the two modes of thinking: faster and slower. We think fast when our brains run their habitual routines to come up with the answer, but sometimes the situation is not as it appears superficially and we end up with, for instance, petrol in our diesel cars. But the contradiction here is that the Kata coach tries to teach us the correct routines to run through, the routines that are flexible enough to allow us to spot the gaps by consciously slowing down our thinking. This is a phenomenon worth understanding and is well explained in *Thinking Fast and Slow* (Kahnamen, 2012). The broad steps of the Kata approach are to:

1. Understand the direction.
2. Grasp the current condition.
3. Establish the next target condition.
4. PDCA toward the target condition.

So, by trial and error, we extend our threshold of knowledge by changing only one condition at a time.

Six Sigma/DMAIC Formal Projects, Project Management

In the context of deployment vehicles, the distinguishing feature with the traditional formal project approach is just a matter of timing and pace. The same steps can be followed, and indeed the same tools can be used in a three-month Six Sigma Green Belt project or in a 3-day Kaizen event. A Kaizen event is a way of applying Lean, single-piece-flow to the problem-solving process with a minimum delay in handing over data, conducting analysis, taking action, and checking results.

CONTROVERSY CORNER: "WE ARE NOT READY FOR SIX SIGMA"

This is an often heard quote in the operational excellence world. So, how do you know if you are ready for Six Sigma? Firstly you have to ask if you mean a Six Sigma "program" or even becoming a Six Sigma company like General Electric. Secondly, ask if your processes are ready for Six Sigma. This is much easier to answer from a technical point of view as you can conduct stability analysis and capability analysis (SPC, CpK) to see if your processes are in control (statistically) and able to meet the customer requirements without excessive defects. If either of these indicators suggest you need improvement, then a Six Sigma-type approach will be required because, in theory, there will be no special causes to use the investigative approach on (like 5 whys). You don't need Six Sigma per se, but the approach to common cause variation will require many of the tools, so for convenience, you may want some process specialists to have those skills. Much can be done with basic operating conditions to achieve stability, but after 15 years of someone saying they are not ready for Six Sigma, it may be time to ask the questions, "at what point will you be ready?"

The Six Sigma brand tends to get in the way of the real purpose of the tools. Some people don't like the elitist nature of the "belt system" where Green Belts might be seen as inferior to the Black Belts. As a change agent you need to be able to see beyond that and identify if the tools are going to give your organization a performance advantage. Have you reached the limit of process knowledge yet? Do you fully understand the levers to pull to get the desired output? Sometimes it's hard for people who are invested in a process to admit that this is the case. We see this a lot.

Regardless of whether your organization is ready for Six Sigma, as a change agent, you should be. The thinking behind Six Sigma is invaluable in your line of work, even if you don't do Six Sigma projects as the classic program approach demands.

Fraser

Strategy Deployment

In the TQM arena, a distinction is made between Policy Management and Daily Management or breakthrough verses continual improvement. Policy Management (or Strategy Deployment as it is more commonly known) includes all the breakthrough or step-change improvements that go into the Annual Plan and usually end up as projects. Daily Management is the collective effect of a large number of small, rapid improvement activities that over time deliver huge benefits.

Strategy Deployment has been a hot topic of business since the Japanese gave us the term of Hoshin Kanri, the literal translation of which is "direction management," and key to this process is the engagement of all people involved to set the deployment methods and buy-in to the plans. So much of what passes for strategy deployment misses this point. The overall aims of the business are set at a high level but these are then discussed and devolved at all levels before plans are sent back up for review. This "catch balling" process continues until all parties have agreed on the targets and the methods of achieving them. I've been involved in a number of incarnations of this and it is hard work and requires a significant commitment of time to do it right, especially in a large multilayered, multiunit organization. Even when this was done reasonably well, it still lacked a real hard financial edge.

Often when the plans are made they don't get down to the "how?" question. Say we want to incrementally improve the yield from one of our processes, we might see a line on a plan saying *Improve yield on process X.* "How are we going to do that?" you may well ask. "A Project Team will be set up," comes back the answer. "And what exactly are they going to do?" you ask innocently (it's always the killer question and usually you know the answer). If they come back with, "Improve yield, of course" or some made up waffle, you can be pretty sure your job is secure for the foreseeable future. All too often the senior team gives out annual plans and targets without having a reliable and repeatable means of achieving those plans. This is where you come in. You need to be able to suggest the most appropriate methods of achieving those goals, including what specific tools and techniques may be needed at each stage as the need arises. These should be the go-to methods familiar to the whole business. We've covered some of these above but in the next chapter, we'll look at some of the more detailed ways we can drive improvement at this lower level.

CONTROVERSY CORNER: WHEN MORE IS LESS

So, you have carried out the initial diagnosis, identified any improvement opportunities, and you have selected a deployment vehicle. Leadership is highly enthusiastic about the program and benefits identified have become promised benefits, ideally to be delivered yesterday. You and your team are now overloaded with projects, but you are all motivated so you will work on all these topics and give 110%.

But is this the right thing to do? You are probably aware that not all projects will deliver (remember the 30% drop-off rate mentioned in the OGSM paragraph in Chapter 2*), so you indeed need some project reserve. But how much can you cope with? Yes, you have embarked on a multi-year program and there is no quick fix, but this does not mean that selection and sequencing do not matter.*

In fact, our experience is that overburdening project teams is one of the main causes of slow delivery. This is mathematically supported by Little's law.

John Little, based on his study of queuing in banks, published in the early 1960s the law that now bears his name. It states that the length of a queue is equal to the product of Throughput and Leadtime (how long it takes from start to finish). It is abbreviated as WIP = T × LT. A consequence is that the lead time (time spent in the queue) is directly correlated to the amount of Work In Progress as LT = WIP/T.

In other words, the more projects (assuming a constant capacity in the team), the more time it will take to deliver. This result is illustrated in Figure 5.5.

The appeal of sequencing to deliver benefits more rapidly is easily understood. Yet we tend to forget this when defining programs and think that we need as many projects as possible to deliver more.

A key strength of Agile Thinking is this philosophy of "Focusing on less projects at each stage but acting decisively on the selected few will ultimately deliver more."

So when you reach the stage of program planning, make sure that you focus first on a few projects and get the resources that will deliver fast. You will have to resist leadership pressure. They will want to know when the financial benefits will be delivered. You will have to promise ambitious timelines on the selected few projects and resist the urge to add more projects by showing that accumulated cash flow will be higher in the case of a sequenced program.

Hervé

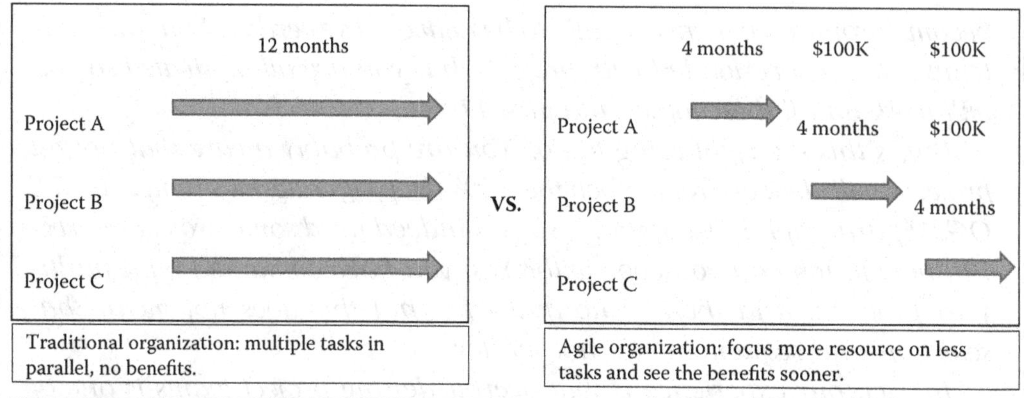

Figure 5.5 The benefits of focusing on the rapid delivery of a limited number of projects.

Summary

Very often in change programs much attention and fanfare is given to the development of "The Program." All too often the same level of attention is lacking when it comes to thinking about how to successfully deploy "The Program." Giving people the what-to-do without the how-to-do-it can be demoralizing if they don't have the wherewithal at their disposal to successfully complete the task.

Setting up the organization to support a change is a vital step, and it requires much attention and some detailed planning around the personnel involved, the stakeholder management, and the overall approach. As much as possible, any change must be led by the operational or functional teams, and it should not be seen as an initiative driven by a support or project organization. The role of that organization is vital in bringing the expertise, helping in setting standards, and giving an overall direction of travel.

We have discussed the broad approach to deployment activities in this chapter, and next we will get into some more of the detailed tools and techniques that all organizations need to have in their armory.

Get started on your Chapter 5 learnings – reflecting on the aspects of cultural change that I am supporting

I. *Assessing our change efforts against a model approach*
   a. *What change management model(s) will I use?*
   b. *What aspects of the model(s) are working well?*
   c. *What aspects of the model(s) are the weakest?*

- d. *How can I influence leaders to improve the application of the model(s)?*

II. *Assessing the balance of our "results vs. culture change" efforts*
- a. *What efforts are change agents making to change the culture?*
- b. *What efforts are change agents making to change results?*
- c. *Is the balance right based on the current situation and maturity of the organization?*
- d. *If not, what will you do to influence a change?*

III. *Assessing the capability and capacity of the change team*
- a. *What is the balance of the team's efforts in "doing" or in creating "multipliers" of change?*
- b. *How would you assess the capability (i.e., passion, energy, enthusiasm, credibility, and influence) of the team to create "multipliers" for change?*
- c. *How would you assess the capacity (i.e., number of people and time available) of the team to create "multipliers" for change?*
- d. *What action will you take to address any shortfalls?*

Chapter 6

Improving

Fraser Wilkinson

> The biggest room in the world is the room for improvement.
>
> **Helmut Schmidt**

Introduction

One of the more well-known traps in improvement circles is believing that the application of analysis tools constitutes improvement. The important lesson is that improvement in the current state only comes about by moving to a better future state. This does not require the use of any particular tools, but tools can aid us to be more effective, efficient, and sustainable in our improvement efforts. It is not the intention to give a detailed account of each of the tools available; there are many of those available already (e.g., both authors have used *The New Lean Toolbox*, Bicheno & Holweg, 2023, a lot during their career). This chapter sets out to explain how tools should fit into the change agent's overall approach.

So, let's be clear that just using tools is not improvement. Improvement is improvement. Tools are there to help us better perform the tasks of improvement. Tools help us put structure and order into our thinking processes. They provide a common language, "pass the ten centimeter, left-handed forceps please, nurse." Think of those tools we use to build the factory and those we use to help us run the factory. We don't need the cement mixer to help make our products once the factory is built, but we may need a tool like Kanban to help keep down WIP or a visual management board to aid day-to-day communication and decision making. In this chapter, we will

DOI: 10.4324/9781003486022-6

explore the nature of an improvement culture and how we can utilize methodologies, tools, and techniques to drive our improvements.

A Framework of Improvement Activities

We should all know by now that maintaining the status quo in business is a death knell for all but a few highly specialized industries whose main value proposition is their history and heritage. The pace of change is such that no business can rely on sporadic or happenstance improvement for survival. We must have a systemic approach to continual improvement of all areas of the business. I am grateful to John Bicheno (Bicheno & Holweg, 2023) for introducing me to a very useful framework (Figure 6.1) that should help all change agents in quickly assessing the current condition regarding how improvements take place in an organization.

All too often I hear that, "we are doing continual improvement" because some people have ideas and these get implemented. Of course, this is a fine start but it's not sufficient. Simply relying on people to have "light bulb" moments will inevitably lead to the lights going out for good. The passive approach finds itself somewhat systemized in the classic suggestion scheme with forms to fill in and boxes to put the forms in. There is nothing wrong with that as long as the system is governed well and recognition/rewards stimulate

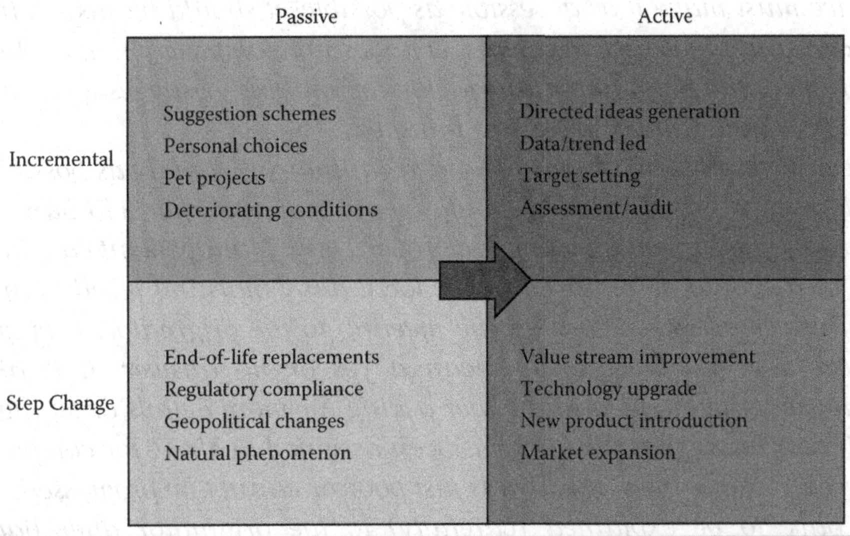

Figure 6.1 A Continuous Improvement framework (see The New Lean Toolbox, Bicheno & Holweg, 2023. Internal text by authors).

activity, but these systems are notoriously difficult to run well and sustain. So, "passive" means improvements are not part of an "active" system. An active system would be one driven by goals that continually stretch performance such as the daily and weekly monitoring of charts and the active deployment of tools and techniques to maintain and improve the process.

Finally, I have seen a site using the number and quality of suggestions as one of the inputs of the individual performance appraisal. Quality might be somewhat subjective, but a number of suggestions are not. The aim is not to artificially get a high number of suggestions, but to make everyone understand that thinking about and suggesting improvements is just a normal part of every job. A more active approach, on the other hand, would look to set a specific challenge to a team that is aligned with a company goal and then let them generate ideas relevant to achieving that goal. If we then make this way of working part of our production system and require a certain number of these events to happen over a year, then we now have an active improvement approach.

HERVÉ SAYS: SPEED IS THE KEY TO A GOOD SUGGESTION SCHEME

Suggestion schemes exist in various shapes and sizes. They can be paper-based or IT-enabled. Their complexity can vary. My personal preference goes for the simple paper-based ones on the shop floor on the grounds that we must make it as accessible as possible: it should be easy to input an idea. But the vehicle (paper vs IT) does not completely matter. In my experience, the most important factor for making a suggestion scheme take off is how rapidly ideas are handled.

Feedback must be given to the idea initiator as rapidly as possible. A good practice is that no idea should be unanswered after 24 hours. This should not be an issue if using the proper Daily Management cadence: a new idea should be reviewed in the local daily morning meeting and a first answer passed back after the meeting to the originator. Giving an answer does not necessarily mean a yes or no answer. It is about acknowledging the idea and either asking for more details or letting the originator know that the idea has been assigned to Mr. X for completion by week Y. Sometimes, the idea is just poor or cannot be progressed. This will have to be explained (carefully) to the originator after having thanked them for the idea.

And simple ideas have to be implemented as soon as possible. Otherwise, originators lose faith in the system and stop putting forward suggestions. And this is especially true in the early days of the system. A lot of people on the shop floor will be pessimistic when you announce a shiny new scheme. You will have to pay attention (and possibly have set aside resources) to make a few quick wins and show people that they can change their work environment and benefit from giving ideas.

Similarly, we can distinguish between step-change activity and incremental activity. Buying new equipment, developing new processes, and installing new systems should all give a step change in performance, but again, if we only do this when our equipment or systems fail, then it is a passive approach. Doing it because we have identified that is the way to grow our business or improve profitability in line with strategic aims then becomes an active approach.

I see the job of the change agent as being to assess the current activities against the improvement matrix and to move the organization further toward the active quadrants. By doing this, you will start to build in some longer-term capacity for continual improvement. Adding specifics around which methodologies, deployment vehicles, and tools and techniques to be applied would make this a really powerful engine of change and the core of a "Company (Toyota?) Way."

The TQM Legacy – Stability, Improvement, and Step-Change

Let's remind ourselves about the principles of TQM we discussed in Chapter 2 and expand on how we can better describe a system that encompasses and integrates Stability, Continuous Improvement, and Step Changes (or Innovation). With these three elements, we have everything we need to drive operational improvements. In Chapters 7 and 8, Hervé will take us through the steps needed to control process stability, but let's delve a bit deeper into why I like to separate CI from Stability and indeed from the subject of problem-solving as well.

Problem-solving and CI are often seen as being interchangeable terms, and indeed, both can be said to have the same starting point – a gap or deviation from a standard or a desired condition. What elevates a CI system from a problem-solving system is the way in which an organization captures and manages those gaps and applies a level of management control to the selection, resourcing, and closure of those gaps. It is the governance of closing those gaps that a CI system seeks to impose. A distinction should also be made between a deviation from a standard or "normal" situation, which will require a backward looking, investigative approach, and a deviation from a desired condition or a gap that we have created by stretch target setting, which will usually require a new, future change to be made to close the gap or indeed a combination of both. Not all problem-solving requires a structured approach, as many small issues can just be addressed as they arise, but that requires an organization where the mindset is to fix things as they arise. When we have a "walk-by" culture, this won't happen automatically. A good friend always insists that you check the cleanliness of the bathroom in a restaurant before deciding to eat there. Similarly, in a work setting, if the bins are overflowing and the workplace is cluttered with mess, it would be hard to believe it could produce consistently excellent product. The workplace faithfully reflects the attitude of management.

As we have seen in the previous chapters, we may employ diagnostics, data mining, surveys, polling, market analysis, etc., to first gain a better understanding of the current situation before we embark on root cause analysis or the application of novel ideas. So, I see problem-solving as an integral but discrete element of both CI and stability through a daily management approach. Both of these also have their own distinct problem-solving approach based on SDCA or PDCA cycles (Figure 6.2).

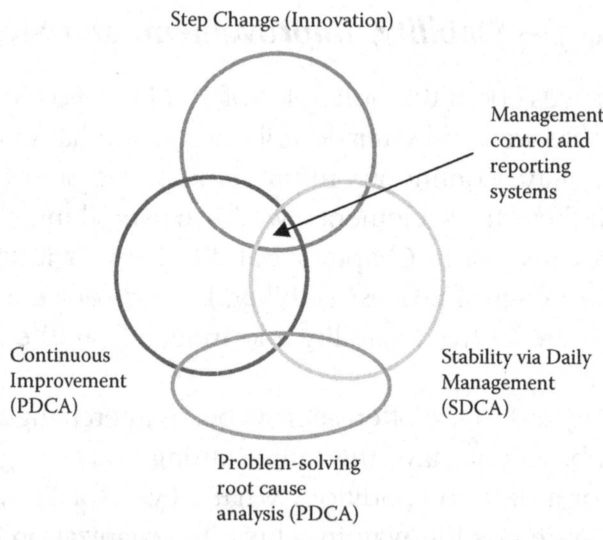

Figure 6.2 A model of operational excellence.

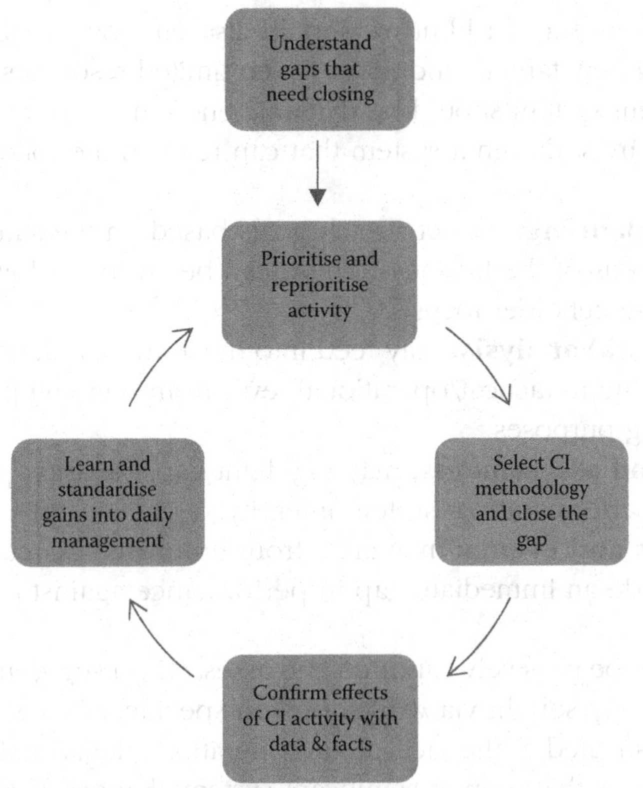

Figure 6.3 A generic Continuous Improvement system.

A CI system therefore sets out the elements to be in place to drive an overall governance for improvement activities (Figure 6.3). This includes the governance elements needed at each level of the business. When an organization has effective management control and reporting systems, information flows both ways in terms of closing gaps at all levels, from strategic to shop floor operations. Systematically identifying and closing gaps becomes the focus of management attention, and not just reacting to problems as they arise.

A CI system must be dynamic and flexible, but also rigid enough to keep the focus on longer-term, strategic goals. It must balance the annual planning targets with issues and incidents that arise during normal operations. It must always follow the PDCA cycle at an organizational level.

Plan

The starting point for the CI system is the collection of potential performance gaps to close. These performance gaps will be arising continually in the form of deviations from standard but we should also employ a regular (annual) cycle of setting new target conditions. Given limited resources to close gaps, the management system should be dynamic enough to not overburden the resources. We must design a system that can react to the following inputs:

- **Annual planning:** we set stretch goals based on the strategic and tactical needs of the business. These can be customer focused or business/stakeholder focused.
- **Trend (data) analysis:** may feed into the 1 annual planning process or be at a more tactical/operational level from ongoing performance monitoring purposes.
- **Audits and assessments:** may highlight gaps or risks (potential gaps) in performance or system integrity.
- **Incidents and events:** may arise from unforeseen circumstances and provide an immediate gap in performance against a standard or norm.
- **Ideas:** can be passively captured and assessed via suggestion schemes or proactively sought via workshops on specific subjects. Ideas that can be instigated at the tactical and operational levels fall into the CI system. Ideas that require significant system changes or CAPEX fall into the Step Change Innovation loop.

Regardless of how a gap is identified, prioritization of opportunities is required. Some of these gaps will fall into the arena of problem-solving, and others into analysis and improvement activities.

Do

Each gap that has been prioritized should be assessed to establish what standard improvement methodology should be applied. Many organizations will struggle at this stage because they haven't got a clear set of methodologies to apply. Change agents must articulate this need, and a suggested list will include:

- **Root cause analysis:** problem-solving and investigation.
- **Project management:** solutions are known but need deploying.
- **Process analysis:** diagnostics, value stream mapping, etc.
- **Human performance analysis:** behavioral/cultural change.

- **Active idea generation:** focus novel ideas on a discrete gap to close.
- **Toyota Kata approach:** short cycle rapid iteration of PDCA.

From the above activity, root cause and countermeasures are identified and control mechanisms are applied. Estimate the confidence in reaching a true root cause (Appendix 4).

Check

Confirm the effects of implementing the countermeasures via monitoring of lead and lag KPIs, Go-see activities, surveys, observations, and fact gathering. After countermeasures are applied, you should estimate the level of effectiveness of the countermeasures (Appendix 4).

If the gap is closed, move to the Act stage. If the gap is not closed, investigate if the approach (root cause or investigation) was at fault or the deployment was at fault. Too often we try another approach first without considering that poor deployment may be to blame.

Schedule further planned activities to check 3, 6, and 9 months after the deployment. Build checks into audit and assessment routines.

Act

Once gains are confirmed, standardize the control mechanisms into daily management activity (Chapters 7 and 8). Learn from the application of the methodologies and improve competence and confidence of practitioners. Grow the level of maturity of the CI system itself.

Celebrate success and capture and share knowledge throughout the organization.

The SDCA and PDCA Cycles in Problem-Solving

Problem-solving requires the application of two connected but distinct cycles: the Standardize, Do, Check, Act (SDCA) cycle and the Plan, Do, Check, Act (PDCA) cycle (Figure 6.4). The SDCA cycle is required to ensure process stability or the maintenance of process outputs to the desired specifications. This SDCA cycle is described in the Daily Management system in Chapters 7

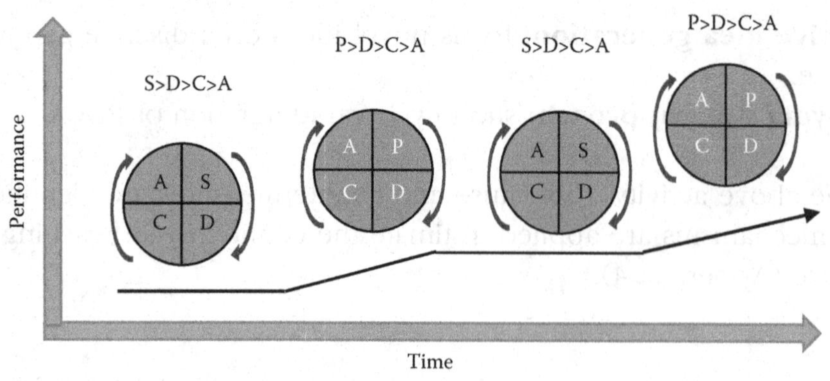

Figure 6.4 SDCA and PDCA loops working in tandem.

and 8. The primary problem-solving element of DM is the response to deviations in process inputs or outputs in order to regain control. The SDCA cycle is designed to capture previous root cause analysis or potential failure and potential root cause analysis and the subsequent control mechanisms that have been applied. The most common type of document to do this would be a Failure Mode and Effect Analysis (FMEA). Not many organizations explicitly make the link with using the FMEA as a first step in problem-solving activities. If FMEA is only taken out when the auditor arrives, then you are missing a huge opportunity to integrate management tools into a living system. None of the methodologies or the tools and techniques we discuss in this book should be applied in isolation from each other. Look at the inputs and outputs associated with each and build a picture of how they should form a self-reinforcing system.

The key control mechanisms are captured in a document (e.g., Control Plan, Maintenance schedules, etc.) that also defines a Reaction Plan when deviations arise. For the majority of the time, we aim for the SDCA cycle to be only a Do and Check interaction when we have no deviations. When deviations arise, we move to Act and investigate if it is the standard is at fault or the operation of that standard. If the standard needs to be adjusted, we then make the change, and having retrained and checked competencies, return to the Do and Check interaction.

The first stage of problem-solving is therefore to check if these standards or control mechanisms are still in place, adequately applied, and effective at the time the deviation was detected. Only when we have ensured all standards were satisfactorily designed and applied should we then instigate the PDCA cycle of problem-solving on an unknown root cause. So much of our problem-solving activity is directed at problems that already have a known root cause and known remediation activity. This is often a failure of knowledge management systems. How we capture previous problem-solving activity and make that valuable knowledge easily known to future teams is a key activity for Excellent organizations.

The next level of improvement involves capturing these repeating deviations and applying deeper root-cause investigations and actions. In reality, we may have reached the practicable limit of further elimination of root causes, and so we capture the remaining known risks and how we deal with them in a document such as an FMEA or risk register. If we make an informed decision to accept the remaining risk due to current constraints, we should not continue to waste time in further root cause analysis.

The Purpose of Tools and Techniques

Some tools help with analysis and planning of changes and others help in maintaining stability. Over the years, hundreds of tools and techniques have been developed, but a lot of these are designed to aid the diagnostic and analysis of problems and not to be applied on a continuous basis. We can usefully categorize tools into their basic functions in order that we are clear about what stage of improvement we are in:

- Diagnosis of the current condition (situation appraisal).
- Analysis of cause and effect (past conditions).
- Analysis of the future condition (positive future condition).
- Analysis of risk (negative future condition).
- Prevention and/or detection of risks (control current condition).

What the above list starts to look like, then, is very close to a generic methodology such as described in Chapter 2, and that's no coincidence. Methodologies are a logical sequence of steps and some, like Six Sigma and Shainin, include specific tools, but others are more open such as A3 Thinking and the basic PDCA cycle. All of them, however, have a "Do" or "Improve" stage whereby we must make a change and verify with data what the effect of that change is.

As seen in Chapter 3, diagnostic tools can help to pinpoint a problem or an opportunity before it comes to the attention of management. Other active approaches are related to an analysis of risk, either in our existing processes or in scenario planning. Many times in business there is a failure to identify these risks and indeed some risks can almost never be anticipated. These are the things that come and bite us unexpectedly and are usually of a strategic nature, but there are some tools to help with this and they usually involve variations on the SWOT (Strengths, Weaknesses, Opportunities, Threats) and PESTE (Political, Economic, Social, Technological, Environment) type matrices or even some very complex data analysis and scenario modeling tools that are beyond our expertise but can give great insights.

The Problem with Problems

Problems are like little diamonds, so the saying goes. If we solve all our problems and collect the diamonds, we'll be better off. Indeed, in the Toyota Way, Liker (Liker & Meier, 2006) puts problem-solving at the pinnacle of the operational triangle and it is undoubtedly one of the key competencies in world-class companies, but not all problems need to be solved. Can we "dissolve" a problem instead? Will things improve if we do nothing: simply by attrition or a changing environment? Maybe we can take away the subject of the problem by a change in technology, materials, product, or person. Problems always have a certain subjectivity attached to them, and only if somebody recognizes a problem can it be classed as such. What you consider a problem may not be in accord with what others view as problems. What if we can "resolve" the problem through dialog and a greater understanding of the situation and change peoples' minds, or, indeed, have our own minds changed?

Problem Definition and Problem Statement

From Figures 6.5 and 6.6, we can clearly see that a problem can be described as a deviation or gap from a standard or desired condition. In each of the four-item cases, common cause performance, special cause performance, new target level, and common cause specification, we must first describe and quantify the deviation or gap. Be clear on what the *subject* of the deviation is. Too broad a subject (like energy usage in a factory) will need to be broken down into a more granular form. This is not just to help with managing the problem-solving resources, but to enable a clear root cause to be established. By narrowing the focus, we can also narrow down the gathering of facts that are relevant to helping get to the root cause. If we have a set of facts relevant to two or more root causes and they are not demarcated, it becomes harder to

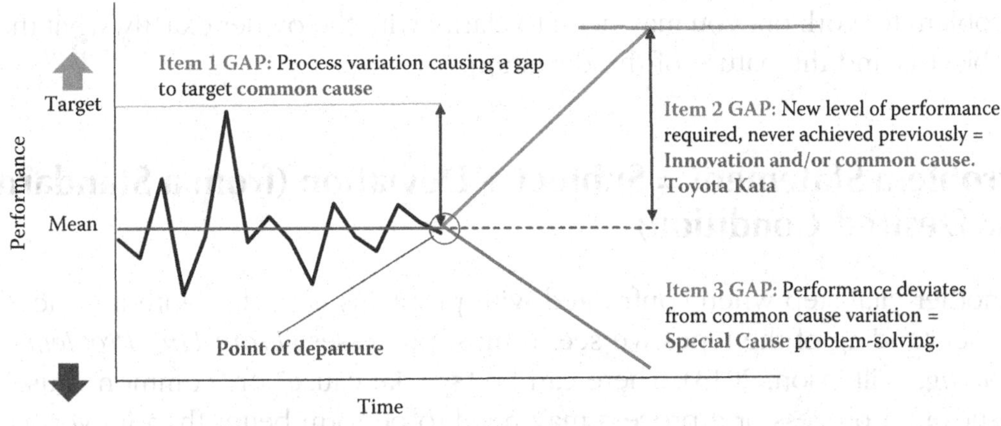

Figure 6.5 Defining problems in terms of a deviation (gap) from a performance target.

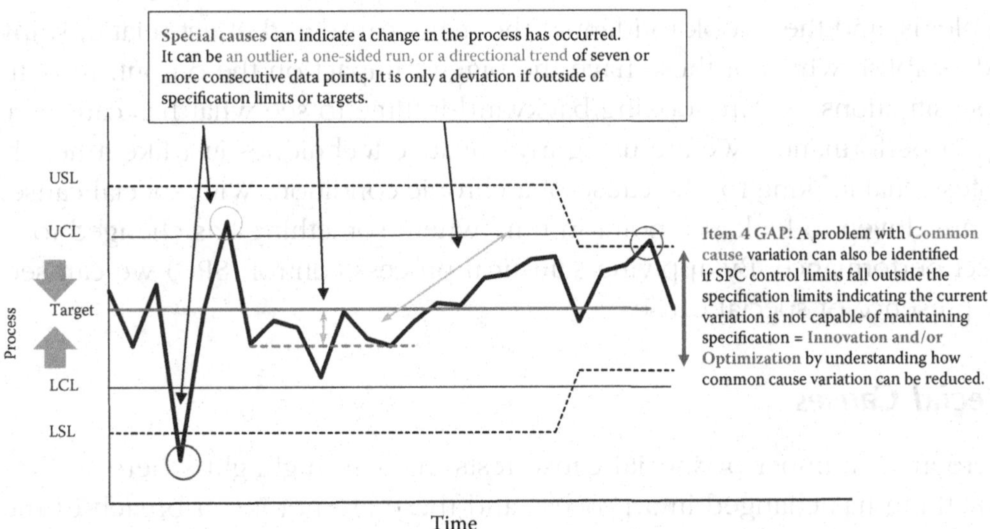

(UCL) Upper Control Limit, (LCL) Lower Control Limit as dictated by natural variation (normal distribution).

(USL) Upper Specification Limit, (LCL) Lower Specification Limit as set by customer requirements.

Figure 6.6 Defining problems in terms of a deviation from a target specification with upper and lower limits.

assess potential root causes against these facts, since we must be able to explain how a *potential* root cause explains the verified facts we have. So problem definition is not just a management activity but a vital part of the root cause analysis process. Time spent on problem definition is never wasted although it can be hard for people who don't understand the full process to be able to see the value of this activity at such an early stage. If you are given a problem to work on, you may need to clarify with the owner exactly what the subject is and the nature of the deviation.

Problem Statement = Subject + Deviation (from a Standard or Desired Condition)

Another vital step when confronted with problems is to start with a basic understanding of the types we see in most processes (*Front Line Problem Solving*, Wilkinson, 2013). There can be "special cause" or "common cause" issues in a process or a process may need to perform better than it ever has done on its best-of-best days. Certain analysis tools are better suited to special cause investigations, and these look to ascertain the cause and effect chain and get to the "root cause." Others are more applicable to common cause problems, and these look to identify the many cause and effect relationships and establish which of these have the biggest impact on the output. In both these situations, we are looking backward in time to see what has caused a gap in performance. We are using investigative techniques just like a health professional looking for the cause of a chronic condition. With special cause, we are driven to look at a point in time where something has changed to affect performance. By applying statistical process control (SPC) we can see the presence of special causes.

Special Causes

There are a number of special cause tests that can highlight where something has changed in a process and these are not just a breach of the control limits. These tests rely on probability to identify the difference between random variation and variation arising from a specific phenomenon. The chance of a data point being higher or lower than the preceding one is roughly 50/50, so we can use this to help identify if a process has changed. Depending on how confident we want to be we can set the rules accordingly. What is the probability of eight points in a row being above or below the preceding ones if we only have random variation at play? If you do the math it's about 0.004%, which means you can say with a certainty of 99.996% that something has changed in the process and drift is occurring. If you require more or less certainty to act, then increase or decrease the number of points in a run that trigger action, and you will alter the probability of detecting a true special cause.

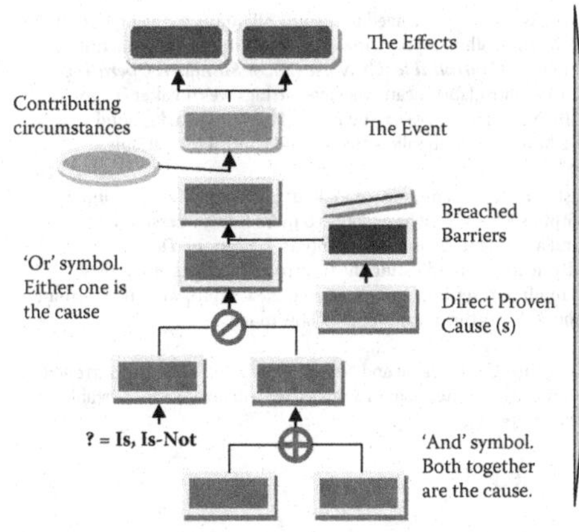

The event map is used to capture only the verified facts (subject + deviation). This may be sufficient for problem-solving. Where we have an unknown cause and it is necessary to find it to take meaningful action, we then move to IS, IS-NOT analysis (the problem specification).

Once we have completed the IS, IS-NOT by asking the open questions, we can then start to test possible causes. Does the possible cause explain or verify (V) the IS and the IS-NOT condition? When it does not explain any of the IS, IS-NOT conditions, can we eliminate it (X) or do we need further explanations to verify(?)

	Is	Is-Not	Changes	Distinc-tions	Possible causes			
What?					X	X	X	V
Where?					X	?	X	V
When?					X	V	X	V
How much?					V	V	X	V
Trends?						?	X	V

Figure 6.7 Special cause strategy.

There are many standard rules that have been set to determine if special causes are in play, and these can be easily referenced. Only if we apply SPC rules can we enact our Out of Control Action Plan (OCAP). Many people confuse OCAPs with a Reaction Plan. I know it's a technical point, but it is worth getting right. A Reaction Plan is initiated as part of a Control Plan when certain adverse conditions occur, and they may be associated with an OCAP if SPC is in place, but not necessarily. See Chapter 8 for more on SPC rules (Figure 6.7).

Common Cause

As we have said previously, all things exhibit variation, including all of our production and service outputs. The modern world is built upon the concept of the interchangeability of parts. Until such time as we started to standardize parts and have the capability to manufacture them within a defined tolerance, we were reliant on craftspeople to make individual items with fettled parts that fitted together in only that item.

No matter how good our processes are, we will always see variation. This can become a problem if the tolerances we require are sometimes tighter than the process can consistently achieve and we create defects. In studying a process, we must first identify and eliminate as far as possible all special causes through investigative and preventative means, as these will also cause defects in most cases. After that, we may need to reduce variability in order to ensure we have a process that is statistically capable of achieving the tolerances required. We can only do that if we can identify what inputs (X's) control the outputs (Y's). Only by controlling input variables can we control

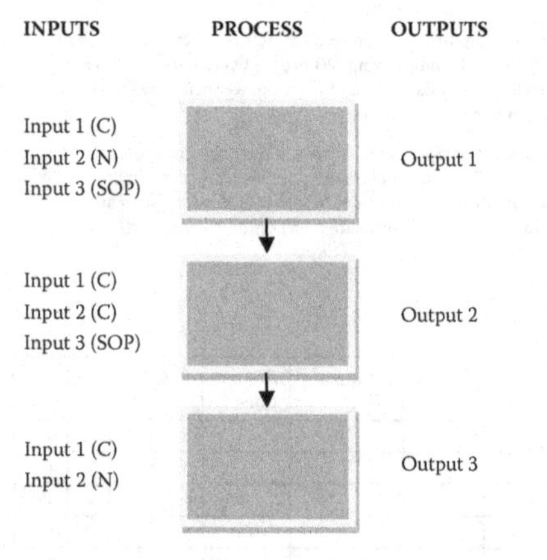

In the common cause strategy, we need to identify all inputs to the process at each step. Only by controlling inputs can we control outputs. Once identified, we categorize them as ***Controllable*** (C), ***Noise*** (N), or ***Standard Operating Procedure*** (SOP). Controllable means we have settings we can alter (High-Med-Low, 1–10). Noise factors we can't control (Humidity, Background radiation) or we have an SOP to follow that should control the variable.

We can then use statistical techniques to look for correlation between input settings and output settings if we have data. To more fully understand relationships and any interactions between inputs, we can use ***Design of Experiments***. By deliberately adjusting the Controllable inputs about their maximum and minimum settings and measuring the Output, we can determine which inputs most affects the outputs and by how much.

Finally we look to turn Controllable and Noise inputs into SOPs (or controlled variables). By eliminating unnecessary variables, we will create a more stable process with less tampering.

Figure 6.8 Common cause strategy.

the output variable. This is what Six Sigma was developed to do. We identify all potential causes of variation via a fishbone diagram (Ishikawa), and using expert knowledge we judge which are likely to have the biggest effect on output. Then we test the theory by data analysis or preferably by a design of experiment to fully understand the cause-and-effect relationship. We can then say with a degree of certainty what the inputs need to be to get a consistent and in-specification output (Figure 6.8).

New Performance Level

Another situation may require us to look forward in time. For instance, if we need to reach a new level of performance, then we need to do something we have never done before. We can't simply will ourselves to run faster or jump higher. We need to train ourselves over time to develop new techniques and strategies and to build new capabilities. Toyota refers to this process of striving for a new target condition as Kata. Kata is a reference to the practice of martial arts that requires constant repetition of stances, forms, and moves in order to train the body to perform these as a matter of routine. In Toyota, the routine taught is the scientific method of problem-solving based on the PDCA cycle. The main focus is to rapidly change only one thing and immediately check results. Don't produce a long list of to-dos, because once you have changed something the starting condition has also changed and future planned changes may be redundant. This method is often referred to as short-cycle improvement. Speed is of the essence and failure is an expected part of the process as you rapidly try out new approaches (Figure 6.9).

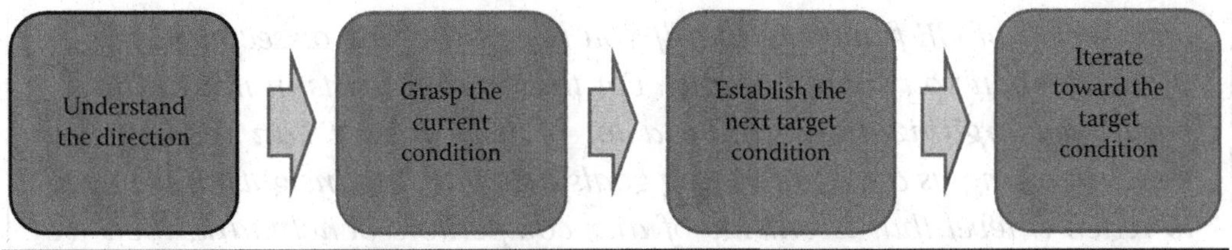

Figure 6.9 Steps in Toyota Kata (see Rother, Toyota Kata, 2010).

In a highly regulated medical device carton packing section, I was involved with a kaizen team that used the Kata approach to reduce the number of people required to pack the final products into kits. Much of this was manual operation with some semiautomated label application. We had dispensation to try out many different configurations of benches, machines, and work allocation, including constructing slides and temporary tool holders from cardboard, tape, wood, and suitable office supplies. It was great fun and got everyone involved in coming up with ideas we could easily try out. We would do a run of 45–60 minutes and time the throughput and the station cycle times, then review and modify and do the next run, and so on until we had a new layout designed. We then handed this over to the engineering department to put into a more durable form. This took the number of people from 5 down to 3, and these were then freed up to carry out further kaizen activities.

As a new consultant in a bakery, I casually mentioned that after observing a process I thought it may be a good idea to move a large, fixed mixing machine to the end of the line. To my surprise, the next day it had been moved and rewired into the position and the operators were already seeing the benefits. I was more careful with what I said after that, but it taught me the power of rapid Act and Check activities even though the Plan part was based on little evidence. Sometimes you have to give things a go and see what happens. In the bakery, there was very little downside if things hadn't worked out, and I think the operators would also have had something to say if the idea was too controversial.

CONTROVERSY CORNER: BENCHMARKING MATTERS

I've heard it said that benchmarking is not part of the lean philosophy and that to benchmark means you are somehow limiting your ambition. I can understand why purists may take that stance. If you have your strategy right, then you always strive to maximize those areas of performance that drive you toward that true north. I've also heard

Jack Welch of GE fame say that if you're not the first or second in your industry, then you should get out. For those non-purists in mid-industry positioned organizations (quite a lot of us!), then I can recommend benchmarking as a way of setting goals and gaining insights. If we need to reach a level that is outside of any competitors benchmark, then we need a more radical approach. Sometimes the best we can do is catch up in certain areas, and benchmarking can help with ideas on how to do that. Benchmarking in your industry is good, but benchmarking outside can sometimes be more revealing. In both cases, the naysayers will tell you it's not a level playing field, and you can't make direct comparisons. They are correct up to a point. What you should be able to do, though, is explain what it would take to beat those benchmarks, however unrealistic it may appear at first. If you ever wanted to be first or second, then you need to know the size of the challenge.

Fraser

Understand Your Problems

The above section on the nature of problems only scratches the surface of the whole problem-solving universe, but I believe it is vital to first have a good understanding of what type of problem you are presented with. All too often I observe people trying to apply inappropriate tools and techniques to a problem because they have been on a problem-solving course that does not make the distinctions we make above. Fishbone diagrams *can* be used to help get to special cause, but they are certainly not the most efficient or effective means. When we brainstorm during fishbone exercises, we mostly try to get the possible root causes out onto the chart. How do we then decide which of these is the real cause(s)? By voting, by consensus, or by who shouts the loudest? If we start with an event (the special cause), then we should create an event map (5 whys) that describes the direct proven causes and not all possible causes. If we don't know the direct proven cause, then we should seek more facts. Only when we come to the point where we decide this is a common cause problem do we need to use the fishbone as the starting point for a more statistical-based approach to solve the problem. This I why I always recommend to start with the A3 Thinking approach: it's the Swiss Army knife of problem-solving.

HERVÉ SAYS: 5 WHYS IS THE BEST TOOL … AND THE MOST DANGEROUS TOO

I have a love/hate relationship with 5 whys.

On the one hand, 5 whys is one of the best tools in the Continuous Improvement toolbox. It is, along with 5S, one of the easiest tools to deploy on the shop floor. And despite its simplicity, it can significantly contribute to engage the workforce and create the foundations for a learning culture.

On the other hand, root cause analysis is an art that requires a lot of practice. If you are not careful, 5 whys will create the illusion that anyone can do a good root cause analysis after 5 min of training. The truth is that a good analysis will unearth the complex network of causes behind apparently simple events. By handling events through 5 whys, only one branch will be investigated but not the others. And 5 whys might even be used to push the blame to another department. Depending on who fills the 5 whys, you can end up with "because maintenance did not maintain the equipment properly," "because purchasing went for a cheaper supplier," "because manufacturing did not inform maintenance that there was an issue," and so on … .

So use 5 whys wisely. Limit its usage to very simple problems. And when coaching 5 why users, keep in mind the root cause tree and ask for several 5 whys on the same problem to explore all the branches (e.g., for a customer complaint, always ask at least two 5 whys: why did the defect occur and why did we send the defective part to the customer). These multiple 5 whys can ultimately be joined together to demonstrate that problems have many causes and to bring your students to using full root cause analysis tools such as Event Mapping.

At a Lean Conference in 2019, I was privileged to hear Dan Jones (of Lean Thinking fame) reflect on 30 years of research and application of lean. In his closing remarks, he re-emphasized the absolute importance of the A3 Thinking approach as probably the most important learning from Toyota. Not only does it provide a simple means of applying the scientific method of problem-solving, but within Toyota it also provides the vehicle of discovery. When used as a tool to aid the mentoring of problem-solving, it gives a means to allow people to practice the thinking required, make mistakes, and reflect on those learnings. I am convinced that in many organizations we want to try and be good at all of the so-called lean tools, yet if we had spent all our efforts on developing problem solvers and the problem-solving culture, the businesses would have been in much better shape than they are otherwise.

Simple concepts like cause-and-effect relationships (the 5 whys) and fact gathering sometimes get lost in the sexy stuff. It seems like everybody knows about the 5-why concept, but if you ask them to do it you see that it is not easy for most people. I have been guilty of seriously *overestimating* the ability of very experienced engineers to conduct simple 5-why analysis. And when you ask them to gather facts to help solve a problem, they also struggle to distinguish the relevant facts (only relating to the Subject + Deviation) and to organize those facts into a useful format. After all, if you ask people to gather the facts surrounding a problem, then there will be thousands of them. Kipling's six honest men serve us as well as they served him in this regard.

> *"I KEEP six honest serving-men*
> *(They taught me all I knew);*
> *Their names are What and Why and When*
> *And How and Where and Who.*
> *I send them over land and sea,*
> *I send them east and west;*
> *But after they have worked for me,*
> *I give them all a rest."*

We use this in a structured way via the IS, IS-NOT analysis (Kepner & Tregoe, 1981). We ask questions regarding the What? Where? When? How Many? and Trends? relating to the problem definition to compliment the Why questions in the event mapping. Who is responsible is also covered, but not who to blame. Who can give us the facts and be responsible for taking countermeasures to prevent reoccurrence of the problem.

We consistently observe that people tend to either be too simplistic or they overcomplicate problem-solving. This is often a fault of the training they've been on as they try to apply it to all problem types. In this book, we are striving to give the reader a means of assessing situations before taking action. By showing you some of the pitfalls, we hope to set you thinking about what further skills you need to develop so as to have a consistent and structured thought process to apply in all circumstances. Much of the work we do with clients is about getting them to think differently about the problems they encounter. To do this, people need to be exposed to multiple problem types over many iterations and many years. Remember the false learning curve from Chapter 2 and how superficial knowledge of the buzzwords can be what passes for learning in the early stages of change.

We can therefore think of problem-solving falling into the following categories:

1. Just do it.
2. A deviation from standard – apply SDCA for known root causes.
3. A deviation from standard – apply PDCA on an unknown root cause.
4. A deviation from a desired condition of the current state (a created gap) – apply a combination of root cause analysis and Toyota Kata type approach.
5. A deviation from a desired condition beyond the current state – apply radical change, redesign, new technology, novel applications (Research & Development arena).

Selecting Problem-Solving Methods, Tools, and Techniques

It is easy to get confused with the number of problem-solving methodologies, tools, and techniques, and which situations lend themselves best to these. Figure 6.10 shows a decision tree to aid in selecting the most relevant given an appraisal of how the problem is presented. As the problem solver grows in experience, it will become obvious which is the most effective approach.

The four standard root cause problem-solving methodologies we recommend are:

1. The 3Cs
2. The A3 Thinking method
3. The Define, Measure, Analyse, Improve, and Control (DMAIC) method
4. The Toyota Kata approach

All are applications of the PDCA cycle. The 3Cs is the most widely applied method for most low-level problems and can be a very powerful day-to-day tool to capture problems that can be solved at the local, shop floor level. A3 Thinking should be the default method for more structured, in-depth problem-solving that may require more time away from the production line. The full DMAIC method and tool set is reserved for the application of common cause problem-solving (<5% of operational problems) that may

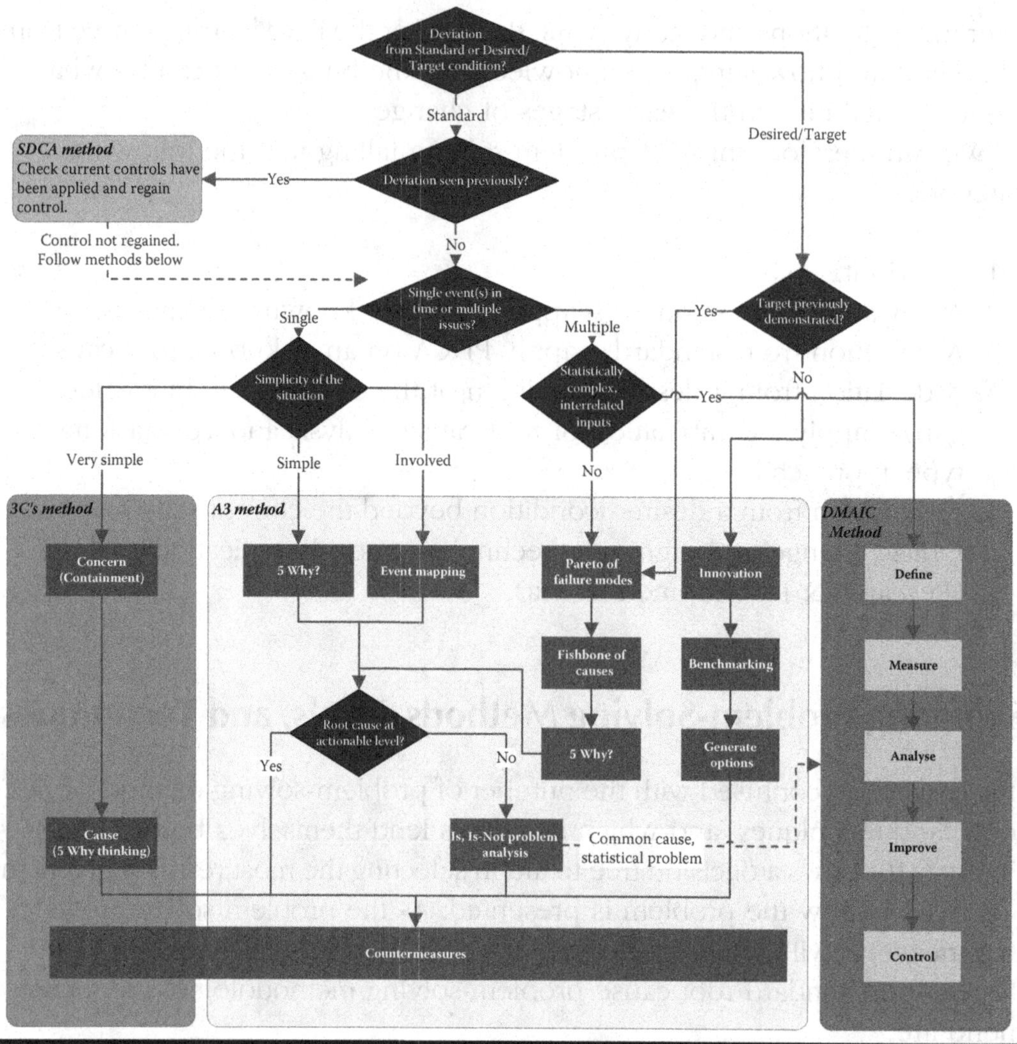

Figure 6.10 A decision tree for selecting problem-solving methodologies and common tools.

require the use of advanced statistical techniques and dedicated teams of experts (Table 6.1).

Concern, Cause, Countermeasure (3Cs)

This is a very simple technique that can be used for capturing and focusing attention on low-level problems, for instance at the daily or shift level. Capture the Concern as a subject + deviation. The cause can be established with the 5 whys thinking tool. Decide on countermeasures and who will implement by when. These should be captured in a simple table format as

Table 6.1 Comparison of problem-solving approaches based on a statistical (SPC) analysis

Special cause	*Common cause*	*Kata*
Investigative approach	Interaction approach	Iterative approach
Fact driven	Data driven	Innovation driven
Looks back at events and seeks to prevent recurrence	Looks back at cause-and-effect relationships and seeks to optimize multiple inputs	Seeks novel applications, one factor at a time with short-cycle feedback.
Tools: 5 Why, Event Mapping, IS, IS-NOT	Tools: Fishbone, Data plotting, Multi Vari studies, Main effects plots, hypothesis testing, design of experiment	Tools: One-factor experiments, benchmarking, idea generation

Table 6.2 The 3Cs problem-solving format

Date/ Ref.	*CONCERN (Subject + Deviation)*	*CAUSE (5 why thinking)*	*COUNTERMEASURE (Containment actions, prevention actions)*	*Who*	*When*	*Status*
						⊕
						⊕

shown in Table 6.2. If 3Cs do not prevent the deviation from recurring, then instigate the A3 Thinking method.

A3 Thinking Basics

The A3 Thinking method can be applied universally to problem-solving whenever root causes must be investigated or new actions taken to close the deviation. A3 Thinking is a seven-step method and the main points of each step are shown below:

1. **Background**
    - Short problem description.
    - Who is the customer/stakeholder?

- What is the impact of the problem on the customer?
- Specify costs, link to business targets.
- What containment measures are set during problem-solving?

2. **Understand the problem**
    - What is the problem exactly?
    - Quantify and visualize the gap (time plot) as the difference between the desired and actual situation (deviation from the standard or desired condition).
    - Breakdown the problem into the underlying sub-problems or processes via Pareto analysis.
    - Indicate the contribution of each sub-problem to the total gap.
    - Focus and prioritize: which sub-problem or process has priority and will be addressed first?
    - Where lies the point of cause of this sub-problem or process?
    - Gather facts (what? where? when? how much? trends?) and complete the IS, IS-NOT analysis if required.
    - Use diagnostic tools such as process mapping, surveys, audits, and assessments.
3. **Formulate the target**
    - Formulate the SMART target (Specific, Measurable, Achievable, Relevant, Timebound).
    - Be specific regarding the WHAT? (= selected sub problem = deviation).
    - Who, timeframe and which target to address?
4. **Analyze the root cause**
    - Provide the rationale of the analysis.
    - Use root cause analysis tools such as 5 whys or why tree.
    - Include the direct proven cause and effect chain from root causes to actual occurred problem.
    - Describe where the system failed, e.g., direct proven cause, breached barriers, and contributing circumstances.
    - Test potential root causes against verified facts.
    - Include results of any statistical analysis (DMAIC) of root cause.
    - Estimate the confidence in finding true root cause.
5. **Countermeasures**
    - For each root cause determine potential countermeasures that prevent recurrence.
    - Assume each countermeasure measure is a hypothesis that must be proved.

    - Follow the hierarchy of control mechanisms: 1. Eliminate root cause, 2. New barrier (a. Error Proofing, b. Automation, c. SPC, d. Standard Work.)
    - Estimate the effectiveness of the controls.
6. **Confirmation of effects**
    - Verify the effectiveness of the selected countermeasure against the SMART target.
    - Indicate whether a new A3 should be started to close remaining parts of the problem gap.
    - Compute the realized impact (financial benefits).
7. **Remaining issues and follow-up**
    - Describe how each countermeasure is sustained as part of the Daily Management SDCA cycle and whether these are confirmed via core tool review (Process Flow, FMEA, and Control Plan or equivalents).
    - Indicate sharing and learning opportunities.
    - Capture the output of all problem-solving in a local repository.

The DMAIC Steps

All of the tools used in Six Sigma already existed in the quality improvement arena, but the power was to bring them together under the DMAIC process and put the focus on distinct projects that have a significant monetary value. However, the basic steps are still worth repeating since they can be applied outside of a formal Six Sigma program, and indeed many people are being training without the organizational infrastructure associated with a formal program. Although in my experience the results are disappointing in terms of results and competence.

- **Define:** The project's purpose and scope are defined. Background information on the process and customer is collected.
- **Measure:** The goal of the measure phase is to focus the improvement effort by gathering information on the current situation.
- **Analyse:** The goal of the analysis phase is to identify root cause(s) and confirm them with data.
- **Improve:** The goal of the improve phase is to try out and implement solutions that address root causes.
- **Control:**The goal of the control phase is to evaluate solutions and the plan and maintain the gains by standardizing the process, and outline steps for ongoing improvements including opportunities for replicating the benefits.

Just like the Lean approach, Six Sigma starts with the Customer and what is of most value to them. When you know what they require, you can translate these into Critical to Quality (CtQ) items, and from there the process leads you to understand which process inputs have the most effect on these output CtQs. Once you have proved the cause-and-effect relationship, then you standardize and control variation in the inputs and so control the variation in the outputs. The equation below describes the fundamental relationship for controlling outputs. Y = the primary output to be controlled, and this is a function (*f*) of the inputs (*x*). (See also the Common Cause Strategy in this chapter.)

$$Y = fx^1, fx^2, fx^3 \ldots \ldots, \text{etc.}$$

The result should be a satisfied or hopefully delighted Customer and more efficient production process due to less waste. This is also the aim of Daily Management, and both are extremely complimentary.

Additional tool usage within the A3 or DMAIC method is also shown in Appendix 3.

Hidden Problems

Sometimes the diamonds available to us are very well hidden. We don't know we have a problem or an opportunity to improve because it is buried within a mass of data. With the emergence of the Internet of Things (IoT), the data available to an organization will rise exponentially. Data analysis tools, if used appropriately and with skill, can uncover cause-and-effect relationships that are not recognized by the process "experts." We applied statistical data analysis tools (from Six Sigma) to a download of all the data points we could get from one of our operating units. This quickly showed that we had unrecognized inputs that were having a big impact on the process outputs. This made the management team sit up and take notice. With renewed interest, further analysis showed that several long-held assumptions were in fact wrong, based on the available data. But, like any good data sleuth, we also had to question the measurement systems themselves starting from first principles. This part of the analysis uncovered many potential areas where we could not fully rely on the data.

When these initial findings were presented back to a senior team, those who were less well disposed to engaging in a Six Sigma approach suggested we could have uncovered these insights by more shop floor engagement. Shop floor engagement in problem-solving is to be encouraged, but it won't tell you the famous "unknown, unknowns."

HERVÉ SAYS: BEWARE THE ROOT CAUSE MASQUERADING AS A SOLUTION

Sometimes people will say the root case of a problem was because something was not in place at the time of the deviation. The solution is to add in this thing that was missing, maybe a check, an inspection, or a new system. Of course this may help in the future, but strictly speaking it is not a root cause since it could not have "failed" if it was not there at the time. We must only include verified events and facts at the time of the deviation or event. We class this action as a new barrier to the problem happening in future. If this barrier then fails, we can include it in the next root cause analysis as a "breached barrier." People are tempted to shoehorn in pet projects this way.

Countermeasures and Solutions

All of the improvement methodologies mentioned in this book have a stage that requires us to make a change. We must do something different to avoid getting the same results. We talk a lot about solving problems, but maybe a better terminology is that we are only implementing "countermeasures" to the current situation. A solution represents a finality, a permanence, something we can put in place and forget about, yet in time, most solutions become redundant. Thinking of the actions we put in place as temporary countermeasures opens our minds to the need to constantly review the present system for improvements. It is an ever-restless state of semi-stability that we require. Too stable a system may have too much inertia to change, and all too often the source of that inertia is in our own heads. The young and inexperienced in any field may recognize that the old guard are implementing the countermeasures they've become accustomed to, and so we should be alert to the possibility of new paradigms.

CONTROVERSY CORNER: SIMPLE SOLUTIONS TO COMPLEX PROBLEMS

The kind of problem-solving required in most production areas will predominantly be the kind that can be tackled with a reductionist approach. In other words, we can break down the problem into smaller, more discrete chunks and work on these individually as they will have distinct root causes. Paint defects are a great example. We can categorize these into a Pareto chart and work on the most important first.

Reductionist approaches, however, can be less effective when we have complex interactions and relationships that can be the root cause or be contributing circumstances to those root causes. If we take the problem of world hunger and break this down, then if we provide food for every person in need every day, we will eliminate world hunger. So why have we not done this? Even if we manage it for a week, a month, or a year, would it address the root cause of unsustainable local food supply for all in need?

So the idea of looking for the simplest solution to complex problems is attractive because we are naturally drawn to the least resource intensive options. We like to take the easy route. And there is merit in applying the least complex root cause analysis tools to a complex problem, but they don't always work that well. If we apply the 3C's (Concern, Cause, Countermeasure) to a problem with multiple root causes, interactions, and contributing circumstances, then we will fall short on the countermeasures applied.

So there remains some controversy amongst the problem-solving experts. My advice is to always look for the simplest analysis and countermeasures whilst having in mind that more complex analysis and countermeasures may be needed. That's why a master problem solver must understand the full range of tools available.

Fraser

In broad terms, most countermeasures are designed to either eliminate the root cause(s) of a problem or put in place a barrier to detect and prevent the cause(s) becoming an event. In the Daily Management system (Chapters 7 and 8), we term this as preventing a deviation from becoming a defect. This

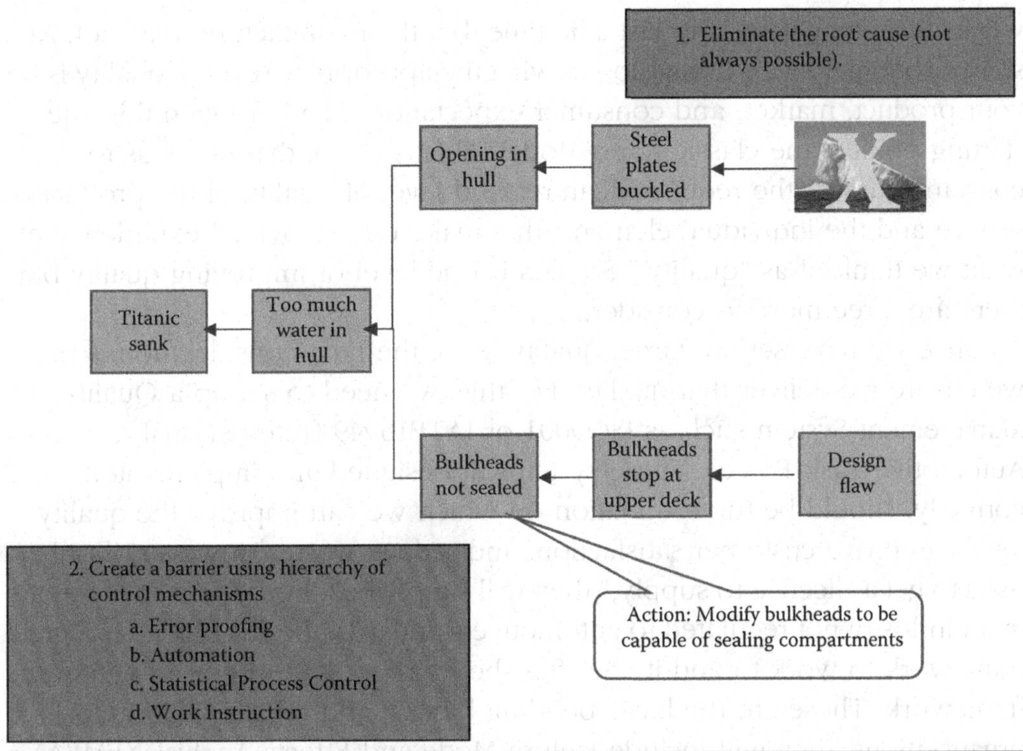

Figure 6.11 How to view countermeasures and relate them to the root cause analysis.

holds true for all of our primary measures of business performance: Safety, Quality, Delivery, Cost, Morale, and Environment (SQDCME) when we start to think of a defect as a nonconformance to the expected or specified outcome of a process. Some tools are more suited than others to help with each of these categories, although I don't think there are any exclusively applicable. In the next section, we will focus on a few specific tools that can help with analyzing and improving the Quality, Delivery, and Cost dimensions in particular (Figure 6.11).

Quality

Much has been written about the importance of quality, and some would even see the pre-eminence of quality as a goal. But as we know, quality can be both subjective and situational. Do you need to have your lawnmower built to the same quality and with the same traceability of parts as a Boeing 787 Dreamliner? Probably not, but you would like it to last more than a few weeks. You may want it to last a lifetime, but the manufacturer may not. And so, we soon get into a discussion of what the appropriate level of quality is for your product, market, and consumer expectations. To help with this, the starting point is the classic Kano Model. This is a tool that helps us to constantly assess the required features and level of quality of the product or service and the individual elements that make up the overall experience of what we think of as "quality." So, this is one level of improving quality but there are three more to consider.

Once we have set the target quality level, the next consideration is how we ensure we deliver that quality. For this, we need to set up a Quality Management System such as ISO9001 or IATF16949 (International Automotive Task Force). These systems, if designed and implemented correctly, should be the foundation on which we can improve the quality levels, improve customer satisfaction, and reduce waste. However, if only used to get a "licence to supply," they will simply be a burden. Even if you are in an industry not regulated to automotive standards, the IATF16949 is a great framework to work to and it specifies the "core tools" to be used within the framework. These are the basic building blocks, and for the majority of organizations, they will include Failure Mode and Effects Analysis (FMEA), Measurement System Analysis (MSA), SPC, and Control Plans (CP). If a quality management system is operated correctly, it will drive improvement through the constant use of these self-perpetuating tools.

At the next level, quality is improved by the application of specific tools that help us establish the root cause of quality problems, and many of these have been discussed previously. Many common cause problems require more advanced tools and techniques to establish cause-and-effect relationships and interactions, and the Six Sigma toolset is an ideal starting point. Most of the more advanced tools require considerable expertise to use in real-life settings, as there are usually underlying assumptions on the data sets that need to be fully understood. Depending on how critical the decisions to be made from these tools are, I would recommend you seek expert help. The basic 7 Quality Tools are also of great importance here and can be taught easily as part of the problem-solving process (Appendix 8).

And finally, for the last couple of decades, the use of Design for Manufacture tools has been the mainstream in many industries. Making the product as robust to the manufacturing process as possible is the aim. If we try to eliminate as many of the possibilities for error as we can, then quality will be improved as a result.

Delivery

Delivery performance is the result of the entire order-entry, planning, scheduling, and production system, and as such, improvements must start at the system level. The two main methods for analyzing delivery performance at a systems level are Value Stream Mapping and Theory of Constraints. Understanding the fundamentals of supply chain dynamics and the critical importance of the effects of statistical fluctuations coupled with inter-dependent events (almost all production environments) can lead to some counterintuitive realizations. Schedule less product through your plant and get more out? In Chapter 1, we discussed how at a certain point in the loading against maximum capacity of each unit, you will see a sharp deterioration in delivery performance; the magic number seems to be about 85% of maximum capacity, but this changes dependent on the level of variation in processing times. As a change agent, you will need to study this phenomenon.

Of course, just like quality, the next level is to apply root cause analysis tools to try and reduce the amount of variation in the system. A composite measure of production effectiveness is OEE (Overall Equipment Effectiveness), which looks at Quality, Speed of Work, and Availability of a particular piece of equipment. Analysis of the root causes of each of these will help drive performance, but there is a caution. Whatever the OEE performance, if the equipment is loaded beyond ~85% of mean capacity, delivery performance will still be compromised. OEE should also only be used on capacity constrained or bottleneck equipment.

Cost

There is good reason why cost is lower down the hierarchy of goals than quality and delivery in more enlightened companies. Firstly, better quality and delivery performance will reduce unnecessary costs and may make for a more attractive value proposition to customers, therefore improving the top line. Second, cutting costs can be detrimental to higher-level goals. This sounds obvious when stated here, but in the often unconnected and chaotic world of business functions and continual minor crises, it can be easily forgotten. A focus on value-in-use models can help with this.

The two aspects to be considered in any focus on cost are the demand and the commercial elements. Understanding why we have costs, especially in services, in the first instance can lead us to consider alternatives and the potential to eliminate or reduce demand at source by focusing on demand generation. Once we have a true picture of demand then we can consider the commercial elements and value-in-use.

The Future of Improvement

We, as humans, are increasingly becoming the most fallible part of the business operation, and yet without us no business would survive very long, at least until such point as artificial intelligence (AI) and robotics become dominant forces. Even now we have algorithms that can make better decisions about our lives than we can ourselves (Harari, 2017).

In most organizations, AI will undoubtedly become one of the most powerful improvement tools we have. The advent of Industry 4.0 and IoT will have a huge impact on how we compete with rivals even as algorithms today try to outdo each other in the stock markets. If my great-grandchildren ever read this work, they would be laughing at our pathetic attempts to improve things by *ourselves!* No wonder we were so slow to change anything if we didn't use AI. Until such time as the machines take over, however, we will all continue to make mistakes; we miss or perform incorrectly about 1 in 33,000 actions. That doesn't sound too bad until we think about how many tasks and operations we perform every day. Some mistakes, failures, and inadvertent actions can actually lead to breakthroughs and insights like the invention of the glue used on Post-It Notes® but let's stick with improving our operations by cutting down on mistakes or making our systems more robust to those mistakes.

CONTROVERSY CORNER: SURVIVORSHIP BIAS

Beware of the interpretation of data. Many biases exist. An interesting but maybe less-known one is survivorship bias. It is a selection bias that occurs when the data you look at are a particular subset of a wider pool.

A famous example from World War 2 is the research that was carried out to identify where armor should be added on Navy planes. A team at Columbia University gathered data about bullet impacts found on returning planes and built maps of planes showing impacts. Some people allegedly wanted to recommend to reinforce the areas that had received the most bullets. But statistician Abraham Wald counterintuitively explained that the Navy should instead reinforce areas with the least bullet impacts. He had understood that bullet impacts were probably uniformly distributed across a plane during dogfights. Planes that returned were the lucky ones where the least critical areas had been hit. On the contrary, the absence of bullet marks on returning planes on, e.g., fuel tanks meant that such a hit was most likely lethal. Looking at a sample consisting only of returning planes was an example of survivorship bias.

So be especially aware of this bias when exploiting data from employee or customer satisfaction surveys. Most of these surveys are only collecting data from the planes that came back home. Very often they will not consider the planes that did not come back home, i.e., employees that left or customers that stopped buying. Whilst it is more difficult to access this type of information, businesses should attempt to collect this valuable data through, e.g., employee exit interviews or capturing reasons for enquiries not converted into orders. Ignoring them will make you overestimate the company's performance and you will miss critical opportunities for improvement. For example, your lead-time might be a bit too long for a market segment, so you would lose customers in that segment. If you only ask customers that have decided to buy from you, the message you will get is that your lead-time is acceptable, so you will not work on that problem.

Hervé

What Is Industry 4.0?

This expression refers to the fourth industrial revolution, a phase characterized by cyber physical systems enabled by communications technology, sensors, or computer learning, for example. The first revolution is said to be the widespread use of mechanization and steam power, the second was the internal combustion engine and the use of oil and gas, and the third was the age of electronics. Things are indeed moving fast: technology becomes better and better while its cost rapidly goes down. IT-driven systems can acquire, process, and analyze more and more data. These gadgets are wonderful, but can they help us achieve operational excellence? They can indeed be of great help in the following areas:

- Defining the normal state, i.e., the optimal process parameter combinations
    - AI can identify within the jungle of available data which parameters have a positive effect on a final product characteristic. Although

humans can do that clumsily with techniques like Shainin, for example, AI will be much faster. And human reasoning is no match when effects of combined parameters are investigated.

- **Anticipating problems**
  - Industry 4.0 allows us to visualize parameters that start to drift. Whilst paper-based control charts do that as well, automated alerts are useful when process parameters to monitor are too numerous.
  - SPC is powerful, but in my experience is difficult to sustain when analysis has to be done manually. SPC software is now linked to the process and removes the burden of data entry and calculations, thus allowing focus on data analysis

- **Detecting problems earlier in the process**
  - For example, using continuous monitoring/measurement devices, high-definition defect recognition cameras rather than relying on human inspection.

- **Finding causes of problems more rapidly**
  - Never in human history have so many data been available so easily. Often a simple analysis in Excel will help find the incorrect process parameter, a task that would have taken us hours or days 30 years ago.
  - The downside of availability is that data might swamp us. Moreover, some issues are the result of adverse combination of several process parameters, which are difficult to detect for a human analyst. Fortunately, Industry 4.0 brings us Advance Analytics and Machine Learning: computers can now detect which parameters cause problems much better than human analysts.

Increasingly, automation and the application of inexpensive sensors and monitors will be used to prevent costly mistakes. Augmented reality devices will blend the real-world view with advanced graphics to help us in every task. Maintenance technicians will be directed to and instructed in routine tasks and parts will be ordered as used. Meetings will become slicker and more effective as they are run by our office assistants (mobile devices and apps) who will communicate in a network to take the next steps and keep us focused on tasks. Analytics will be more automated and directed by company strategy, informing us constantly of where we need to dedicate our attention. Every aspect of our performance will be monitored, and improvement opportunities will be highlighted. We will be valued by whatever the machines are not yet capable of. Deciding right from wrong, moral judgments, and the application of empathy and sympathy. Maybe we'll come to the point where our very imperfections are of the highest value to society and the organization.

Recently Toyota has started to re-think its robotization strategy in some of its production facilities. They will only apply robotics after they are sure the human team will be augmented in the long term by the use of automation. Until machines can learn and re-organize for themselves, the human element is still required.

As we've seen in the discussion on the common frameworks, new movements come along regularly. Sometimes these frameworks rehash old ideas or collect together a slightly different set of thought processes than the last ones. Very few are truly new ways of running an organization. At the time of writing, for instance, Agile is very much of the moment. Agile was first proposed by a group of software developers who saw the disadvantage of the traditional way of commissioning and developing software solutions. In most cases, a very tight specification was agreed upon at the start of the project, and the software was only released for use when all features were tested and working fully. The disadvantage of this is that it does not allow for an easy reconfiguration if new features are identified. It also assumes that those specifying know exactly how the software will be used. A good analogy comes from the design of pathways in new building schemes where the architect tries to predict where people would walk. The more agile approach is to allow people to move around and see where the paths should go before laying them.

The agile approach allows for the creation of minimally viable products that can be tweaked and adapted as users discover what is needed or not needed. Can this idea be transferred to a traditional manufacturer? Only if the product can be modified easily after sale, and that's usually not the case. The part of the agile approach that is being applied in traditional settings is the way the project is managed through the monitoring of actions that can be done in a specified timeframe or a "sprint." These "sprint" meetings attempt to keep the focus on delivering smaller chunks of the whole in order to reach the end goal on time. Neither of the authors has any practical experience of this approach, so we'll keep an open mind, but it does not appear to be such a radical departure for project management as it does for product development.

What the agile example shows is that these novel approaches will continue to arise and the change agent must be willing to investigate with an open mind whatever comes along. There will be pros and cons to each. So, whatever you think about the picture painted above, we can be sure the future of improvement is already with us: it's just not evenly distributed.

CONTROVERSY CORNER: TECHNOLOGY SOLVES ALL OUR PROBLEMS?

It is tempting to believe that industry 4.0 will solve everything. This topic is very hot and many companies make money selling 4.0 solutions. But all these tools will have to be designed with a purpose and with a clear understanding of the process and the relationship between process parameters and product characteristics. They have to be approached with the Golden Triangle and Daily Management cycle in mind (see Chapters 6 and 7). If the Daily Management ground work is not done before implementing these 4.0 solutions, they will just be a set of expensive tools that might gather dust.

Hervé

Summary

We've seen in this chapter that it is easy to confuse action with improvement. In the early days of the Lean movement, we talked of the "happy mappers"; people who were content to busy themselves with mapping processes, systems, and entire value chains but never made the next step of improvement. Current state must be translated into future state via a transition plan. Completion of the plan improves the performance. Analysis is necessary but not sufficient. You must understand the improvement frameworks that exist in your business and assess if these are also sufficient. Leaders must ensure that everyone is contributing to improvement and that your role is also about development of others. Once we have been through the improvement loops, we must next focus our attention on the sustainability of performance improvements, the subject of the next chapter.

Get started on your Chapter 6 learnings – practicing problem-solving skills

I. *Defining problems*
   a. *How do I assess a problem to identify if I am using the best method to find countermeasures (special cause, common cause, or innovation)?*
   b. *How do I select a suitable team to work on a problem?*
   c. *Have I got a good problem statement with subject and deviation clearly articulated?*

II. *Finding the true root cause of a problem*
   a. *Have the team gathered all the relevant facts and are they organized in the Is, Is-Not framework?*
   b. *Is there a logical why tree structure showing the interrelationships between cause and effect?*

III. *Proposing, evaluating, and selecting countermeasures*
   a. *What process can I use with the team to select the countermeasures that address each root cause?*
   b. *What level of confidence do I have in the effectiveness of the countermeasures selected?*

IV. *Creating integration*
   a. *How can I model the interactions of all the methodologies, tools, and techniques used in this exercise (inputs and outputs)?*

Chapter 7

Sustaining Improvements with the Golden Triangle

Hervé Duval

Entropy can never decrease over time for an 'isolated system.'

The Second Capital Law of Thermodynamics

Introduction

So, we have just applied the improvement approach as explained in the previous chapters, and we solved a problem. This is great. Now how are we going to prevent the problem from coming back?

The second law of thermodynamics taught me that chaos will always win, it is only a matter of time. This statement is empirically backed by my experience of trying to get my son to keep his bedroom tidy. The second law is concerned with the direction of natural processes and states that entropy can never decrease over time for an isolated system. It also asserts that a natural process runs only in one sense is not reversible. For example, heat always flows spontaneously from hotter to colder bodies, and never the reverse, unless external work is performed on the system.

The key (and depressing) consequence of the second law in our working lives is that any standard that we create will degrade over time unless external work is performed to maintain the system. Fortunately, a simple tool, the Golden Triangle, can help us to provide this "external work to maintain the system." Here is what this triangle looks like (Figure 7.1):

 DOI: 10.4324/9781003486022-7

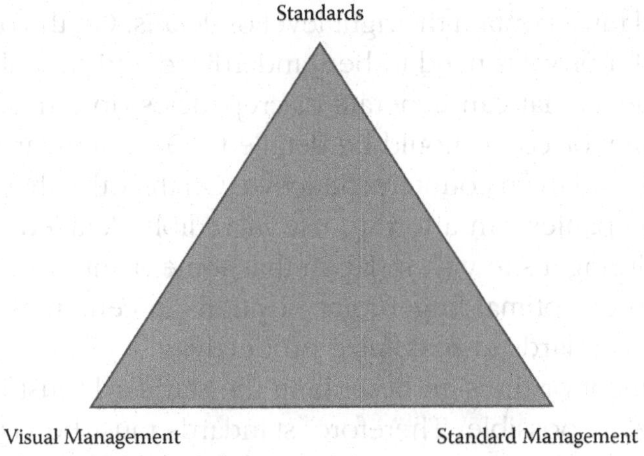

Figure 7.1 The "Golden Triangle."

The First Vertex of the Golden Triangle: How to Write a Good Standard ... and Why It Is Not Enough

Once we have found a solution to a problem, the first thing that most CI professionals will rightly think of is "let us create and deploy a standard," i.e., a description of the most efficient method to perform a task. Not only can standards help sustain improvements, but they are also the base from which the next improvement cycle will start. Taiichi Ohno (father of TPS) famously said that "without standards, there can be no improvement."

Most readers will be familiar with standards, so I am not going to explain in detail what standards are and why they are important. I would, however, like to share a few points that I learnt about standards that work:

- Standards must be created by those who are going to use them. It increases the chance of the standard being adhered to. Standards are most important in organizations that work shift patterns to ensure consistency between teams. This creates the need to put together representatives of the two, three, or five shifts that will apply the standards. It is not always easy to arrange in practice. If it is not feasible, you will have to give the task of writing standards to opinion leaders as teams often consider that the way they have always worked is the best conceivable way.

- A standard must contain the right level of details. On the one hand, not all steps of a process need to be standardized and described in detail. Only elements that can generate discrepancies (in terms of safety, quality, time, or cost) should be detailed. "Over-standardization" is pure waste and even counterproductive. On the other hand, extremely mature companies can afford to use incredibly detailed standards. I was told during a site visit in Japan that some plants had introduced a description of optimal finger joint positions in certain assembly operation standards to maximize productivity.
- The document or the sign describing the standard must be as easy to understand as possible. Therefore, standards must be visual. A 14-page procedure is not a good standard as no one is ever going to read it, let alone memorize it. Ideally, standards should consist mostly of pictures or drawings.
- Most standards describe what needs to be done or controlled. But very few explain what should be done if a deviation is detected. A good standard includes a reaction plan (also sometimes called OCAP for Out-of-Control Action Plan if we use sound statistical methods). For example, if a standard describes how an operator should measure a chemical concentration and what are the control limits, it should also describe what the operator should do if the concentration is too high or too low.

Deploying a standard is necessary to sustain benefits, but it is far from being enough. Most companies have ISO-certified Quality Management Systems based on standards. Yet most of these systems fail to deliver sustained continuous improvement. So, it would be naive to conclude that the job is done once standards have been implemented.

Chaos and degradation can be slowed down by understanding why standards fail. So let us discuss the reasons for failure and strategies to uphold standards. Employees can either unconsciously or consciously not follow a standard. In this first case, employees might not be aware of the standard. Either they have not been properly trained or they have forgotten. People need to be trained and reminded of the standards. The best way to do that is to ensure that standards are displayed. This is not about displaying on the wall a 10,000-word procedure. It is about visual management. And you must constantly check that standards are understood and used. This is standard management. In the latter case, standards are also often consciously ignored.

The most common reasons for consciously ignoring standards are:

- **Ignorance:** They might know the standard, but not why it is important to comply and what could be the impact of not following the standard. It is therefore important to include this information in the training and visually where the work happens. For example, rather than just telling people to switch lights off when they leave rooms, it is often beneficial to display little posters informing them of the cost of lighting.
- **Practicality:** A standard might not be practical or even great in theory but impossible to follow. This issue will be avoided by ensuring that users are involved in the design of standards. Stating the obvious (but you would be surprised by how often this piece of advice is ignored), standards must be tested before being communicated and enforced. Piloting the standard in a small area is usually a good idea.
- **Negative mindset (e.g., disengagement, "not invented here" syndrome, laxity):** These are usually signs of a cultural (and therefore a leadership/management) issue. This can sometimes change if opinion leaders can be swayed. But it is not a great starting environment.
- **Desire to innovate or to perform:** Sometimes people will do things their way because it is better (or they think that their way is better).

CONTROVERSY CORNER: YOU DO NOT HAVE TO BE JAPANESE TO FOLLOW STANDARDS

During a tour of one of our European plants, visiting Japanese engineers were surprised by how much safety guarding we had put on our production lines (as this made operating and maintaining the line more difficult). We explained that we needed guarding to prevent employees from accessing machines and risking hand injuries. Our Japanese visitors then suggested that we remove guardings, paint a line on the floor and tell people not to cross it. Whilst this solution works in Japan, it is unlikely to work in Europe, as our relationship to standards is different.

For many years, I complained about the fact that our Western culture was making my job more difficult. I then realized that the Toyota plants outside of Japan were employing local people, and yet they managed to create this culture of standards. Three of the plants I had supported have a Toyota plant less than 25 km away, therefore hiring from the same employment pool. And yet the plant cultures are massively different.

So whilst national cultures matter, the key is to recruit people with the right attitude towards standard work. And above all, it is the responsibility of the leadership to promote standard work, build a system that will ensure adherence to standards, and walk the talk, as we will see in the rest of this chapter.

Hervé

In all these cases, management often ignores the fact that standards are not followed and usually only takes action after a major issue (accident or quality problem) is investigated. Another advantage of always thinking in terms of standard work is that it is a great paradigm for root cause analysis. Failure is often analyzed through technical lenses. But this is not enough. The first step in analysis should not be root cause investigation (only use this for unknown causes), but an investigation into known controls such as operational standards. Are the standards satisfactory, and are they being followed?

EXAMPLE: THE GOLDEN TRIANGLE APPLIED TO ROAD SPEED LIMITS

To improve road safety, we are told to avoid speeding. Without a standard, this would be a rather vague instruction. Therefore, all countries define maximum speed limits. Can we guarantee that every driver will remember the standard, whatever the road he is on? Probably not, which is why the standard (i.e., speed limit) is visually depicted on road signs. But defining speed limits and displaying them is not enough to guarantee that all drivers will comply. It is therefore necessary to confirm that standards are complied with, which is done using speed cameras.

Removing any element of this golden triangle will degrade results. Not having defined speed limits would be very dangerous. Not having road signs makes it much more difficult to comply with speed limits the moment you start driving in areas you are not familiar with. And removing speed cameras will cause drivers to increase speed.

So, whilst creating Standards is the most well-known of the three elements in the Golden Triangle, Visual Management, and Standard Management are equally important to ensure that our improvements will not drift.

The Second Vertex of the Golden Triangle: Visual Management

Any plant or business will operate hundreds or even thousands of standards. These standards range from a simple set of numbers such as min./max. range of values (e.g., the standard for this chemical bath's temperature is 38°C +/−2°C) to a procedure of several pages. Moreover, standards may constantly evolve. It is therefore impossible to try and remember the content of every standard. Yet, all employees should know every standard relevant to them.

Turning standards into something visual is the solution. Ensure that all your displays, whether digital or analogic, are color-coded to reflect the limits within which your parameters should evolve (e.g., the 38°C ±2°C from the previous paragraph). Paint the floor to materialize the number of parts that you need to be available at any time rather than hoping that people will remember.

Visual Management also helps a new employee or a temporary worker to pick up the essential points of standard work, thus allowing them to be rapidly able to operate with a guaranteed minimum level of performance, especially around safety and quality.

Finally, compliance with standards must be regularly audited. Traditional auditing takes a long time. One must check the content of procedures in large physical folders or IT systems. It is therefore impossible to exhaustively audit a quality manual. But compliance with a visual standard can be assessed immediately. To maximize chances of spotting abnormal conditions, visual management should be deployed to ensure that anyone (even new employees) can spot deviations.

An example of how Visual Management can help spotting abnormalities is colour coding of valves. Opened valves that were supposed to be closed (or the other way around) are a common cause of problems in factories, especially in process industries. Whilst it is possible to determine whether a valve is open or closed, how do you know that this specific valve's normal position is being open? You do not want to have to look for that information in a huge folder listing all the valves in the factory. Even searching a slick IT system might be time consuming. But this information can be made readily available by using

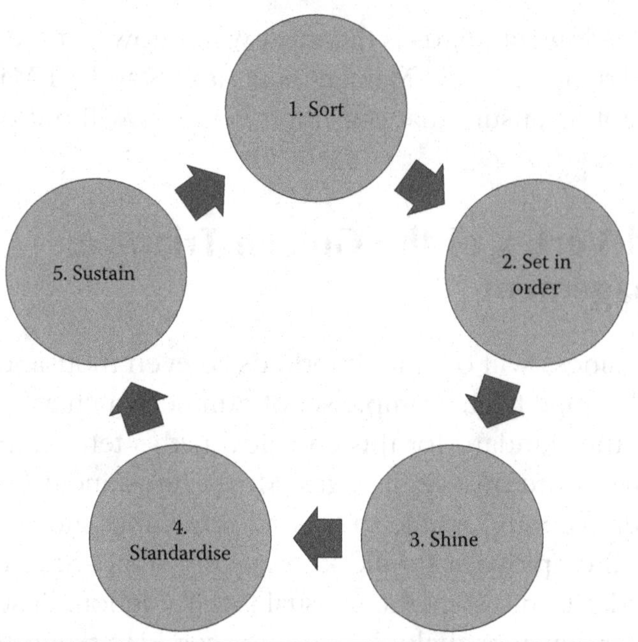

Figure 7.2 The 5S system.

the visual factory concept. If you define a color code (e.g., red = normally closed, green = normally open, yellow = partly open), you can spot immediately any deviation.

To consistently achieve this level of visual factory, one needs a process. 5S is a great 5-step process to do this (each step's name starting with S, hence "5S") (Figure 7.2).

The steps are the following:

- **Sort:** This is about removing anything unnecessary from the area in scope. Clutter is a source of accidents and mistakes. A clutter-free environment makes completing tasks easier. At a basic level, it is about removing obsolete parts or clutter that have nothing to do with the area. In some advanced examples of 5S, even buttons that are not used are removed from control panels.
- **Set in Order:** Once all unnecessary items have been removed, remaining items must be placed in the best possible location, i.e., easy to reach, close to the point of use. Once this has been done, the correct location should be marked/labeled to ensure that items are always returned to the right place. A classic example is the tool shadow board (see picture 7.3).

- **Shine:** This step is about cleaning the area and the equipment, and they should be returned to pristine condition if possible. Japanese say that "cleaning is inspection." Cleaning increases your chances of spotting problems (during the cleaning operation itself, but also to make deviations easier to spot). Once the first 3 "S" have been completed, the workplace has significantly improved, and it gives the team a great feeling of achievement. Unfortunately, many 5S efforts stop after 3S and slowly wither. What 3S has done is give us a standard with some visual management. We need to put in place the Golden Triangle to make the effort sustainable. The fourth and fifth steps are therefore about putting in place Standard Management.
- **Standardize:** In this step, we need to put in place the operational standards that ensure the workplace is in a state that supports flow and reduces waste. Cleanliness and tidiness are important in themselves and can bring order and safety to the workplace, but the aim is always to prevent hindrance to flow. These activities must support the standard work elements of standard operations, standard sequence, standard work-in-progress (WIP), and standard outcome. We need to think about applying the hierarchy of control mechanisms to our standards. Can we error proof our workplace organization? We call this "unbreakable 5S." If we need a tool at a workstation, then maybe we can chain it to the machine. Can we eliminate the tool by redesign? Can automation alert us to an out-of-standard condition? Again, standard work is the least effective control mechanism.
- **Sustain:** The last step is ensuring that users of the area sustain the optimum condition for flow and waste reduction and drive further improvements in results. This will usually be through team leaders' and managers' checklists and routine go-see routes. It could also be through more formal 5S audits, but feedback should always be given in person.

Figure 7.3 is an example of outcome of the first four steps.

5S is a great tool that immediately appeals to people new to continuous improvement. "Doing a 5S" is rewarding as changes in the workspace can take place very rapidly. The approach easily engages people involved in the process. But there is a major pitfall that new practitioners must be aware of. It is very tempting to start 5S-ing the world. Most of us have seen pictures of

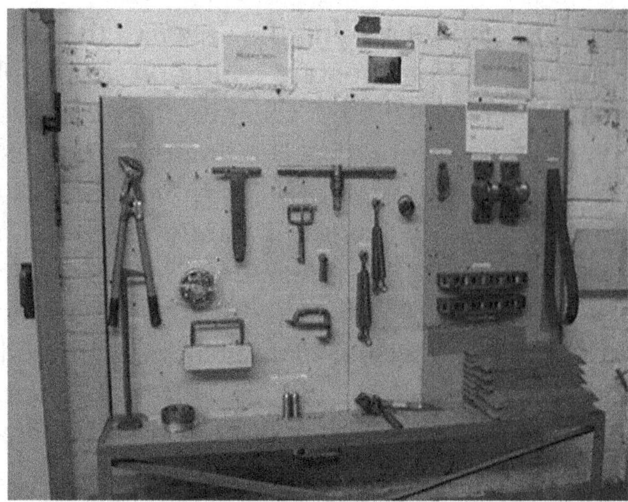

Figure 7.3 Shadowboard example. (Courtesy of Tata Steel India.)

offices where the position of the stapler is marked with tape on desks. This is very visual, but it is missing the point. 5S must be done for a purpose, not for the sake of making things more visual. We want to make processes as visual as possible so that they are easy to follow, and deviations are immediately spotted to avoid degrading process effectiveness and/or efficiency. What is the risk associated with having a stapler not in place? Is this really going to lead to productivity loss? Is this one of the biggest problems you had to deal with? This type of naïve enthusiasm for the form of 5S rather than for its substance is what earned in some places the nickname "clean coaches" to our newly trained Lean coaches. Case Study 3 has a lot more on deploying 5S.

Visual Management also provides easy to implement solutions that help avoid investing in expensive technologies as illustrated by the following example. I had lunch in Nagoya in a restaurant run by three old ladies. There were many small rooms and tables, so I was wondering how they were keeping track of table availability during rush hour. Some of the European engineers in our group speculated about the existence of some hidden hand-held devices. When we reached the till, we found out that the three old ladies were simply using a laminated map of the restaurant with small magnets indicating occupied tables.

Another aspect of Visual Management is visualization and communication of performance. This setup is usually called a "war room" when used to pilot operational performance improvements. Figure 7.4 is an example of such a war room.

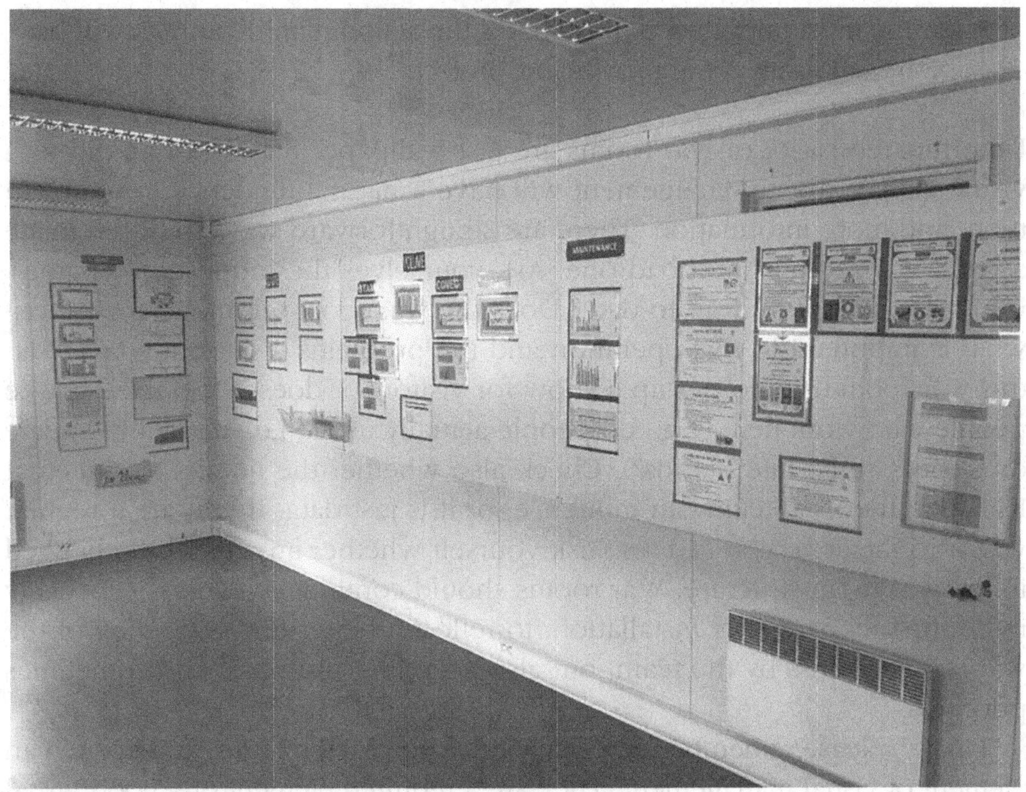

Figure 7.4 War room example. (Author's own photo.)

> **EXAMPLE: HOW 5S IMPROVES PERFORMANCE: THE VISITOR WHO SPOTTED A LEAK**
>
> *I once visited Tata Steel India's rolling mill in Jamshedpur. With the support of Japanese consultants, the place had become a notable example of visual management. The cellar under steel rolling mills is traditionally an extremely dirty area full of oil and grime. The cellar of that mill was so clean that I, a mere visitor, was able to spot the beginning of a leak which was then subsequently corrected. In any other mill, it would have been impossible to spot this deviation, which could eventually have led to a breakdown.*

A good war room will display the following for each KPI:

- KPI graph (including performance and target).
- Gap analysis (why is there a gap between the target (or 100%) and the KPI). This usually takes the form of a Pareto.

- For the most important gaps, what is the action plan? Ideally, it will be expressed as an A3 improvement project.

Unfortunately, a lot of war rooms are just wallpaper instead of an aid to visual management. Management will have a natural tendency to generate more and more information. There are straightforward ways to differentiate a good war room from a bad one. Ask yourselves these questions: Is the information displayed up to date? Does the war room tell me a story about what is important to this operation and the problems it currently faces? Is this war room used to put up a show for visitors or does it feel used by the people who work here (e.g., do people actually use it, i.e., manually update on papers and white boards?). Check also whether the graphs track actual KPIs that the local team can influence, or if is just data. If you are a regular visitor to the area, you can also ask yourself whether anything has changed in the war room structure. War rooms should continually evolve, especially in the first months after installation, to reflect a better understanding of the war room process by the team, but also changing problems and sometimes priorities.

Finally, please remember that war rooms are visual metrics, and as such an element of visual management. They are a required element of a good visual management system, but they are not the only visual management required. They might be a good way to introduce visual management, but visual management does not stop there.

To sum up, visual management has many benefits and leads to better performance when used in conjunction with standard work, provided management avoids the classic pitfalls of information overload and command and control. The following diagram summarizes the benefits of a comprehensive visual management approach, and how they lead to better performance, as well as pitfalls that need to be avoided (Figure 7.5).

CONTROVERSY CORNER: THE PITFALL OF COMPUTERS IN WAR ROOMS

I have seen many teams considering automating/digitizing their war rooms. Some companies even sell IT solutions for digital war rooms. Digital cockpits can indeed have benefits in the case of distributed teams, sites, or lines. But this is just a cockpit and not a war room.

The main grief we get from paper war rooms is that it takes time to get the data. If it really takes time to update your war room boards, then you are quite likely having one or two problems. It maybe takes time to calculate KPIs, in which case it is indeed worth automating calculations (but not the displaying). You might also have too many KPIs and should do a bit of pruning. Moreover, using pen and paper creates a much greater sense of ownership. Picking the red pen or the green pen is also part of a ritual. Who feels truly responsible for a KPI that is displayed on a computer screen? A Japanese Sensei said that "thinking comes through the arm."

Finally, the beauty of pen and paper is that it makes a war room very flexible. If you need to change priorities or have an idea to improve your daily management process, you just need to get another piece of paper or board. It might take a bit longer to modify your IT solution.

Hervé

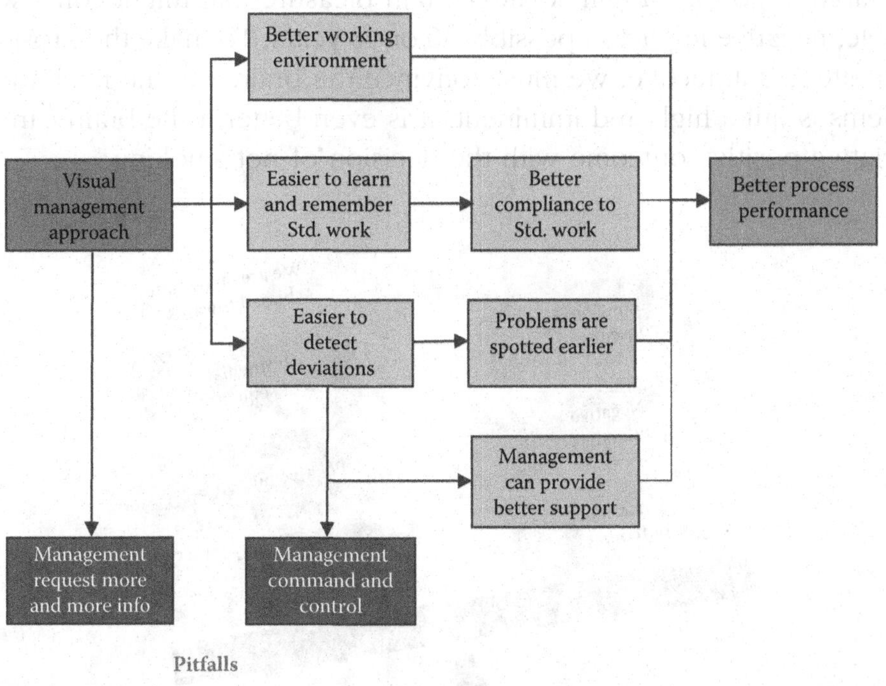

Figure 7.5 Benefits and pitfalls of visual management.

The Third Vertex of the Golden Triangle: Standard Management

You will only have successfully implemented a standard if your employees do the right thing even when you do not watch. Standard Management is about constantly checking that your system is working as intended and is not degrading.

To understand why standards are not followed, one needs to understand how the human brain works. Why do some doctors smoke? They are in the best position to understand how dangerous this habit is. The answer lies within our brain. We unconsciously make decisions based on three factors: impact of decision, likelihood of impact, and timing of impact. This is not a bad set of input data, but unfortunately, we are wired to take risks when impacts have a longer-term effect and are uncertain. Research shows that our perception of risks is skewed: we underestimate likelihood and size of impact of negative outcomes and overestimate potential gain and likelihood of success of positive outcomes. Our bias is illustrated in Figure 7.6. In other words, our proverbial smoking doctor's risk-taking brain thinks that it is acceptable to go for an immediate, certain pleasure that might come with a possible, negative impact in possibly 30 or 40 years. To make the prospect of a cigarette less attractive, we must convince the brain that the likelihood of problems is quite high and imminent. It is even better if the brain can associate a positive outcome with the decision of not smoking.

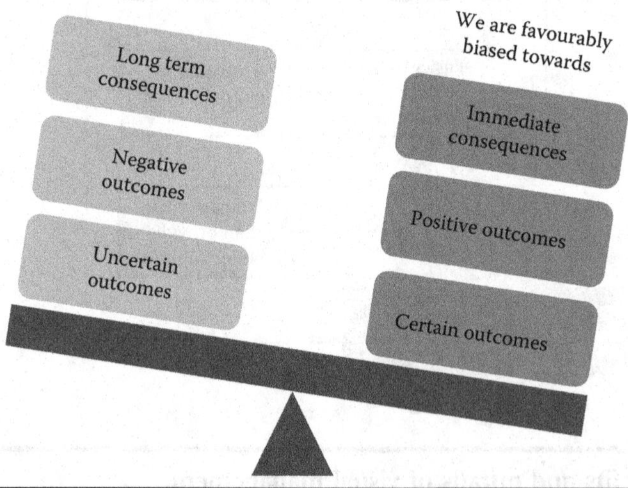

Figure 7.6 The human bias for action.

If we go back to our operations, standards are usually perceived as a constraint (negative outcome, no one likes constraints). Our employees' brains are constantly considering the benefits of not following the standard, which would give them an immediate and certain benefit (less work, less time, less constraints). If the only barrier is the distant prospect of a possible (but not certain) negative outcome in the shape of being reprimanded in a few days, weeks, or months, the odds are that some people will take the risk.

FRASER SAYS: CONSEQUENCES, CONSEQUENCES, CONSEQUENCES ... .

When we undertake proper root cause analysis of why standards are not followed, we see that there are usually a competing series of consequences that drive behavior, both negative and positive, short- or medium-term and certain or uncertain impacts. Individual have to balance these drivers and take a view about the best course of action. Sometimes the bias is for self-interest to dominate the decision making (if a blame culture exists). These type of risk assessments are something we have to do all of the time and are usually only done mentally and informally. Only after the event do we take time to look for what would drive someone to not follow a standard – sometimes with severe consequences. If we can encourage this type of formal analysis, then leaders will be more aware of how their attitudes and behaviors can drive undesired behaviors in those who undertake the work, putting pressure on individuals to make the wrong decisions. This can only be done with the individual(s) involved since each person has his own opinion on the perceived consequences of their actions at the time of an event.

The logical consequence of the principles mentioned in the previous paragraph is that we must (if possible, immediately) make people feel (if possible positive) consequences through standard management. Having involved people in the creation of the standard is obviously a good way to give them a positive feeling when following standards. If people see that you check that standards are complied with, they are more likely to comply. This process of checking is called *confirmation* of the standards.

CONTROVERSY CORNER: "… A KIND WORD AND A GUN"

Change beliefs and mindset to change behaviors or change behaviors to change beliefs and mindsets? As many companies failed to change behaviors, a lot of clever people explained that we should have started to directly change beliefs and mindsets first. This trendy theory is very nice and appeals to the good side of our managerial instinct. Unfortunately, it is very difficult to ask people to change their beliefs. It is a bit like looking at someone in the eyes and telling him "be motivated!" or "vegetables are good!" and hoping that this would change his beliefs. On the contrary, I suggest that we first let people no option but to display the required behavior (after having explained why this new behavior was important). Of course, adherence will initially be superficial. Over time, people will rationalize the new behavior and ultimately consider that it is their own decision. I would argue that latest advances in neuro-science support my point: research indicates that repetition of action could re-program the brain, thus explaining "the acquired taste" effect. As we keep on doing something, we start to perceive this action as normal and more acceptable. My theory is that companies that failed to change behaviors lacked the will to enforce standards for long enough. It does not mean that we should not try to win hearts and minds, but let us keep in mind the Al Capone quote from The Untouchables: "You can get further with a kind word and a gun than you can with just a kind word."

Hervé

Confirmation works on several levels:

- At a basic level, you will confirm that things are happening. This is very much "command & control" but might be necessary, either because maturity is low or because the consequences of failure are catastrophic. In one of the Indian construction sites I visited, safety representatives had to do a daily tour to ensure that there were no safety issues on the site. They had to email every day pictures taken during their tour to the central health and safety team, which confirmed that the tour had taken place.

- At a more advanced level, you will want to confirm the quality of the work or the effectiveness of the control mechanisms and not just that the planned action has taken place. During a visit to a Japanese automotive subcontractor, I noticed a part painted in pink. This part was intentionally defective. It was regularly put back on the line to check whether their control system would stop it before it reaches the customer.
- At a systematic level, you want to ensure that people who are supposed to do these confirmation checks can and will do them properly. The level above them should therefore confirm that the confirmation process works. This is called Layered Process Audits. Everyone from the bottom to the top of the organization is involved in some form of confirmation as illustrated in Figure 7.7.

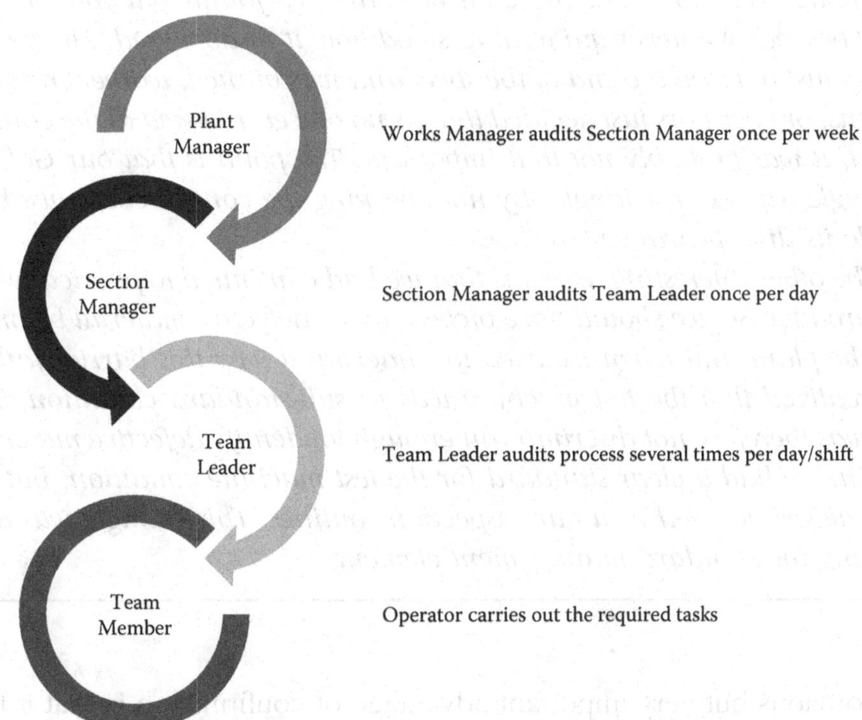
Plant Manager
Works Manager audits Section Manager once per week
Section Manager
Section Manager audits Team Leader once per day
Team Leader
Team Leader audits process several times per day/shift
Team Member
Operator carries out the required tasks

Figure 7.7 Layered process audits.

EXAMPLE: THE TECHNICAL MANAGER WHO THOUGHT HE HAD CRACKED THE PROBLEM

Before being introduced to the beauty of the Golden Triangle, I naively believed that finding technical answers was the key to ensuring a good process outcome. I learnt in an expensive way that it is indeed necessary to define the right technical standard and make it visual, but it is unfortunately not enough. After a rather clever technical analysis, we were able to determine which pretreatment bath concentration limits guaranteed the best paint adhesion results. We therefore created on the shop floor a control chart on which operators would report said concentration every shift (i.e., we put a standard in place and made it visual). I was persuaded that we had nailed the adhesion issue and that we will never again have a customer adhesion complaint. Yet, after a few months, we started to receive numerous complaints about adhesion issues. By the time we had solved the problem, we had received 42 complaints and had to pay $300K to our customer. What had happened? When we went to check the control chart, we found out that it had disappeared. We never quite understood how it disappeared. Maybe the graph just reached the end of the sheet and was binned, workers ran out of pens, or operators just decided that as no one ever looked at the control chart, it was probably not that important. The point is that our Golden Triangle was not a triangle. By not checking the control chart, we had made its disappearance possible.

The other interesting aspect is that we had continued to physically test the product. So, we should have picked up the defective material before it left the plant. But when we tried to understand why this barrier failed, we realized that the test machine was in sub-standard condition. The test was therefore not discriminant enough to identify defective material. Again, we had a clear standard for the test machine condition, but we had never included it in our inspection routines. This triangle was also missing the standard management element.

A less obvious but very important advantage of confirmation is that it forces managers to spend more time on the shop floor. Barriers between managers and shop floor operators are often very high. Many operators think that managers live in an ivory tower and do not understand the real work.

Managers often spend too much time in front of a computer in their offices. By bringing managers to the shop floor, confirmation increases their knowledge of the processes they are running. Moreover, it forces them to take interest in practical issues faced by operators, hopefully leading to improvements. This is a great way to show respect, an important aspect of the Toyota way.

At this point, take a short pause in your reading and have a think about a significant quality failure you experienced in your own operations. The odds are that you might have had a standard in place, but you missed visual management or standard management (or both).

Summary

Any implemented solution will degrade over time. It is possible to make solutions more robust by following the golden triangle concept, i.e., ensuring that the solution is based on a managed, clear, and visual standard. Having a standard is fundamental. The standard should be built by those who do the job and be as simple as possible, while also including what to do if a deviation is detected. 5S is an important tool to improve visual management in your workplace. Finally, the concept of confirmation of standards will help you to keep your processes under control and at the same time will show your respect for people.

The next chapter will dive deeper into how we can use the Golden Triangle as part of a systematic approach to stabilize our operations.

Get started on your Chapter 7 learnings – practicing the Golden triangle approach

I. *Reflect on a past improvement activity that was not sustained*
   a. *What was the current situation (at the start) and the countermeasures deployed?*
   b. *How were clear standards developed, amended, or reinforced?*
   c. *What type of visual management or visual factory controls were deployed?*
   d. *How were these standards updated, controlled, and communicated to ensure future adherence?*
   e. *What was the root cause(s) of the failure to sustain the improvements based on the Golden Triangle elements?*

II. *Reflect on a recent improvement activity to assess the likelihood of sustaining the improvement long term*
   a. *Was the current situation adequately described via the three elements of the Golden Triangle?*
   b. *Were the current standards thoroughly reviewed in light of the improvement required?*
   c. *How were these standards updated, controlled, and communicated to ensure future adherence?*
   d. *How robust are the visual management or visual factory controls?*
   e. *How likely is it that this improvement will be sustained?*
   f. *What elements of the Golden Triangle can be strengthened and how?*

III. *Reflecting on a current live problem I'm working on*
   a. *Have you gathered all the facts to adequately describe the current situation?*
   b. *Have you adequately reviewed all of the current standards associated with the process/problem?*
   c. *How will you amend or create new standards to ensure adherence from those conducting the work?*
   d. *What actions do leaders need to take to ensure the Golden Triangle is effective long term?*
   e. *How will you assess the ongoing effectiveness of the standards?*

Chapter 8

Sustaining Improvements with the Daily Management Cycle: An Approach to Make Problem-Solving Systematic

Hervé Duval

> If you can't describe what you are doing as a process, you don't know what you are doing.
>
> **W. Edwards Deming**

The Golden Triangle is the tool that will sustain a solution to a given problem. So we can now find a problem, deploy solutions, and sustain them. This is great. Deploying this approach is a great way to increase Operational Excellence maturity in areas where initial maturity is low and customer risks are limited.

However, this approach can feel "whack-a-mole" to a certain extent. It is reactive, which is not acceptable in sectors where customer risks are high such as automotive, food, or pharmaceuticals. Businesses operating in sectors with high potential customer risks cannot afford to wait for problems to happen and solve them very professionally. Such businesses must have a systematic approach that would allow us to proactively identify and solve potential problems before they happen (and such an approach would of course include the Golden Triangle to sustain these solutions).

This approach has many names. It is sometimes called Daily Management (DM) and is often described as a cycle (Ando & Kumar, 2011). As it is derived

DOI: 10.4324/9781003486022-8

from the automotive quality approach, we are going to illustrate the concept of DM in the field of product quality improvement. But DM can be applied to any process, physical or not. We will illustrate at the end of the section how the same concept applies to other types of issues, such as safety performance or production line availability.

Defining the Daily Management Cycle

Improving quality of an operation starts with identifying the customer requirements. We can then define what are the process parameters windows and process conditions needed to deliver the product characteristics required by the customer. Once we know what standards we need to follow, we can apply the Golden Triangle to sustain them. There will always be issues and deviations, so we need to spot these deviations and address them. Finally, we must capitalize on knowledge that we have just acquired when we solved the problem. The cycle that I have just described is what we call the DM cycle. Let us have a closer look at each step of the cycle (Figure 8.1).

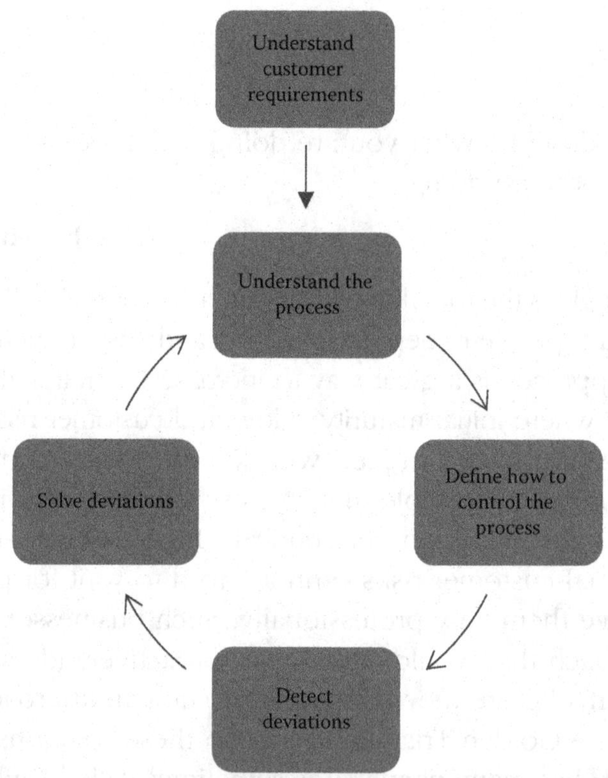

Figure 8.1 The Daily Management cycle.

Step 1: Understand Customer Requirements

The customer requirements we are trying to identify here are what product characteristics are important to the customer, and what numerical limits are given to each of these characteristics. Every single product characteristic that is important to the customer must be defined. A target value is not enough. Each characteristic should also have a tolerance assigned to it. Ideally, all these requirements should be captured in a document called a Service Level Agreement (SLA) to ensure that they are easily accessible and that performance against each of the characteristics can be tracked. This agreement can be the basis for a regular review with external paying customers but also internal customers along the value chain.

The importance of this step should not be underestimated. It is tempting to assume that we already know these requirements and that we could skip this stage. In many industries, norms define unequivocal customer requirements. For example, if a customer mentions DX53 to a steel supplier, he is not talking about a droid from Star Wars but indicates with only four letters and digits what are the minimum and maximum yield stress, ultimate tensile strength, and elongation values that the product will need to meet.

Unfortunately, workplace reality is not always as neat. Customer specifications might be vague or ambiguous, sometimes because the customer does

Form SLA
Rev 01
Effective Date : 09/06/14

Service Level Agreement
2014

Customer Department :- __End Customer	**Supplier Department :-** Statapult operations

Requirement related to Products/Services

	Sl. No	SLA Parameter	Unit of Measurement	Base Level (Period)	Target Level (Period)	Actual Performance											
						April	May	June	July	Aug.	Sept.	Oct.	Nov.	Dec.	Jan.	Feb.	Mar.
Production /Quality Delivery parameters	1	Quality (range)	ppm	200	150	210	230	145									
	2	Delivery	On time in full	90%	95%	96%	95%	97%									
	3	Production	Lead Time	14days	10days	15	12	10									
	4	Cost	Reduction %	-	5%	2%	2%	3%									
	5	Safety	LTA	2.00	0.00	0.00	0.00	0.00									
Service parameters	6	Complaints	No.	5	0	0	0	0									
	7	Supplier dev.	Training days	20	45	3	4	4									
	8	Tech. response	Time	48hrs	24hrs	30.00	20.00	26.00									

	Apr	May	Jun	Jul	Aug	Sep	Oct	Nov	Dec	Jan	Feb	Mar
Customer's Remarks :	Quality concern	Quality still a concern	Work on Tech response time									
Suppliers Signature	A Ball	A Ball	A Ball									
Customers Signature	C Roe	C Roe	C Roe									

Figure 8.2 An example of a Service Level Agreement (SLA).

not know precisely what is acceptable and what is not. Also, customers might have passed their specifications to sales or sales engineers but not everything reached operations. In this case, completing the SLA is a valuable exercise. Additional service or support requirements are also in scope. SLAs should also indicate such requirements as packaging, stillages, lead times, customer technical support, complaint resolution, and so on (Figure 8.2).

Step 2: Understand Our Own Process

Once we have defined precisely what customers want, we can define what are the critical elements of the manufacturing process that need to be under control to deliver these requirements. The key principle driving us here should be that quality cannot be inspected into the product, it must be built in. We should aim to reduce product characteristics (final) inspection and instead monitor the process parameters that ensure we achieve the desired outcome. So, we must understand the relationship between process parameters and product characteristics. Ideally, we would not even need to check the final product if we are confident about our process parameters. In real life, we must tend toward this situation, but in-process inspection of the finished product is often unavoidable.

Some manufacturing processes can be quite complex so the number of elements that need to be under control can be high. The following two-step process is a wonderful way to focus on the most critical elements.

Step 2.1: Creating the Product Characteristic Matrix

In the first step, you will assemble a team of people who are familiar with the manufacturing process. You need to ensure that it is a good mix of experience and knowledge, both practical and theoretical. This team's task is to define which process step has an impact on which product characteristic. Impact can be intended or unintended. The Product Characteristics Matrix (PCM) is an easy tool to capture this information (Figure 8.3).

For a given product characteristic, simply mark in the matrix if a given process step has an impact. Mark with an "I" if the impact is intended or with a "U" if the impact is unintended (i.e., whether the process step impacts the characteristics even though it has not been designed with this aim). For example, annealing a steel strip is commonly used to achieve the right mechanical properties. An intended impact on mechanical properties should therefore be recorded in the annealing step of the matrix. But a side effect of

Product Characteristics Matrix											
Version date											
PCM Team :	**Mr X, rs Y, ...**										
Process Section	**Entry**	**Process 1**		**Process 2**			**Process 3**				**Exit**
Subsection	A	A	B	A	B	C	A	B	C	D	A
Section number	21	22		23			24				25
Sub section number	5	05	15	5	15	25	05	15	20	25	5
Part number	C	-	-	-	-	-	-	-	-	-	-
width	-	-	I	C	-	-	-	-	-	-	-
gauge	-	-	-	-	I	-	-	-	-	-	-
surface quality	C	-	-	-	U	U	-	-	-	-	-
coating thickness	-	-	-	-	-	-	-	-	I	-	-

Figure 8.3 Example of a Product Characteristics Matrix. Legend: I = intended, U = U = unintended, C = check or inspection, S = take a sample.

annealing is that the strip width could be reduced by a few millimeters. Width is an important product parameter, so an unintended impact on width should be recorded in the annealing step of the matrix.

It is not unusual that this exercise triggers debates as people might disagree on the impact of a given step. This is usually proof that the exercise has been valuable; that is if the team finally reaches a consensus on the eventual answer or designs an experiment to determine who is right. If you leave the room without an agreement or a way forward, you have missed something. Do not hesitate to challenge "experts" to ensure that they just do not repeat myths or half-truths. Be sure that what they say is based on science; either theory, or even better, actual tests. Another valuable outcome of the exercise is that less experienced team members will learn about the process if it is a complex one, e.g., with chemical and/or physical interactions.

The last stage of the PCM creation is to record where checks take place with a "C" in the matrix or an "S" to indicate a sample is taken. As Deming stated, one shall not pass defects to the next operation. Controls should therefore take place in the process step where the defect can occur. Unfortunately, controls often take place right at the end of the process.

Figure 8.4 illustrates a process where all checks take place at the end of the process. This creates a risky situation where defects could be generated early in the process and be passed on, which is wasteful.

Figure 8.5 illustrates a process where checks take place as early as possible in the process, guaranteeing that defects are immediately detected.

Once the PCM is complete, it contains a number of boxes marked with Is, Us, and Cs, usually too many to explore in detail. This is where the team needs to

Product Characteristics Matrix

Version date

PCM Team: Mr X, rs Y, ...

Process Section	Entry	Process 1		Process 2			Process 3				Exit
Subsection	A	A	B	A	B	C	A	B	C	D	A
Section number	21	22		23			24				25
Sub section number	5	05	15	5	15	25	05	15	20	25	5
Part number	-	-	-	-	-	-	-	-	-	-	-
width	-	-	I	-	-	-	-	-	-	-	-
gauge	-	-	-	-	I	-	-	-	-	-	-
surface quality	-	-	-	-	U	U	-	-	-	-	-
coating thickness	-	-	-	-	-	-	-	-	I	-	-

Figure 8.4 PCM of a process with poor control sequence.

Product Characteristics Matrix

Version date

PCM Team: Mr X, rs Y, ...

Process Section	Entry	Process 1		Process 2			Process 3				Exit
Subsection	A	A	B	A	B	C	A	B	C	D	A
Section number	21	22		23			24				25
Sub section number	5	05	15	5	15	25	05	15	20	25	5
Part number	C	-	-	-	-	-	-	-	-	-	-
width	-	-	I	C	-	-	-	-	-	-	-
gauge	-	-	-	-	I	C	-	-	-	-	-
surface quality	C	-	-	-	U	U	C	-	-	-	-
coating thickness	-	-	-	-	-	-	-	-	I	C	-

Figure 8.5 An example of PCM of a process where controls are in the right place.

decide which area has the most impact on the problem. Once this is determined, the team can start the second step, which is to determine what can go wrong and what needs to be done to prevent these problems. In plain English, this is a risk analysis. Quality experts call this Failure Modes and Effects Analysis (FMEA).

Step 2.2: Completing the FMEA

The format of an FMEA is fairly standard as it has been a requirement of quality systems for many years in automotive and aerospace sectors. It is a table in which each line is a Failure Mode (the risk). Columns correspond to four main blocks, corresponding from left to right to describing the risk, characterizing the risk, stating what we are going to do to reduce the risk, and eventually recharacterizing the risk once actions have been completed. In more detail:

Describing the risk: the main columns for each risk are:

- Where in the process can the risk happen? Capture here the relevant process step in alignment with a process flow chart.
- Which deviation would cause the risk? Describe what could go wrong.
- What problem will it cause? Describe the impact of the deviation.
- What control systems are currently in place to either prevent or detect this potential deviation/defect?

Characterizing the risk: this step is about scoring to help prioritize. The main columns in this block are:

Three scores (between 1 and 10) for:

- **Severity (SEV):** How big is the potential impact? (10 most severe)
- **Occurrence (OCC):** How likely is the problem to happen? (10 most severe)
- **Detection (DET):** If the problem happens, how likely is that it will be detected? (10 least detection)

A Risk Priority Number (RPN) between 1 and 1,000 is calculated as SEV × OCC × DET.

Although there is an element of subjectivity in the scoring process, it should be kept as objective as possible. This can be achieved by using standard scoring tables such as those in the IATF16949 automotive standard and can be easily accessed online. Be aware that a higher RPN does not always translate as a more serious concern. Severity should always be the first point of interest, so action may be needed on any high-severity items (9 or 10 scores typically). An owner and a deadline must be recorded in the FMEA wherever action is deemed necessary. Finally, as actions progress and are completed, Severity, Occurrence, and/or Detection, and therefore RPN, will reduce. The new scores should be recorded in the final four columns (Figure 8.6).

Completing the FMEA as a team will give you consensus on what is important to deliver what is expected by customers of this process, internal or external. The FMEA is also a great way of prioritizing what needed resources or capital spend. Senior leaders should always be asking to see if projects and capital spend are impacting on FMEA scores. This is an example of integration thinking (remember our discussion on the Malcolm Baldridge model in Chapter 2).

Key Contact/Phone Herve Duval					Core Team Fraser Wilkinson, Herve Duval, Iain Davey										FMEA Prepared: By F Wilkinson
Process No.	Process function	Product output characteristics	Potential Failure Mode	Potential Effect(s) of Failure	SEV	CLASS	Potential Cause(s) / Mechanism(s) of Failure	Current Process Controls Prevention	OCCUR	Current Process Controls Detection	DETECT	RPN	Recommended Action (s)	Responsibility & Target Completion Date
10	Load Statapult	10.O1 Ball is freely released from the cup	10.O1 Ball is not released freely from the cup	**Customer Complaint**	8		10.P1 Ball cup interface friction/resistance too high (sticks)	None	3	None	8	192	Create Standard Work to check the ball cup tolerance at every changeover and instruct operators not to use excess force to seat the ball	FW July 2014
20	Tension the Arm	20.O1 Correct elastic tension when arm drawn back	20.O1 Correct elastic tension outside of tolerance	Increased variation in product	7		20.P1 Angle of 177 Deg not achieved	Visual indicator	7	None	8	392	Backstop to be installed	Completed
					2		20.P2 Elastic not within the strength tolerance	None	2	None until elastic breaks	9	36	Transfer risk of elastic break to the MTI/Failure Reduction Study	FW July 2014
30	Release the Arm	30.O1 Correct velocity of the ball on exit	30.O1 Velocity of the ball on exit too high or too low	Increased variation in product	5		30.P1 Variable time of elastic under tension	Cycle time	7	None	5	175	None	
					3		30.P2 Variable friction generated at the release point	None	8	None	9	216	Create Standard Work for relaese technique	
					9		30.P3 Consistent force exerted on holding down the statapult base	None	8	Visual	7	504	Create Standard Work for holding down base	FW July 2014
													Fix the base to the floor	FW Oct 2014

Figure 8.6 Example of the FMEA logic for risk management.

Step 3: Define How We Are Going to Control Our Process

Once we understand the process and the risks, we can define what needs to be put under control to secure the desired output. We can identify which product characteristics and which process parameters need to be under control. The list of all the things that we need to control is the Control Plan (Figure 8.7).

The ultimate sophistication would be to put all key process parameters under control so product characteristics would in theory not even need to be controlled. Of course, this remains a theoretically ideal scenario: in reality, all businesses will need to continue to somehow measure product characteristics. Stopping the end-of-line product quality checks before process parameters are under control would invariably lead to unbearable levels of customer complaints. Nevertheless, this gives us an ideal situation to aspire to. It is worth noting that the cost of quality in Japan is mostly spent on preventing defects from occurring, whilst in the West most of the cost of quality is spent on controlling products to stop defects from reaching customers.

So how can one control a process? One can make it physically impossible for a deviation to occur. If it is not possible, any control mechanism will be a variation on the concept of standard work to reduce the risk of deviation occurring.

Department: Statapult Operations
Process Name: Statapult

Rev. No. 001
Date : June 2014

Prepared by: F. Wilkinson
Approved by: H. Duval

Form No. :
Rev. : 04
Effective Date : 10/6/2014

			Characteristics				Methods						
Process Number	Process Description	Machine/ Device	Source (PFMEA/ R&O/ MoU)	No	Product (Output)	Process	Product / Process Specification	Evaluation Method	Sample		Control Method	Responsibility	Reaction Plan (Doc. Ref.)
									Size	Freq			
00	Statapult operation	Cup	PFMEA/SLA	10.O1	Ball is freely released from the cup		Within range specified in SLA	Tape measure and Spotter	1	All shots	Trend Chart (X-MR chart to identify special causes)	Recorder	Immediately feedback to Operators and mark up control chart with assigned cause
		Cup/Ball	PFMEA	10.P1		Ball cup interface friction/resistance	As per Operational Standard OS001.Fig.1 2 mm larger ball diameter than cup diameter. Do not use force when seating ball in cup - Standard Work SW001	Vernier calipers/Go-NoGo Gauge	1	Every setup and changeover	Record on Setup and Changeover Checksheet CCS001. Confirmation of SW001	Operator/Team Leader	Quarantine ball for QA investigation and draw new ball from Stores. Check tolerance of new ball and cup
		Elastic band	PFMEA	20.O1	Correct elastic tension when arm drawn back		As per Operational Standard OS001 Fig. 2. +20mm to +25mm deflection on10 gram to 20 gram increase. No damage on the edges.	2x 10 gram weight and ruler	1	Every 1000 shots or 2 weeks whichever is sooner	Trend Chart (X-MR chart to identify special causes)	Team Leader	Change elastic band if out of tolerance or damaged
		Statapult base	PFMEA	30.P1		Consistent force exerted on holding down the statapult base	As per Standard Work SW001. Place maximum weight on the base before releasing the arm	Confirmation check	1	Each operator every month	Daily/Weekly confirmation sheets and Layered Audit system records	Team Leader/Production Leader	Instruction by Team Leader in correct method for holding down base.
		Statapult base	PFMEA	30 P4		Pins and/or cup not in specified positions	As per the Product Definitions Sheet PD001	Visual against template	1	Every setup and changeover	Record on Setup and Changeover Checksheet CCS001	Team Leader	Reset the pin and/or cup positions
		Base amd Tape	PFMEA	40.P2		Mis-alignment of the base and the measuring tape	As per Operational Standard OS001 Fig. 3. +/- 2 deg from centre	Laser sight and rule	1	Every 1000 shots or 2 weeks whichever is sooner	Record on Setup and Changeover Checksheet CCS001	Team Leader	Call Engineering support to re-align the tape measure
		Statapult	PFMEA	70.P1		Cycle time of each shot has too much variation around 15s mean	Within range specified in SLA	Stopwatch	1	Every 100 shots	Trend Chart displayed in workplace	Team Leader	Feedback to Operators

Figure 8.7 Example of a control plan.

The safest control mechanism is error proofing. If we want to make sure that it is impossible to use fuel in a diesel tank, we should design nozzles and fuel fill shapes in a way that makes it impossible to insert the wrong nozzle. We could, for example, use a triangular nozzle for diesel fuel and a square nozzle for unleaded fuel.

But error proofing will not always be possible. So, a different control mechanism must be put in place. Most control mechanisms will be based on human standard work, i.e., putting in place standards describing how to best set and operate a machine, in which range process parameters should be, and so on. Standard-based control mechanisms can be implemented rapidly and are quite flexible. On the downside, humans make mistakes.

This raises the question of automation of control mechanisms, also known as machine standard work. Automation strongly reduces the risk of human mistakes (not removing it completely, as programmers also make mistakes). Unfortunately, automation also has several downsides. The first one is cost. Automation also takes time to be implemented. It can make further

Table 8.1 Summary of control mechanisms

Type of control mechanism	*Pros*	*Cons*	*When to use?*
Error Proofing	No/low cost Ease of implementation	None!	As much as possible
Human Standard work	Flexibility Limited cost	Risk of human error Requires time and effort (training, confirmation audits)	When the manufacturing process is bound to evolve often
Machine Standard work (automation)	Significantly reduces the risk of human error	Lack of flexibility costs	When impact of mistake/deviation can be very costly e.g., Process industries

improvement more difficult to implement. And it potentially leads to a decrease in knowledge as the software becomes a black box over time.

Table 8.1 provides a summary of pros and cons of each control mechanism. A comprehensive hierarchy of controls is described in Appendix 5.

Using Control Charts

A specific but especially useful type of standard work as a control mechanism is the use of control charts, which are a key tool of Statistical Process Control (SPC). A control chart is a display of measured values of a process parameter or of a product characteristic. Standard work here is about plotting at regular, predefined intervals values of key process parameters and/or product characteristics. Representing visually these values helps to keep them within specification: producing the chart will highlight deviations, but also trends.

A few triggers are present on a control chart. Predefined action is taken if one of these triggers is met and should bring the process back under control:

- A control chart must include reaction limits, which are more stringent than specification limits. If measured values cross-reaction limits, action must be taken so that specification limits are not reached. These actions must be defined in an OCAP (Out of Control Action Plan) rather than being improvised when parameter drifts are spotted.

Example of OCAP instruction: "add x liter of acid Y at concentration Z if pH reaches reaction limit."

- If a run of 8 points all above (or all below) the central line is observed, it is extremely likely that there is something wrong with the process. Again, an OCAP should be in place to ensure that reactions to this type of run are standardized and effective.

SPC is an easy, inexpensive, and visual method that works very well. It is also a way to involve the shop floor teams in process control activities. SPC is a subject that we are unable to fully explore in this book, but we highly recommend you investigate study options. Rules to detect special causes are not standardized, so you should reference which ones you adopt (Table 8.2).

Table 8.2 An example of Joseph Juran's rules for detecting "special causes" (Duran, 2017)

One of one point is outside of ±3-sigma control limits
Two of three points are above 2-sigma control limits
Two of three points are below −2-sigma control limits
Four of five points are above 1-sigma control limits
Four of five points are below −1-sigma control limits
Six points in a row increasing
Six points in a row decreasing
Nine out of nine are above or below center line
Eight points in a row on both sides of center line, none in zone C

Measurement approaches can be ranked from the crudest to the most effective:

- **Level 0:** No measurement is taken. Product will reach the customer, even if it is out of specification.
- **Level 1:** A spot measurement of a required product characteristic is taken. This is usually done at the end of the line. For example, the final product dimensions might be measured, and the product will be rejected if not compliant. More rarely, intermediate product characteristics will be measured at some stage during the process. This will help detect deviations, but the process will still generate defective products until a deviation is detected.

- **Level 2:** Continuous measurement. Process parameters and/or product characteristics are continuously monitored. The signal coming from the continuous measurement device is usually displayed on computer screens. It is important that the screen also displays specification limits and control limits, i.e., from which value do we need to do something to bring the process back under control? When possible, it is always preferable to build alarms in your software as we should not rely on human beings being able to spot 100% of deviations.
- **Level 3:** Close Loop Control. This solution consists in coupling a measurement device with the line automation system, thus removing the need for human intervention. The system will automatically modify the process parameters to ensure that product characteristics are optimal. This obviously requires a particularly good understanding of the process and usually requires a mathematical model linking process parameters and product characteristics (Table 8.3).

Table 8.3 Summary of measurement maturity levels

Measurement maturity level	*Where is deviation detected?*	*When is deviation corrected?*	*Downside of approach*
0 – No measure	Not detected	Not corrected	No control of process
1 – Spot measurement	At the end	Through rework or new production	Does not prevent occurrence of defect
2 – Continuous measurement	Potentially immediately	Potentially immediately	Initial cost still relies on human intervention
3 – Closed Loop Control	Immediately	Immediately	Initial cost

FRASER SAYS: STANDARDS AND PROCESSES DETERIORATE NATURALLY

Closed loop systems don't work well in organizational settings. We must open them up to external forces if we are to avoid a deterioration. Constant attention to a standard or process is required. This can be through process confirmation checks or by an SPC-type approach that looks for a deterioration using a set of statistical rules. A more proactive way is to set targets for process improvement in the stability and capability indices.

Whatever the type of control you have selected, you must be sure that the results of the measurements can be trusted. Common issues with measurements include:

- Measurement devices drift over time. Therefore, having a calibration process in place for all key controls is important. A good calibration procedure will describe how to calibrate, but also the frequency and an owner. The Golden Triangle should be in place for the calibration process: date of validity of calibration and owner of the equipment should be clearly labeled on the device so that anyone can raise a request if calibration is not carried out at the required frequency.
- Measure imperfectly describes what we need to measure. For example, if you get a reading for an oven temperature, does the measure reflect an average temperature, temperature in the middle of the oven, or near one wall? How representative is this measured temperature from the overall temperature profile within the oven. If temperature only varies by a few degrees across the oven, it is fine. But if temperature varies more widely, you might need several sensors instead of relying on just one.
- Measure is not always reproducible (two different operators could find a different result when measuring) or not always repeatable (the same operator could find a different result every time he measures the same sample). It is therefore important that you carry out MSA (Measurement Study Analysis), a type of analysis that will confirm whether your measurement devices are capable or not (i.e., in plain English whether you can trust the readings or not). Gauge R&R studies can determine how much of the variation we record is due to the measurement system itself and how much is "true" process variation. If we use a measurement system to certify customer-required specifications (or release criteria), we should always conduct an MSA study (Table 8.4).

Table 8.4 Summary of common issues with measurement

Issue	*Solution*
Device not reliable after some time	Calibration procedure
Measurements do not reflect the important process parameters	Alignment of measurement with FMEA/Control Plan
Measurement not reproducible and/or repeatable	Regular R&R study

Step 4: Detecting Deviations and Acting Upon Them

As discussed in the Golden Triangle paragraph, the Golden Triangle will help you to detect deviations, but this ability to detect a deviation will bring no benefits if deviations are not acted upon. Unfortunately, it is common that these alerts are ignored. The main reasons are the following:

- **Lack of visibility:** Visual alerts are sometimes placed on PC screens that are not always accessed or are in remote parts of the plant. My boiler is equipped with a light that flashes if it disfunctions. Not surprisingly, my boiler is hidden so the only moment I see this alert is when I have realized that the boiler is no longer working. A more useful alerting system would, for example, send me a text message.
- **Lack of knowledge:** People who notice alert signals might not have been trained on the nature and purposes of these alerts. They therefore do not necessarily know to what extent it is important to react, nor what to do.
- **Disbelief:** Users do not always believe what measurement systems report, blaming instrument failure or inaccuracy. This attitude, as well as the ones described in the next two bullet points, derives from our brain's preference for good news and tendency to minimize risk.
- **Laxity:** Some people think that they have enough time to react, thus delaying actions that would put the process back in control. I know a person who continued to drive for a while after their car's oil alert started to flash. She thought that she had plenty of time, drove on for several days, and was surprised when her car's engine seized.

Similarly, cars run out of fuel when their lax drivers overestimate remaining fuel once the small warning light flashes. The same risk-taking behavior will unfortunately sometimes be seen in the workplace.

- **Alert overload:** Some computer systems suffer from alert overload. Windows keep on popping up, to the extent that users no longer notice them. If you are continuously burdened with false alerts, you will eventually ignore all alerts (the same way you end up missing important emails hidden among spam).

A couple of issues could also lead to alerts not being triggered.

First, in some industries, measurement devices are often maintained in a less disciplined way than manufacturing devices (typically in high-volume, low-margin industries). If maintenance resources are constrained, priority will go to "keeping the line running." This can lead to measurement equipment no longer functioning and the lines running without some key measurement devices. This type of abnormal condition must be detected as soon as possible, which is why it is important to include checking critical measurement devices in daily routines of support functions.

Second, there is a risk linked to proxy measurements, which is more insidious. Instruments will sometimes show a reading that is what we expect, but that sensor is not measuring what we think it does. The result is that we are lured into a false sense of safety. This is what I call the danger of proxy measurement. I first became conscious of this issue when exposed to one of our customer complaints. This customer reported that the material he had received was not oiled, which meant that he could not form it into automotive parts in a press. This was initially a mystery, as our records showed that this steel coil had been properly oiled. But the truth was exposed when investigators realized that the measurement of oil deposited was in fact a proxy measure. It was in fact generated by a flow meter that indicated whether oil was being pumped from the oil tank. This had never been an issue. Unfortunately, the electrostatic oiler became defective. So as oil was reaching the oiler, the flow meter was recording that the coil was being oiled when oil was not projected onto the strip but simply falling back in the oil tank and was recirculating. Operators trusted sensors but were victims of proxy measurement (Table 8.5).

Table 8.5 Summary of key principles of deviation detection

Issue	*Solution/Principle*
Alarms are not seen	Make alarms clearly visible and accessible
Alarms are misinterpreted	Train users on causes and consequences of alarms
Users take time to react	
Users do not believe alerts	
Users become lax become of repetitive false alarms	Tackle sources of "false alarms" as they arise
Measurement devices are less well looked after than pure manufacturing equipment	Strict adherence to preventive maintenance plans, including critical measurement devices in DM checklists
Readings are extrapolated from other measurements	Avoid proxy measurements in the design phase of installations

EXAMPLE: THE THREE MILE ISLAND NUCLEAR ACCIDENT: HOW ISSUES IN DEVIATION DETECTION AND REACTION TO ALERTS LED TO PARTIAL MELTDOWN OF A NUCLEAR REACTOR

On the 28th of March 1979, Three Mile Island nuclear reactor number 2 partly melted down. The accident started because of a combination of water infiltration causing a turbine to stop and a significant breach of the Nuclear Commission Regulatory code. However, this could have remained a "near miss" if the deviation detection element of the plant's DM cycle had been intelligently designed. Instead of that, the US faced what is (so far) the second most severe nuclear accident in the global history of this industry, only outdone by the Chernobyl catastrophe. Several of the factors listed above hampered deviation detection and reaction to deviations:

- *Use of proxy measurement: A relief valve stuck open, which caused the coolant liquid to escape, thus leading to coolant system depressurization. The user interface system indicating whether the valve was open or not was a lamp. The unlit lamp was showing that a solenoid was powered, which should normally be enough to close the valve, rather than showing the actual position of the valve.*

- *Refusal to act on or believe in red warning indicators: Even though pressure, temperature and coolant levels should all have alarmed the team, operators chose to trust the valve indicator and ignore these key parameters. It was only when the next shift turned up that the meaning of the unlit lamp was challenged.*
- *Unavailable indicators: A downstream temperature indicator was also showing abnormal values, hinting that the valve was indeed stuck. Unfortunately, this key piece of information could only be read on an indicator located at the back of a seven-foot instrument panel.*
- *Lack of training: The teams had not been trained to understand the meaning of this downstream temperature indicator, so once they finally noticed it, they could not interpret it correctly.*

Step 5: Stopping Deviations

This step is where classic problem-solving takes place. The how has been covered by Fraser in a previous chapter and in more detail in *Front Line Problem Solving* (Wilkinson, 2016). I would, however, want to link problem-solving with standard work. It is important to understand that finding the technical root causes of a problem is not enough. Problem-solving must

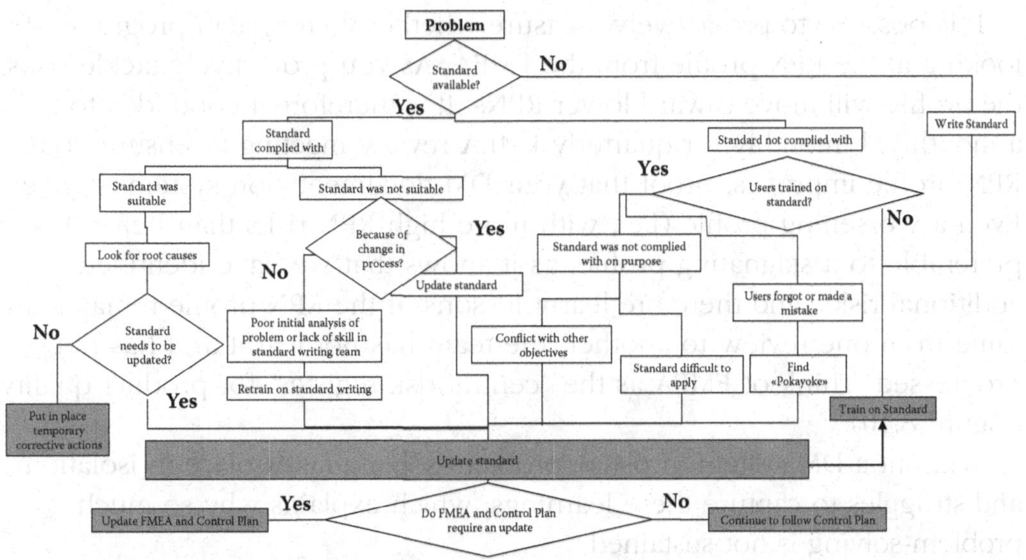

Figure 8.8 Watanabe failure analysis model.

integrate the standard work aspect. Watanabe's analysis is a tool that does just that (Figure 8.8). It is a set of questions that follow a decision tree. The first question to ask is whether there was a standard for the operation that failed. In the absence of a standard, the first action is to create one. If there was a standard, was it followed or not? This will then force you to ask yourself deep questions such as whether the standard was right or not, how people were trained, and so on.

Step 6: Learning from Deviations

Solving the problem of arising deviations does not stop when the manufacturing line resumes production of good parts or when the customer complaint is closed. Learning from deviations only happens if the problem-solving process formally includes a final stage: explicit capture of new knowledge. In other words, after the problem has been fully understood and solved, we need to capture what we have just learnt (what can go wrong, what to do to prevent things from going wrong) in our DM documents.

The DM cycle is a learning loop. FMEAs, Control Plans, and SOPs are elements of a Knowledge Management system, not just some documents that have to be filled in to keep auditors happy. The connection illustrated below closes that learning loop (Figure 8.9).

It is possible to pro-actively measure whether your system progresses by looking at the RPN profile from the FMEA. As you pro-actively tackle risks, the profile will move toward lower RPNs. It is therefore a good idea to hold a monthly, bimonthly, or quarterly FMEA review meeting to ensure your RPN profile improves, proof that your DM documentation system is alive. Even a worsening profile (i.e., with more high RPN risks than before) is preferable to a stagnating profile, as it shows that we have identified additional risks, and therefore learnt lessons. If the RPN profile remains the same from one review to another, the team has not learnt and has not progressed. Think of FMEA as the "central risk register" for product quality (Figure 8.10).

Without a DM system in place, problem-solving takes place in isolation and struggles to capture these learnings, which explains why so much problem-solving is not sustained.

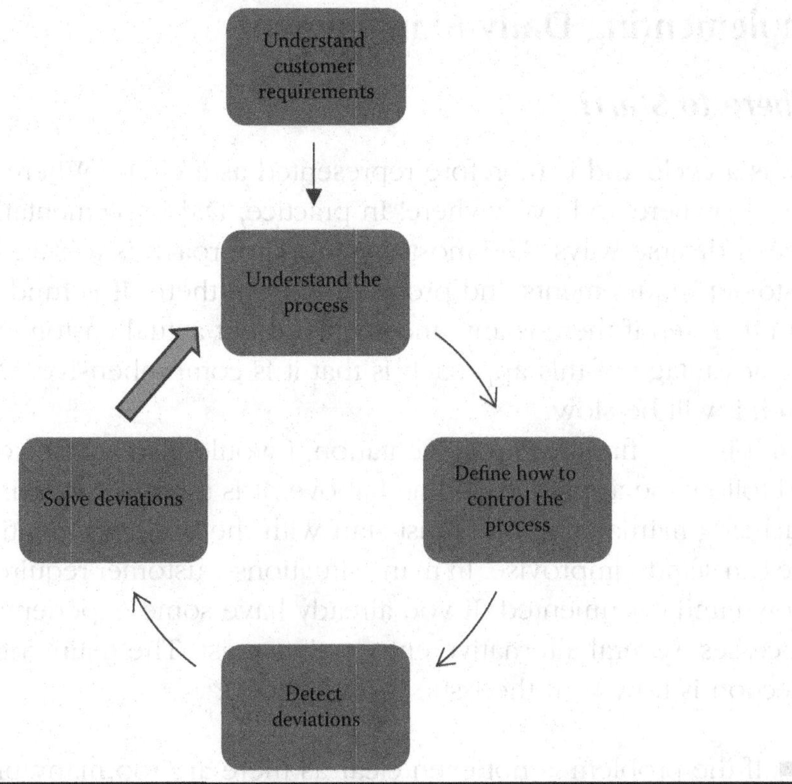

Figure 8.9 The learning loop of the Daily Management process.

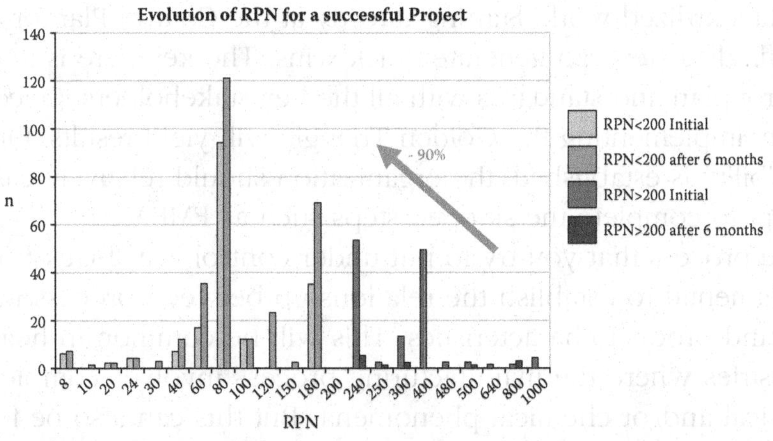

Figure 8.10 Understanding progress made in risk reduction through the use of RPN distribution charts.

Implementing Daily Management

Where to Start?

DM is a cycle and is therefore represented as a circle. Where does a circle start? Nowhere and everywhere! In practice, DM implementation can start in several diverse ways. The most common approach is to start by listing customer requirements and proceeding from there. It is fundamental to start with this step if there is any uncertainty about actual customer requirements. The advantage of this approach is that it is comprehensive. On the other hand, it will be slow.

If it is your first DM implementation, I would also advise you to start there and follow the approach outlined above. It is a bit like learning the piano or practicing martial arts: one must start with the boring, repetitive part before one can start to improvise. In many situations, customer requirements are well known and documented. If you already have some experience in improving processes, several alternative entry points exist. The main criterion for selection is how well the issue is understood:

- If the problem is not even clear as there are too many problems to tackle, it is vital to take a step back and go through the overall DM process step by step.
- If the process is simple and/or understood but performance varies between teams and between periods, the problem can often be solved by standardized work. Starting directly at the Control Plan or Standardize step can generate quick wins. The key here is to build a control plan and standards with all the key stakeholders. Once it is in place, implementing the Golden Triangle will yield results. Once this credibility is established, the organization should relatively easily accept to complete the skipped steps such as FMEA.
- If the process that you try to put under control is a "black box," it is fundamental to establish the relationship between process parameters and product characteristics. This will be common in heavy industries where the manufacturing process involves complex physical and/or chemical phenomena. But this can also be found in smaller-scale industries that use installations such as ovens. I visited a biscuit manufacturing plant that still has a double-digit scrap rate on

its flagship product, even though it has been producing it for more than 50 years. Creating the PCM should be the first step of DM roll out, rapidly followed by an FMEA. This is usually the least favorable DM roll out situation: whilst DM will work, it will take time to make changes as you will need to carry out experiments to prove (or disprove) sometimes contradicting beliefs within the organization as to how the installation works. You might also have to invest in measurement devices, as some key parameters might not be known nor continuously measured.

- Sometimes the optimal process conditions are already known, and standards describing how to achieve a good output already exist, and yet problems still occur. This usually comes either from the fact that standards are incorrect, or people do not comply with standards. In the first case, we will need to check our understanding of the process (see the first alternative entry point). The second case is a clear illustration of an absent or weak Golden Triangle. If people do not comply with standards, it is because the system allows them not to comply. So, the first step in this case is to put in place or reinforce the Golden Triangle.

These scenarios are summarized and visualized in Table 8.6 and Figure 8.11.

Table 8.6 Daily Management actions to address deviations

Scenario	*Identified problem*	*What to do next? Which DM tool/step?*
"Low maturity"	"I do not know" or "we have too many problems"	Follow full DM approach on a few parameters, starting with identifying what is critical to the customer and what parameters need to be put under control to deliver what is required. Do not try to write a full FMEA or standards for everything, target a few critical issues and widen the scope progressively after your first improvements.

(continued)

Table 8.6 ***(Continued)*** **Daily Management actions to address deviations**

Scenario	*Identified problem*	*What to do next? Which DM tool/step?*
"Lack of discipline" Variations in performance	Impact of key process parameters on output is understood (at least by some experts or experimented operators) but: ■ Results can vary significantly by week/month. ■ Results can vary significantly between teams. ■ Solutions are found but are not sustained. ■ Crisis can be solved by experts who have seen the same problem a few years ago.	It is about discipline Focus on standardization and routine management: 1. Build (or review existing) standards. 2. Put in place/reinforce routine management by: • Reinforcing meeting management. • Reinforcing Visual Management. • Introducing Confirmation (layered process audit).
"Black box" Variations in process output	Teams do not deviate from standards (e.g., on a highly automated lines) but outcome is still not stable. Example: a heat treatment installation where 5–10% of the output has to be retreated. It is unclear why (variations of unidentified incoming material or process parameters?)	Knowledge is incomplete. First, build a team dedicated to understanding the science behind the process (with access to other similar lines in the group/in the industry, using scientific problem-solving approach). Sustain findings and solutions through control mechanisms (SOP, SPC, automation, poke yoke) and routine management (confirmation).
"Sleeping beauty" Stable performance but little improvement	No major problem. Line is stable. Performance varies by less than 10% between teams. However, there is no clear long-term improvement trend. Defect/deviation rate is considered "acceptable."	Improve process capability by upgrading the organization's problem-solving capability: ■ Deviation (Customer complaints, non-prime, incidents) analysis must refer to FMEA, control plans, and standards and lead to chances to these elements.
"The dream"	No major problem. Line is stable. Process capability continually improves.	The process has now very little variation, a very good base to continuously improve.

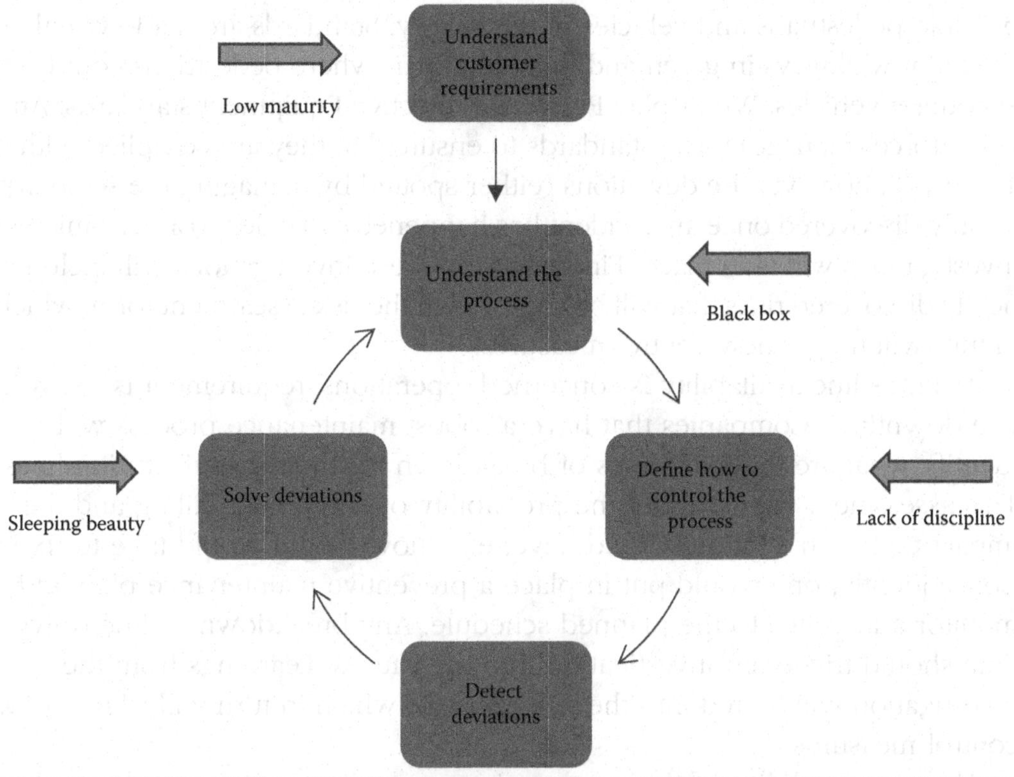

Figure 8.11 A visual representation of where to start or focus DM deployment.

Using Daily Management with Every Aspect of Performance

Experienced readers will have noticed that the DM cycle is an application of the approach described in ISO9001. We have explained in this chapter the DM cycle under the quality performance angle. But the DM cycle applies to all types of performance indicators. To illustrate this, I will briefly explain how the same cycle applies to two other critical operational performance areas, people safety and line availability.

In terms of safety, our employees are the customers of the process of which performance we are trying to improve and sustain. The SLA with our employees is fairly simple: their key requirement is not getting hurt. So, we need to understand the process they work in and assess what can go wrong, i.e., the hazards that they face, and for each hazard, how likely it is to happen and how badly it would hurt them. This is the classic safety risk assessment stage. Once these risks have been identified, we put in place measures to alleviate them. We create standards on several topics. For example, we segregate as much as possible pedestrians and vehicles in the factory. Standards are made visual. We paint walkways in green and highlight areas where pedestrians could encounter vehicles. We display Personal Protective Equipment standards. And we enforce (manage) these standards to ensure that they are complied with. There will, however, be deviations (either spotted by managing the standards or only discovered once an accident has happened). Accident (or near-misses) investigations will take place. Findings from these investigations will include newly discovered risks that will be captured in the risk assessment form, which in turn will trigger new control measures.

As far as line availability is concerned, operations' requirement is to avoid line downtime. Companies that have a robust maintenance process will identify what are the main risks of breakdown for their manufacturing lines. This assessment will consider the probability of equipment failing and the impact that such a failure would have, e.g., how long it would take to fix it. Consequently, one would put in place a preventive maintenance plan and monitor adherence to the planned schedule. Any breakdown or line downtime should trigger an investigation into the causes. Learnings from the investigation will be fed into the risk analysis, which in turn will trigger new control measures.

The transferability of this systematic approach of management can be illustrated with the remarkable transformation that Paul O'Neill led in Alcoa. O'Neill focused on safety to develop a continuous improvement culture in the company. Safety is improved by putting in place a culture and systems of continuous improvement and DM. The organization used these newly acquired skills to improve all other performance aspects (Table 8.7).

Table 8.7 Reference of the Daily Management steps to Quality, Safety, and Maintenance activities

Step	*Quality*	*Safety*	*Maintenance*
Understand Customer requirements	Zero defect SLA	Zero harm	Zero line stop
Understand process	FMEA	Risk register	Risk analysis (frequency and impact of breakdowns)

(continued)

Table 8.7 ***(Continued)*** **Reference of the Daily Management steps to Quality, Safety, and Maintenance activities**

Step	*Quality*	*Safety*	*Maintenance*
Control risks	Control Plans	Safety control plan (not commonly used)	Preventive maintenance plan
Detect deviations (Golden Triangle)	Standard Working Procedures (SWP), Layer Process Audit, Visual Management	Safe operating procedures, safety audits, visual management	Maintenance SWP, finished work audit, Visual Management
Solve problems	Quality investigation, e.g., 8D	Accident investigation	Breakdown investigation

FRASER SAYS: CAN THIS APPROACH WORK IN A TRANSACTIONAL OR SERVICE ENVIRONMENT?

The kind of Daily Management system described in this section is born out of the automotive quality management frameworks, and as such is geared to looking at the control of quality in a manufacturing environment. Usually, when you show the full system to a service industry they baulk at the application of these techniques, and it's true that you can't directly lift all of the lean methods from manufacturing to the service sector, especially in customer service centers. Where it can be used effectively is when you need to have a standard service output such as payroll, end of month reporting, or recruitment. The repeatable nature allows you to identify and control critical inputs. Even FMEAs can be used to capture the ways in which the process could go wrong and how you can prioritize actions against the highest risks (to the customer).

FMEA is particularly under-utilized in the service environment. When designing a new access control system for a large site, we used the FMEA to look at how the system could fail to keep out unauthorized persons and how likely it was that the failure would occur. The team were skeptical at first, but then they saw the benefit of capturing the fears they had about moving to a new system.

P.S., much of the available literature on Daily Management focuses on the daily routines and how we react to problems with countermeasures led at the lowest possible level in the organization. These activities are clearly directly applicable to services as well. The controversy is really about what we call the 'automotive core tools' such as FMEA and Control Plan.

The Hidden Benefits of Implementing Daily Management

The DM cycle obviously directly drives improvement, but it also has several benefits that drive improvement in a less visible but equally important way. DM drives knowledge management, fosters collaboration, and improves process understanding and employee engagement.

The DM cycle is a terrific opportunity to manage knowledge. Many companies are at risk because knowledge is in people's heads or pocket-books (this is called tacit knowledge in knowledge management theory). These experts call it "experience," explain that "it takes time to acquire," and often fail (willingly or not) to pass it to their colleagues. But when people leave the organization, tacit knowledge is lost. Therefore, it is key to turn this tacit knowledge into explicit knowledge, i.e., knowledge that can be expressed in words, numbers, or formulas.

A Bit of Theory on Knowledge Management: The Nonaka Model of Knowledge Accumulation

Professor Ikujiro Nonaka developed the concept of tacit and explicit knowledge. His SECI model (Socialization, Externalization, Combination, Internalization) explains how knowledge is accumulated:

1. First, knowledge is created and shared by Socialization. People informally exchange ideas and thoughts. Overall, some knowledge is created. The downside of this unstructured approach is that it does not guarantee that different people have the same understanding, nor that all people that need to know have actually been made aware.
2. The next step is to create explicit knowledge through what Professor Nonaka calls Externalization, i.e., the process of writing things down. Writing forces disambiguation. More importantly, it prepares the next step: Combination.

3. Once knowledge is explicit, it can be shared more efficiently with other people. Different elements can then be combined to create new knowledge.
4. This new combined knowledge must be internalized, i.e., users must practice to be fully capable. Through using this new knowledge, they will discover new opportunities and generate new knowledge that they will initially spread through socialization before the spiral movement continues.

This movement is not just a cycle. It is represented as a spiral because every step creates additional knowledge (Figure 8.12).

The visible side of the DM approach is very much about the externalization and combination steps. Writing standards is a fundamental aspect of externalization. But the internalization phase, though less visible in the DM cycle, is key as it makes the difference between a standard that leads to improved performance and a standard that is just a piece of paper that no one cares about.

It is not easy to capture years of experience, and many people believe that it is not possible. I agree that it is not easy, and that you will not be able to simply "download" someone's 40 years of experience on a piece of paper. Beware also of the aura of experts. Some of their certitudes are sometimes

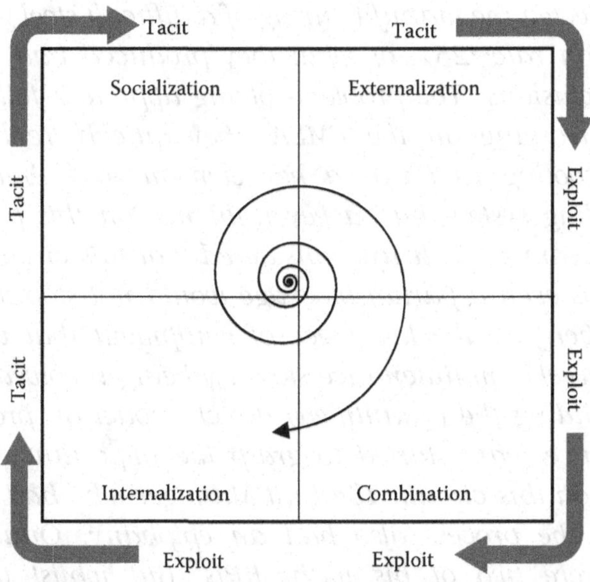

Figure 8.12 The Nonaka knowledge accumulation cycle.

nothing more than just assumptions in which they strongly believe, so one should be ready to challenge them and design experiments with them to demonstrate the validity of their assumptions. Nevertheless, crucial elements of knowledge will be captured in FMEAs and Standards.

The cross-functional team in charge of the various stages of DM, whether it is FMEA, Control Plan, or Problem Solving, will need to work together to reach a consensus. Deployment of a DM approach thus improves collaboration. It allows confrontation of different opinions and sharing of different experiences. Spending a few hours on a FMEA is a fantastic way to transfer knowledge between older and younger employees.

The result of this collective approach is improved process understanding. By taking part in the deployment of the DM cycle, management and employees reach a much higher level of understanding of the process. This usually leads to better-informed decisions.

EXAMPLE: THE UNIT MANAGER WHO DECIDED TO RESTART THE LINE LATER THAN EXPECTED

One of our acquaintances had been asked to support the roll out of DM in a Works producing steel tire cords. Rather than taking the team through classroom training (which usually switches everyone off), he asked them to select a problem that they had been struggling with for years. They selected the manufacturing of a difficult steel grade that had a high rejection rate: 25% of what they produced had to be rejected because of inclusions. The problem-solving approach followed the DM cycle. When working on the FMEA, they quickly realized that the temperature cooling rate was a key element and that the state of the water-cooling system had a key influence on this parameter. The maintenance team had always considered that this circuit was a non-priority item as even a partial blockage would not stop the production line. It was therefore the last piece of equipment that was cared for during the 4-weekly maintenance stop. By being involved in the FMEA and understanding the (quantified) direct impact on product quality, the maintenance team started to grasp the importance of preventive maintenance on this circuit. The Unit Manager who had so far limited knowledge of the process also had an epiphany. Quality and Line Availability were two of his main KPIs. But whilst the impact of overrunning during the maintenance stop was immediately visible, he had never been able to quantify the impact of not completing the full scheduled maintenance program. So, the line always restarted on time after the 4-weekly scheduled maintenance stop, whether all the preventive maintenance tasks had been completed or not (which would have meant a poor-quality performance for 4 weeks when producing certain grades of steel). Having been involved in the creation of the FMEA, his outlook on preventive maintenance changed. By the end of the next 4-weekly maintenance stop, he was confident enough to challenge his manager who wanted him to restart the line on time: they were running late, but he refused to restart the line until the cooling system had been fully maintained. In the 4 weeks that followed, his downgrade rate for inclusion on the grade they had selected remained at 0%.

Finally, the DM approach will help you to assign more optimally your limited resources. As the cross-functional creation of the FMEA will help determine which are the most important risks (and therefore what are the most important tasks to control risks), you will replace low-impact tasks with more impactful ones.

The Importance of Cadence

We have covered in this chapter the building blocks of a DM system. It can be mechanically made to work by just applying the tools. But, as a Sensei once quipped, if we do not put the spirit of Buddha into the statue, it is only stone. The spirit of DM is cadence. It is fundamental that all these activities are done regularly and frequently. Far too often we see big monthly meetings, or even worse, big quarterly meetings, when things should be handled in smaller meetings on a daily and weekly basis.

There are at least three reasons why the cadence of DM is so important. The first one is that we need to detect deviations as soon as possible. The longer between the checks, the more impactful problems will be. The second reason is practice. Whilst all these tools are very simple to understand, one needs to practice to really master them. The first go-see walks can be daunting. It will take at least 30 times longer to become an expert if you schedule monthly walks rather than daily ones. Finally, cadence turns all these exercises into something of a ritual. And rituals are an essential element of a culture. Without rituals that unify groups, individuals drift away from each other. And it becomes much more difficult to sustain a desired culture.

I would suggest that shifting the order of magnitude of frequency will shift the paradigm and create improvement in and of itself. If you have a monthly 2 hr. customer complaint meeting, make it a weekly, 30-min meeting. If you have a 1-h-long weekly meeting, make it a 10-min weekly meeting.

Linking Daily Management with Innovation-Related Processes such as Capital Expenditure (CAPEX) and New Product Development (NPD)

DM is about ensuring that the best-known standard conditions and procedures are applied to guarantee a stable process outcome. Most operations will be very happy with a stable process that is regularly improved through continuous improvement. However, continuous improvement might not be enough to compete. This is where innovation-related processes kicks in, and in particular New Product Development (NPD) and Capital Expenditure projects (CAPEX). A new product or new machine will automatically create instability in the process that you had painfully put under control with DM (Figure 8.13).

NPD, CAPEX, and Manufacturing are often three very well-defined processes that must follow standards. NPD often uses a development funnel with several phase gates. Going through each gate requires that standard conditions are met. The CAPEX process is meticulously defined (usually by the finance function as the most critical activity is alas often trying to get an authorization to spend the money). Manufacturing processes are often the ones where DM is first applied.

And yet, manufacturing a new product or bringing to production readiness a new piece of equipment is for many companies a real headache. The reason

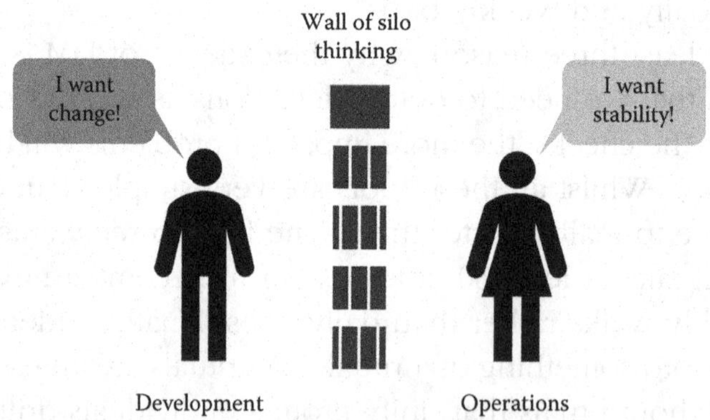

Figure 8.13 Diverging interests between development functions and operations.

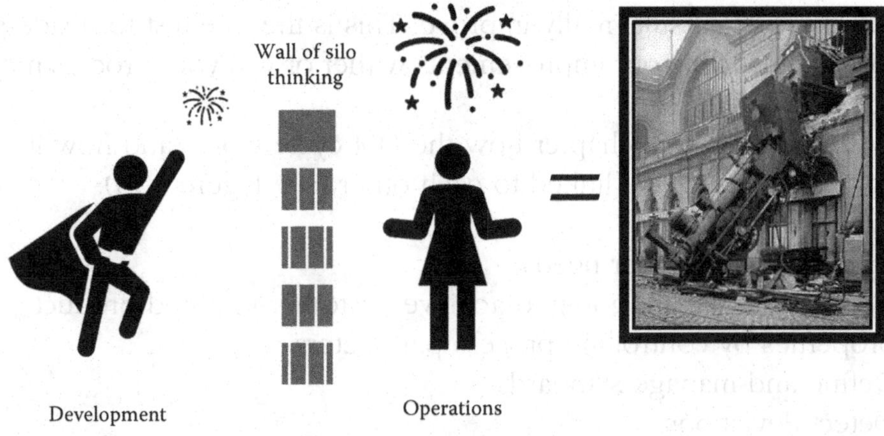

Figure 8.14 The usual consequences of divergent interests between development functions and Operations.

is that the NPD and CAPEX processes, even when heavily standardized and optimized, are not aligned with the manufacturing process. Moreover, operations people are often not involved enough in the development stage. The result is often a disaster. The development teams declare successful completion of the NPD phase. Or the engineers install the new piece of equipment on the new line and then declare their work finished. Sales start taking orders. And Operations must figure out how to manufacture the product consistently or how to use the new piece of equipment (Figure 8.14).

This pitfall can be avoided by integrating Operations' DM requirements in the phase gate criteria. Whether we are talking about a New Product Development phase gate or a new machine, the following boxes must be ticked before going through the launch gate:

- Has the FMEA been updated/created?
- Has the control plan been updated/created?
- Have Standard Operating Procedures detailing this new activity been developed (or have the existing ones been updated)?
- Have the teams been trained on the new standards?

Summary

Sustaining improvement is possibly even more important than improving (and certainly more difficult). Only by making your improvement sustainable will your business results really improve. This is the true test for leaders and CI professionals: will your improvements wither or will your process move to the next level?

We explained in this chapter how the DM cycle works and how its different components are linked to each other (see Figure 8.15):

- Understand customer needs.
- Define how we are going to achieve customer-required product properties by controlling process parameters.
- Define and manage standards.
- Detect deviations.
- Solve deviations and improve the system.

At the heart of the DM cycle is the Golden Triangle (standard work, visual management, and standard management). Visual Management has numerous advantages including:

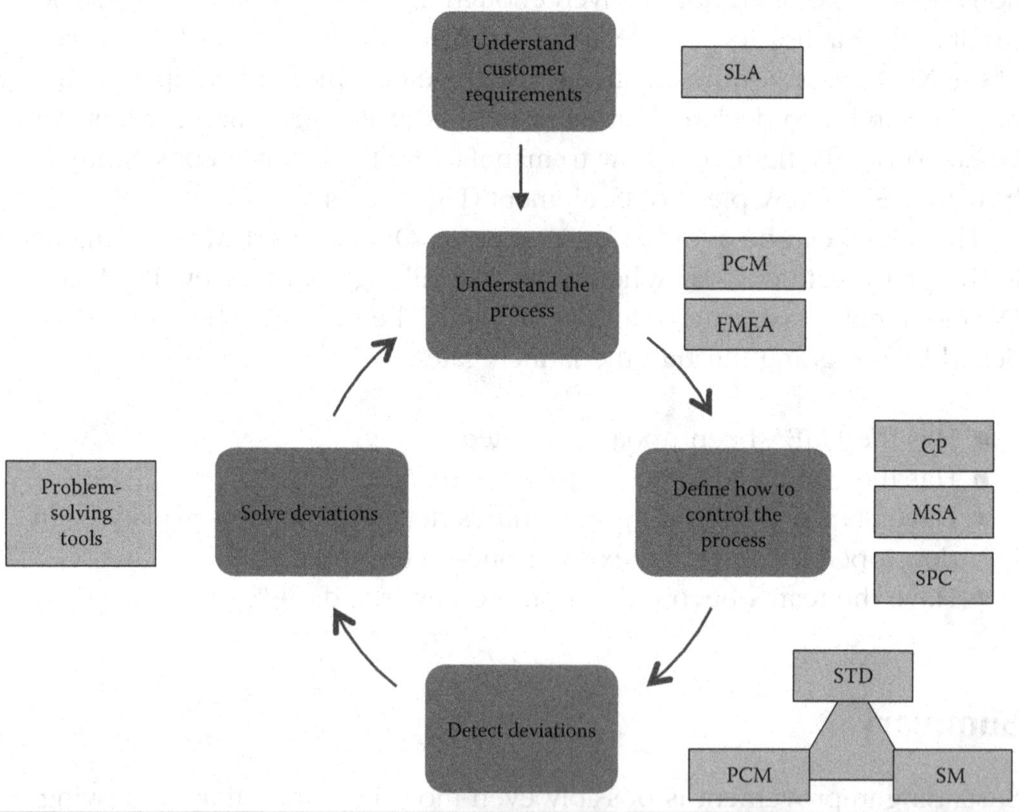

Figure 8.15 Tools used in this chapter related to the DM cycle.

- Making standards known to everyone.
- Facilitating integration of new employees.
- Ensuring standards can easily be audited.
- Making abnormal conditions easy to detect.

The other key aspect of the DM cycle is problem-solving. Deploying a DM approach will allow you to systematically tackle potential deviations of your process. It will also provide you with the start of a Knowledge Management system.

CONTROVERSY CORNER: IS DAILY MANAGEMENT WELL ENOUGH DEFINED?

Daily Management is often initially misunderstood. When Daily Management is first mentioned, it conjures up a number of images (such as war rooms, stand-up meetings, or KPI displays). Unfortunately, the term "Daily Management" does not explicitly refer to process and product control. Moreover, Daily Management is not just daily but refers to repetition at any frequency.

Fraser

So far, we have mostly discussed the tools of problem-solving and DM. A lot of books in the field of operational excellence are about tools. It is important to master the tools. But the truth is that these tools alone will not get you anywhere. Every company has access to these powerful toolboxes, yet most improvement programs fail. This is unambiguous evidence that the problem-solving leader will make the difference, not the tools they will use. So let us examine in the last chapter what it really takes to be a problem-solving leader.

Get started on your Chapter 8 learnings – practicing the application of the Daily Management cycle

I. *Selecting a product characteristic and creating the PFC, PCM, and FMEA*
   a. *What product characteristic will I work on (preferably one with plenty of past incidents)?*

   b. *What did you learn by completing the PFC?*
   c. *What did you learn from completing the process flow steps in the PCM?*
   d. *What did you learn by working with the shop floor experts to fill in a row (or more) of the PCM?*
   e. *What did you learn by completing a row (or more) of the FMEA template with the same people?*

II. *Creating/checking the Control Plan for the chosen characteristic*
   a. *What are the main risks according to the FMEA and do these ring true with the shop floor team?*
   b. *What did you learn by completing/checking the rows in the Control Plan?*

III. *Applying the Watanabe analysis to look for patterns in past investigations into this characteristic*
   a. *What were the conclusions relating to the last three investigations into this characteristic?*
   b. *How do these investigations map onto the Watanabe model and are there commonalities?*

Chapter 9

Building the Capability: Culture, Leadership, and Transformation

Hervé Duval and Fraser Wilkinson

> If you want to build a ship, don't drum up people to collect wood and don't assign them tasks and work, but rather teach them to long for the endless immensity of the sea.
>
> **Antoine de Saint-Exupery**

Introduction

All companies have easy access to the myriad of books describing Lean, Operational Excellence, or the DM cycles, and there are plenty of consultants willing to take the money to help implement these concepts. Yet, discrepancies in results are massive. Even within the same industry, all automotive companies have more or less the same production system deriving from TPS, yet annual surveys on reliability by make and model show significant differences. Financial results also greatly vary. This is proof that tools are not enough. Any car company not using them would go out of business very rapidly. These tools are necessary but not sufficient to ensure success. So what is the missing ingredient?

Those of us who have visited operationally excellent companies have all had the same experience. During the tour, local team leaders would explain

DOI: 10.4324/9781003486022-9

very clearly their roles and how they contribute to the DM system. They explain that they facilitate and train. They might also show amazing examples of problem-solving. We also meet operators who would explain that they have entered more than 50 suggestions in the suggestion scheme.

At the end of the tour, we all end up with the same thoughts: "Their DM system is not very different from ours. But if only I had team leaders and operators like these guys … ." As we are CI-minded people, we might ask ourselves why their team leaders are better than ours. The most likely initial, spontaneous answer: "they have been lucky to have found these few guys." Sensing that they probably have more than the ones we met, we would then switch to: "their HR people are better at recruiting than ours." Eventually, we would have to recognize that these people are the product of that company culture. A culture where people with the right behavior and caliber are selected into positions of influence and leadership where they can be nurtured and developed. And they in turn reinforce that culture through their own behaviors.

Once we have realized that, we can see that the role of the change agent is much more complex and deeper than what we might have anticipated. It is not just about teaching the tools, coaching people how to use them, and being able to report success on a few improvement projects, but more about building a new organizational capability. As we have observed through our own journeys, the challenge laid for the change agent is really about how to ensure that the organization is designed to create these amazingly capable people at all levels in all places. So, in this last chapter, we are going to explore this challenge by asking:

- What culture do we want to create?
- What is the role of leaders in this culture?
- What are the attributes of the problem-solving leader?
- How do leaders change cultures?
- How to influence leaders?

Like most of the topics covered in this work, the literature available on leadership is vast, reflecting the obvious importance of the subject. We won't try and replicate it here, but we will give you some pointers on what a change agent needs to be aware of, both as a leader yourself, and as someone who must influence leadership. The nature of being a change agent means you will need to exhibit levels of leadership in whatever you are involved in. Being out of your comfort zone will be a part of that. You don't need to be able to supply the right answers, but you do have to supply the right questions.

What Culture Do We Want to Create?

If there were a corporate utopia, what would it be? Of course, it would be different for everyone you asked depending on your viewpoint, but if we asked enough people, we would start to see a pattern emerge. We must assume here that the basic "hygiene" factors are taken care of sufficiently to allow space and time for thinking about an ideal state. It is difficult to talk about excellence when the roof is leaking, or people are feeling unsafe or anxious. If you need to go back to that stage, you'll need to concentrate on making positive improvements in those factors first before you can move on to higher goals.

Most people like to feel they are appreciated and are listened to. They have ideas about how the company should operate. Some people prefer working alone, but most of us are sociable and enjoy performing as part of a team. And what better way to satisfy these needs than to challenge people to collectively solve their problems and the problems of the business?

If we could state one key requirement of all operationally excellent organizations, it would be that they have a culture of problem-solving. This means they don't have a culture of apportioning blame or looking for the scapegoat. It would seem to be a natural inclination to look for the poor soul who screwed up and to wash our hands of the responsibility. Until it's our turn to be told *we* screwed up. Just moving away from a blame culture to a culture of system thinking would be a massive improvement, but also a massive challenge to do so. By investigating the root cause of problems in an open-minded way, we can start to see that the vast majority of problems stem from a systemic failure and not the failure of an individual.

How Do We Know That This Culture Works?

Abraham Maslow, the tutelar figure of humanistic psychology, started to highlight in the 1940s the hierarchy of human needs. This concept was famously illustrated by what is now known as Maslow's Pyramid. Maslow's theory is that human needs are ordered and that they must be fulfilled in a given sequence. Fulfilling a higher need is impossible until the previous ones have been addressed. Our contention is that there is a positive correlation between the degree of needs fulfillment and individual performance.

The first levels are the basic needs (food, water, safety, etc.) called hygiene factors. Another consequence of Maslow's Pyramid is that a good working environment and a good salary are not enough to motivate. The fact that these

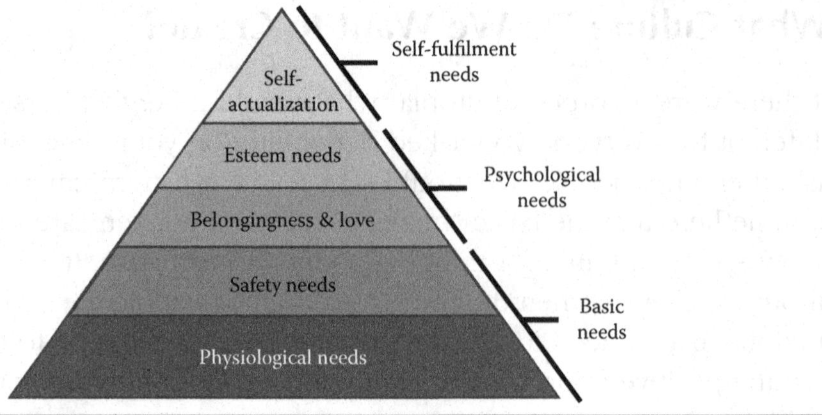

Figure 9.1 Maslow's hierarchy of needs.

needs correspond only to the base of the pyramid means that other needs have to be fulfilled to progress further. Companies where employees are treated like mindless robots and perceived as a cost will never get beyond that point, no matter the pay rises.

So, let us examine the higher-order needs: psychological and self-fulfillment needs. Maslow explains that humans need a sense of belonging and self-esteem that is obtained through accomplishment and self-actualization, which is the highest-order need (Figure 9.1).

A culture of problem-solving ticks all these boxes. Proper problem-solving fosters organizational co-operation. Successful problem-solving generates a huge feeling of accomplishment. The last level, self-actualization, is about autonomy, purpose, and personal growth. Again, all these elements are present in a culture that treats people with respect and lets them improve their own work.

So, beyond the obvious benefits generated by solutions to problems, systematic and widespread problem-solving in an organization fulfills human needs, which in turn creates better performance. In other words, the problem-solving culture creates a virtuous circle.

What Is the Role of Leaders in This Culture?

The role of the leader in this culture is to ensure that the organization builds and sustains the best possible systems to drive toward our goals (Policy Management) and keep our processes stable and capable (DM). A focus on systems ensures we don't get caught in the myth of the "hero leader." Our fiction has always mythologized the hero who by force of personality, courage, and superpowers, can overcome the greatest challenges and lead us to the promised land. On the one hand, we all cheer when the hero wins through in the movie, but is that how great organizations succeed over many years? Civilizations and empires have all had their heroes (and villains), but they also had great powers of organization and systems to ensure continuity. If the Greek and Roman civilizations had only heroes to sustain them, would their legacies have survived for so long and given so many technological and cultural advances?

Maybe we need both types of leadership roles depending on our situation. Heroes can lead us out of a crisis and other leaders look to systems to drive the organization forward. These other types of leaders are often called "servant leaders" because their role is to serve the team or individuals who are the value-adding elements. Is leadership a value-adding activity, a necessary non-value-adding activity, or a complete waste? From a Lean perspective, does the customer want to pay for the suppliers' leadership abilities? We suggest only if they add value. They add value only when they create an environment where less waste is generated.

The role of a leader must then be to serve the higher purpose of the organization by inspiring a vision of the culture required and ensuring the systems are in place to develop people in the right skills, attributes, and behaviors. Leaders must balance these requirements of the hero and the servant leader. Not every leader needs to be a role model of both types, but senior leaders need to recognize the importance of both types in order to deploy them as needed.

The old command and control structures are showing their age now. Millennials are often quoted as the generation who will respond very unfavorably to the older methods of leadership. We must remember this generational divide and be sensitive to the expectations of the younger generations who will of course be our next leaders.

The main role of leaders, then, is to ensure that the right systems are in place to deliver the desired culture and ensure that culture is robust enough to continue when headwinds, great or small, arise. From line stops to value stream redesigns, every aspect of responding to changes should have a well-defined approach, method, and toolset to deploy. Leaders get people fit to respond in well-choreographed sequences of activity to restore a new equilibrium. You could call this the "self-healing value stream."

The link between senior leadership behaviors and the degree of culture change observed can be described in a simple systems loop. The behavior of the most senior leaders is to establish systems that make doing the right thing easy and the wrong thing harder. These systems will then drive the overall behaviors in an organization (culture). Showing the right behaviors should then lead to the promotion of people into positions of leadership where they will continue to make systems easier to use. A virtuous circle is established.

Here is the stark reality of the role of a change agent in many organizations, including most of those the authors have been involved with. Working at the shop floor level of course is essential as that's where the value is generally created. If we stay only at that level, however, the sustainability of improvements is highly unlikely and culture change even less likely. Only senior leaders can establish the necessary processes across the entire organization that will continually improve the process of improvement (Figure 9.2).

Bottom-up approaches will only work if they don't come up against the resistance of the prevailing culture, which is a result of management actions. Where we see great bottom-up engagement there is also a willingness of the senior team to let go of the command and control levers. Responsibility and authority must be devolved down in the first instance. Leaders are unlikely to react well to a bottom-up initiative that threatens the power structures in place. It must be agreed up front what is on the table for change and what is not. An often-quoted example of devolving authority to the lowest level possible is that of David Marquet, a US Naval officer who was tasked with turning around the severely underperforming Santa Fe, a nuclear-powered submarine, in only 12 months.

This being his first nuclear command, he was forced to acknowledge that he could never master the operations in the time period required, so he

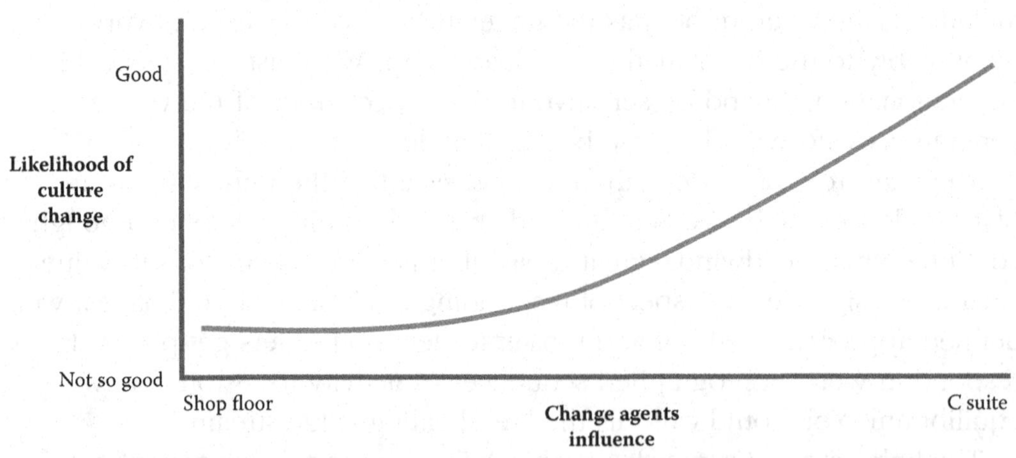

Figure 9.2 The reality of change agent success in driving culture change.

decided to rely on the experience of his officers and men who knew the ship intimately. He vowed to never give another order but instead give the *intent* and let them make the decisions whilst guiding them in the thinking process he would go through as a captain. The result was that 12 months later the ship was awarded the highest inspection marks ever achieved. He had instilled the thinking process of a captain into all aboard the ship. This was a radical change of procedure and certainly lessons can be learned from the example, however, like many great examples, there are contingent factors to consider. Submariners are already a breed with a notoriously healthy disregard for hierarchy but like any military organization, they are also well drilled and trained, spending months at a time in a close-knit group. Take inspiration from these examples, but also consider the hygiene factors already in place before attempting to apply the approach.

The Attributes of the Problem-Solving Leader

History is replete with a cast of hero leaders, and we still appear to be dominated by such types today in all walks of life. Part of the problem is that many leaders see in others the attributes that they possess and are naturally drawn to promoting people with similar attributes. In order to thrive in a world of "strong" leadership, those who want to progress must often adopt the attributes they see in the people in power. At the very worst, we can observe people at the highest level who may be described as narcissistic sociopaths (some say there is no difference between sociopaths and psychopaths).

CONTROVERSY CORNER: SOCIOPATHS IN THE BOARD ROOM?

Much research has been done to try and identify if sociopathic tendencies are more prevalent in the C-suite, and there is some evidence to support this. However, there appears to be a definite gender difference in how people working under these leaders report their support for them. Male leaders with sociopathic tendencies are much better supported than similar women leaders. Women leaders then should not try and ape the male attributes and perhaps the attributes we discuss here are more prevalent in women than men. Not wanting to wade into any gender wars, we will leave it to you to decide if this is the case. The research also suggests that leaders fair better when they display at least some of the attributes that define sociopathy, such as lack of empathy, anxiety, or any sense of guilt or blame. Tough decisions still need to be made, after all.

Fraser

The four attributes we discuss next are what we consider to be those essential to support the systemic adoption of a problem-solving culture and some of the attributes that will alert the change agent to potential danger ahead. Not all leaders will be comfortable with the idea of "servant leadership" as opposed to command-and-control, but it is our observation that these attributes are becoming more prevalent in many organizations, primarily because they are good for business and not just the latest trend.

Fact-Based Decisions

Of course, most people would agree that we need to base decisions on the facts, but in the age of "fake news," it is the role of a problem-solving leader to question where those facts came from. As with data, facts need checking for bias, accuracy, and the effect of the measuring system. Saying something is true with conviction and repeating it often enough can create "facts" from opinion. A healthy skepticism should be cultivated. Getting a well-rounded suite of facts is also essential, and the problem-solving leader must drive this relentlessly through asking the what? where? when? how many? and what trend? questions. Being insistent on fact gathering is the best start to any problem-solving activity.

The danger of these attributes being taken to an extreme is that an insistence on absolute confidence in our facts can stymy valuable progress. Problem-solving leaders must also work in a world of uncertainty, and even "the science" can be open to interpretation. We must encourage our leaders to strike the balance based on understanding the risks involved with making decisions based on incomplete knowledge (which to some extent is always true!). No solution to a problem is risk free, but if a leader involves a team in fact gathering and checking, then risks can at least be estimated and "known unknowns" considered. There are methods developed that do a very good job considering the factors discussed above. In *The New Rational Manager*,

Kepner and Tregoe (1981) offer an excellent set of tools and techniques that, when practiced consistently, will help calibrate the thought processes leaders apply when engaged in problem-solving. We see these thought processes seeping into the culture when senior leaders start to ask for problems to be presented in accordance with these methods.

Leaders must also be conversant with statistical techniques and have an understanding of the nature of variability. Again, this knowledge will guide the critical questioning needed to establish the confidence limits we have in the inferences we make from statistical outputs. Much of the scientific world revolves around the idea of having a level of confidence in the effect of changing an input. No medical treatment is ever declared to be 100% effective because we can never test 100% of the population. We can use the same statistical techniques through hypothesis testing to confirm process changes have led to an improvement, and we can set the confidence level at which we are comfortable to declare a cause-and-effect relationship a fact. The chance of getting an outlier is then a known quantity and we can factor this into our risk assessments. Setting a confidence level we are willing to accept is situationally dependent. How sure do we need to be that the change we make is having the desired effect? That's the nub of the question here. A "normal" statistical confidence level might be set at 99.5%, meaning there is a 0.5% chance that the data we observe is the result of random variation and not the input changes we have made. In business, most people would accept that risk unless there is a direct safety implication.

Risk management is an integral part of leadership in the modern world. Having the facts and statistical data to inform the risk management process is vital. In a world of uncertainty, the best we can hope is that we can stack the odds in our favor by choosing the course of action with the least downside risk and the best upside risk. The caution in that statement is that we delay decision making because we don't have all the facts we would like to have. We should always consider the "do nothing" option to give us a better understanding of the risk involved in delaying a decision. United States General Colin Powel recommends that 80% of the facts are enough, but that may be truer on the battlefield than in business.

As a change agent, we must have a very good understanding of how to gather and utilize facts and data so that we may help our problem-solving leaders to refine their approach. We are looking for effective and efficient problem-solving and decision making by our leaders.

Process Orientated

We talk a lot about "the process" in this book. The modern world is built on process repeatability as we have discussed in Chapter 2, and all international standards are based on a process approach. Operational Excellence models the world over, such as the Malcolm Baldrige Quality Award, require a process view of operations. Processes are often well described somewhere in a quality management system. Six Sigma insists on a process analysis method. And yet, despite the ubiquitous presence of processes, when it comes to business improvement, we so often see that process management is not the first port of call for business leaders. For improvement professionals, it is second nature to think in terms of process improvement, but why is this not the case with more of our leaders? Maybe it's seen as getting in the way of quick decision making, or it's not sexy, or it's only for showing to auditors when they come around again. Maybe leaders feel accountable for the outputs rather than for the process that delivers the output.

What we term a leader in operational excellence is also a process owner. The role of the process-owning leader is to cultivate an intimate understanding of the process that delivers the output. Leaders who are versed in process management will understand the $Y = fx, x1, x2, x3, \ldots$, etc. formula. Where Y is the outcome of the process and it is equal to a function (f) of the inputs (xs). Control the inputs and you control the outputs. This is extremely visible in Japanese companies where a focus on stable conditions and stable standards provides the basis for repeatable outputs, be they quality outputs or time-based outputs (cycle times, lead times, and line balancing). You don't need to have advanced statistical techniques to gain control if you have a high degree of standardization. Is that why Japanese companies are so reluctant to acknowledge the benefits of Six Sigma?

The first, and simplest, step in problem-solving is to ask the "standards" questions: Is there a standard? Was the standard followed? Is the standard correct? In traditional companies, leaders take decisions based on what they believe is happening in the process (without a process focus, incomplete/partial information may be reported to them). The Key rule of problem-solving is to "get the facts." This is not just about numbers but also understanding processes on the frontline. Leaders need to "go, look, see" the process in operation to be able to solve front-line problems.

Leaders must also develop a kind of meta-process view or helicopter view of how processes work in relation to each other. Process improvement without this overarching view can easily lead to local optimization. Leaders need to think in terms of the overall system and how a system has complex reinforcing loops in either a negative or positive way in terms of the output. Leaders need to understand the way performance measurement can drive suboptimization of the value chain. Narrow targets and bonuses based on narrow processes or department goals can lead to "gaming" of the results. It is a brave leader who speaks out against such obvious ill effects of the hallowed performance management system. Human Resources policies and mindsets that seek to drive individual performance through objectives that are set for the sake of setting them, followed by a judgment call on the value of individuals, can contribute greatly to negative reinforcing loops.

So, is process more important than people? This is one of those perennial questions that keep coming up in organizational improvement circles. Let's think of two spectrums: the capability spectrum from high to low and the process design spectrum from poor to excellent. Which one of these is the easier to control? Organizations don't generally set out to recruit the least capable members of the working population (but do try to match capability to tasks), and for very large organizations there is a finite pool of talent to go around. So each large organization will inevitably have a normal distribution of talent in the workforce. The obvious way to overcome the "problem" of a normal distribution of talent is to have very well designed and robust processes. Average people following excellent processes will trump excellent people following poor processes, and in the end that excellent talent will either insist on excellent processes or leave.

Leaders who think and act in terms of improving the value stream by focusing on maximizing the flow of value through the system can avoid the pitfalls mentioned above. Decision making on what process improvements to target can then be made against the objective of improving flow at the value stream level.

Humility and Ambition

So how do humility, ambition, and leadership reconcile themselves in the world of the hero CEO who can single handedly send the share price rocketing? A charismatic leader with a very humble nature and a profound understanding of the importance of systems might be an ideal, although rare, species. The above are two fundamentally different types of leadership, and as change agents we must be able to recognize what type we are dealing with and act accordingly when interacting with each. Of course, different stages of the business life cycle may require more or less of each characteristic.

The C-suite, however, is only a small minority of the leadership population, and most of us will not be having too much to do with those at the top of the world's biggest companies, although leadership types are not restricted to that level alone. We will come across the leader who believes that by their own brilliant character, they can drive through change and make a success of any situation. Maybe for a short time they can, but what is the legacy they leave behind when they move on? Some will employ clever tactics like painting a terrible picture of the state they found the department in when they came to the rescue. They may install favored lieutenants who drive through change and pull out all the short-term stops to make the numbers go their way. Having achieved this feat, they are moved on and celebrated as great leaders. The next person in charge takes the fall for the unsustainable measures installed and the inevitable drop in morale. Change agents can easily get caught up in this situation, and there is no easy answer if you do. If this happens a lot in your organization, then it will tell you a great deal about the attitude of the more senior leaders, and you will then need to reconsider if your role is at all tenable in that situation.

It can be hard to admit that we do not know the answer straight away, that we can't make a balanced decision on the spot, that we feel threatened by the challenges we face as leaders, but if we don't, we'll never get the most from ourselves and from the teams we lead. When we start to see that our role is not about always being at the front, always having the answer, then we are more likely to look to the team around us to gather the facts to aid good decision-making and problem-solving. We believe the best leaders are those that lead from the back. They set up the conditions for the success of the team, and the team takes the credit. They encourage us to "fail trying" and are humble in both their own successes and failures. Most of all, the leaders that drive sustainable processes are those that see themselves as the servants of the team. This type of leader is there to support the teams that make the value flow, the teams that serve the customer, the teams that innovate, and the teams that make an organization excellent.

CONTROVERSY CORNER: SHARE BUYBACKS AND THE HERO CEO

In the US and elsewhere, the practice of a company buying its own shares was illegal until 1982 when the long march of financial deregulation since World War 2 knocked over that sacred cow. When the majority of C-suite

> *compensation is via stock holding, there is an obvious incentive to juice the share price. When the cost of money is cheap, then it's almost a no-brainer for those at the top to borrow and buy back. As an example, between 1995 and 2020, IBM purchased $201 billion of its own shares. That's $201 billion that did not go to investing in the long-term health of the company, its people, and in the wider societal gains the US would get from a technology leader such as IBM manufacturing on home soil.*
>
> **Fraser**

Discipline

It can be tempting to try to shortcut the problem-solving process in order to speed up the timescale to resolution. It is true that experienced problem solvers can indeed be surer of which direction to take the investigative process, but that ability only comes when the process has been applied multiple times (maybe more than 30 times would be a good milestone in a problem solver's development). It is vital for a learner to strictly follow a problem-solving method once it is selected. Leaders must keep problem solvers focused on the steps whilst understanding that it is a non-linear process. It may be necessary to return to previous steps as more knowledge is gained and the problem definition is refined.

Discipline will also increase the chance of success. The risk of not adhering to the process is that we jump to conclusions and propose countermeasures that will not be as effective as they could be.

Discipline supports personal development. The problem solver needs to practice by sticking to the process until mastery of the process is reached. Mastery can be defined as the ability to manage all contingent factors relating to the problem and the context of the problem in order to be able to select the right tools and techniques and be laser focused on the data required and the best way to analyze that data.

Your personal discipline will be noticed by those around you. This will help when you are developing others in problem-solving methods. Self-discipline, when demonstrated in a leader, is a real driver for change. When you see people who can stick to a process or task and who have the self-determination to follow through with tough and emotional decisions, it can be a real inspiration to others. Leaders are not in the business of trying to discipline wrong people into the right behavior. Rather, they should encourage disciplined thought in others. Are your own thoughts as disciplined as they could be? Do you stick to the facts and avoid assumptions or biases? Do your emotions get in the way of following process? Find someone who can give you the feedback you need.

And finally, if we are to sustain the gains from the problem-solving process, we must ensure we have disciplined actions. It is impossible to sustain anything without a certain level of discipline in our people. The DM system described in Chapter 8 codifies many of the disciplines needed to sustain process improvements. The discipline of closing the Standardize, Do, Check, Act (SDCA) cycle can be reinforced by leaders at all levels. The CEO who attends a daily stand-up meeting and asks the right questions on the application of SDCA is showing they have an understanding of the basic stability process management principles and that they value the effort. This is sometimes referred to as the "no hero" mentality. It is much easier to praise those who firefight their way out of a crisis than it is to praise those who are continually preventing the need to firefight in the first instance.

HERVÉ SAYS: DO FOOTBALL MANAGERS MAKE A DIFFERENCE?

In their book Soccernomics, *Simon Kuper and Stefan Szymanski* (Kuper & Szymanski, 2009) *used science to answer the question that every football fan asked himself at least once: do football managers matter? The short version of their answer is that very few do and most teams' final ranking depends much more on their budget than manager ability. There are very few Alex Fergusons and Arsene Wengers.*

I have been wondering since I read that book whether this result holds true for businesses. We unfortunately lack comprehensive studies on the topic. But I cannot help thinking about the first transformation I was involved in. The year was 2005. The transformation that the newly appointed General Manager initiated saved the site that went from being on the verge of collapsing to debt-free in 3 years. The leader got promoted from General Manager of the French site to Managing Director of a small business unit that at some point was making $1 M a week. At the same time, the great 2008 economic crisis hit Europe. The Managing Director retired a few years later and his business unit was closed. Had he suddenly become a poor leader? In the meantime, the new General Manager, a very experienced man, introduced many more changes, but *eventually had to leave the site that was facing significant losses again as the order book had collapsed by 30% because of the crisis. Had he too become a poor leader by moving to this new position?*

The truth is that being a good leader is not enough if you face strong headwinds. The initial transformation of the French site had been a great success. A lot of the credit had to go to the General Manager who initiated it and relentlessly worked to bring the best out of us. But on top of his skills, he was fortunate that the context was one of rising market prices. The transformation allowed us to capture these opportunities. Had we attempted the same transformation just 18 months later, we would have failed. Equally, the second General Manager could have succeeded, had he been appointed three years earlier.

This illustrates the fact that the final attribute of the successful problem-solving leader is pure luck. We are not talking here about the talent that jealous observers could call luck. Great leaders create most of their apparent luck by building a robust and flexible organization. I love this oft-quoted aphorism, "the more I practice, the luckier I get." But we are talking about circumstances that no one can do anything about, i.e., "the fortune or misfortune of wars." Napoleon summarized this in one sentence. He reportedly replied to an aid, when asked to consider an officer for promotion: "I know that he is a good officer, but is he lucky?"

How Leaders Change Culture

In Chapter 5, we discussed the McKinsey change model and the What?/How? connection. These are the basics of how to successfully manage a change in culture, but of course, the reality is much messier than models can depict. There are thousands of articles dedicated to how to change the culture of an organization, yet it proves difficult in practice. McKinsey also recognize this, and they echo our call that the best we can do as change agents is to improve the odds of success. They identify four areas that change leaders must focus their attention on:

- Communicating
- Role modeling
- Developing your team
- Spending more than 50% of their time on the transformation

You can only focus on these tactical areas if you have first defined the end point, the goal, the promised land, the vision, or whatever terminology you choose. Only when everyone in leadership roles understands the type of culture we are aiming for can we begin to apply the tactics as a means of tilting the odds toward that end point. We have defined one very important aspect of the culture we want to create: a problem-solving culture. That's a very simple message that everyone can relate to and has little controversy attached. We would strongly recommend this as a culture change vision.

In the McKinsey change model or the What? How? connection we make the point that if we miss any of the elements, the odds of success tilt unfavorably away. Knoster (search Knoster Change Model) shows this in a slightly different way in his model on the conditions for change, and he suggests what we may observe if we miss any of the prerequisites defined. These are all outcomes we are intimately familiar with (Figure 9.3).

Whilst Knoster's change model is quite straightforward (most of them are!), transformations often fail because leaders either do not effectively manage to build all the blocks described or fail to maintain them in place long enough. In most cases, all the blocks appear to be in place. The company published the vision, company-wide trainings with mandatory attendance are announced, and budgets are allocated. But there will be plenty of urgent things that will conspire to prevent leaders from dedicating time to this cultural transformation. It takes discipline to stay focused on issues of priority for culture change, as these can be very different from immediate operational priorities. Leaders need

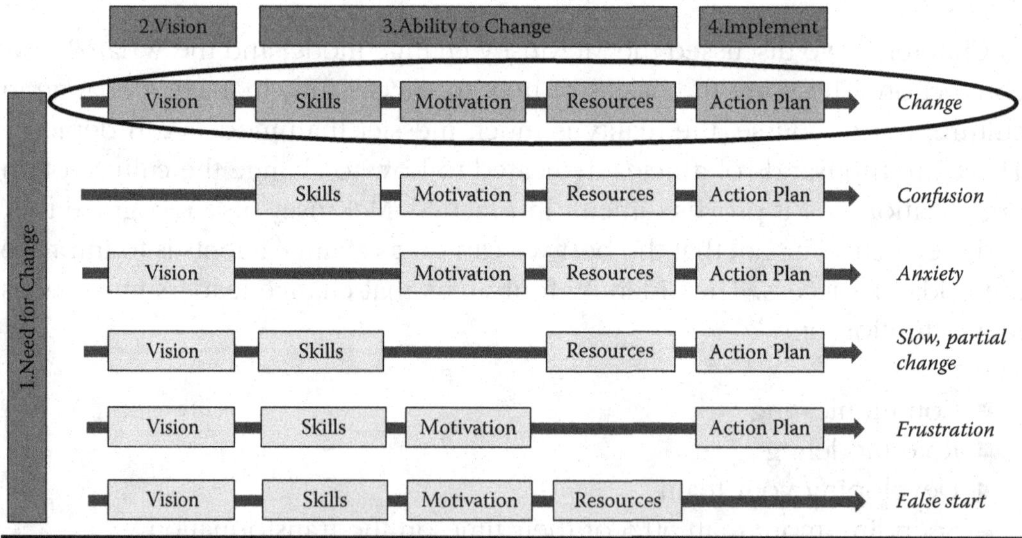

Figure 9.3 Knoster's change model.

to have both results and culture change in the forefront of their minds. This is why Production Systems, Business Systems, or Excellence Systems, no matter how one calls them, are fundamental to sustain performance. Without such a framework to guide leaders and their organizations on a daily basis, the odds are that the necessary long-term work on culture will disappear as focus will constantly be brought back to short-term issues.

We have found one of the best and simplest ways to ensure that enough time is reserved for important things is to use a standard calendar, i.e., blocking slots in the diary for these important tasks such as shop floor visits (Gemba walks), safety tours, waste walks, and stand-up daily meetings. A senior executive we have worked with has also started to only schedule 20-, 50-, and 80-min meetings into their diary to avoid overrun and being ill prepared for the next meeting when there are back-to-back meetings planned. Also keeping a clear diary slot for problem-solving with a team is a way of applying all the change model elements in one go.

Let's take a closer look at Knoster's change model main headings, *Communicate Vision*, *Create Ability,* and *Engage and Implement,* and discuss what we expect our leaders to do within the model.

Communicate Vision

Leaders must define and deploy the excellence vision. A vision should include two elements: the need for change and the end goal. Is there a real crisis to address or are we being asked to make more money for the sake of our shareholders? What does the future look like and feel like? How will I be expected to behave? Will I care about this change? What's in it for me and what's in it for you? All these questions are best answered in a story. Why? Because we all love a story.

There is a $2 trillion a year problem-solving industry called Hollywood that proves we love to hear how people solve problems. In every film, miniseries, box set, book, comic, or reality TV show, there is always a problem to be solved. They all have at their core a story archetype that has to work in uncannily similar ways to have a dramatic impact. And without that dramatic impact, you won't be watching for very long. There is always an inciting incident (crisis) that kicks off the dramatic arc, and if you look closely, it is simply a problem to be solved by the protagonist. Now, if they knew how to solve that problem, then there's not much of a story, so what must they do? They take a journey into the unknown to find the answer. A journey into the woods. At the heart of all great storytelling is a search for knowledge and a resolution.

In the best stories, our protagonist must also take an inner journey of discovery. They must confront their antagonist (who is merely an incarnation of their own fears or inadequacies) and assimilate their own growth with their new-found knowledge to solve the real-world problem.

The age-old "hero's journey" into the woods and back again, complete with the ability to slay the dragon, banish the aliens, reunite the family, kill the shark, find the ark, destroy the death star, and win the boy/girl to triumph (or in tragedy, to fail) is what keeps our attention. There are deep psychological and cultural reasons why this story archetype is so universal, and it reflects the journey of every one of us. We all change as we learn more about the world and about ourselves, and storytelling helps us to live our lives vicariously through our favorite characters to test out how we may feel if confronted by similar problems.

In much of the literature, Toyota A3 problem-solving is referred to as A3 storytelling. Our younger selves didn't quite make the full connection, but when we start to think of the problem solver as our fabled protagonist that we send out into the woods, it becomes clearer. Along the way, they must gain knowledge of the problem, and more crucially for growth, self-knowledge. They may come to realize that they need to approach problems from a different perspective than they have done previously.

We have seen people who can't wait to tell their problem-solving story because they've been on a genuinely engaging journey and discovered something new and important to bring back to the tribe that can help everyone else. The most animated talk of their inner journey as well, and through self-reflection, have been able to identify gaps or blind spots in their problem-solving approach. We think of stories as entertainment, but they are of far more importance than that. Real problem-solving means discovery, and we should ask those adventurers to inspire us with their stories through sharing and learning from in-person events to blogs and videos. Leaders repeat these stories and they become part of our shared culture.

The best leaders tell stories effortlessly and repeatedly, keeping the message consistent. However, if you find yourself repeating the same story by rote, regardless of the context, then you have strayed too far into the role of the well-coached politician, and that's not a good place to be either. We and our leaders must express the excellence vision in a language that engages the head, the heart, and the hand if we are to stand a chance of engaging others in the vision. Occasionally we may need to conjure a little poetry to help in this. It would be nice to think we could all convey our passion in such terms.

HERVÉ SAYS: THE SECRET OF PERSUASION HAS BEEN IN THE PUBLIC DOMAIN FOR MORE THAN 2,300 YEARS

The Greek genius Aristotle is widely credited for having captured the basics of persuasion in the 4th century BCE. In particular, he defined three persuasive audience appeals:

"Ethos" is about establishing credibility. It is important that the audience understands why they can trust you on this topic. The human brain is wired to rapidly assess whether another human is a threat, which must have contributed to the survival of these genes through the ages. In our more moderns time, you are not going to be hit by a big stick by your fellow sapiens if you failed that test, but the first impression is still a defining moment of a relationship. Establishing this ethos at the beginning of an attempt to persuade is vital if you are not known yet. Different cultures will respect different things: academic achievements, awards, experience, money made, humble wisdom, and so on. Understanding what your audience respects will help you to select the right introduction.

"Logos" is about the logical factors. Persuasion attempts should include the facts and figures, but also answer the "what is in it for me?" question. But this is not enough.

"Pathos" is about emotions that you generate in your audience. Emotions incite people to act (and this has been since evidenced by brain chemistry research). An emotional story backing your numbers will considerably increase your chances of successfully persuading your audience compared with a purely logical and cold approach.

So the recipe is simple: let people understand why they should listen to you, have a few shocking facts and figures, and illustrate the data with an emotional story. Concision is key, and metaphors will tremendously help as they conjure up a vision with a few words rather than having to spend several minutes painting the picture.

Is there a "higher purpose" in your organization that you can bring people together with? Don't try to force one upon the organization, but if it's there then use it wisely to connect with the emotional drivers.

Ability to Change – Skills

In most automotive companies and supplier organizations, operational leaders themselves give training to their direct reports. This is possible because they rose through the ranks in companies that have a strong operating system. In most traditional companies, leaders might not be able to give the operational excellence training themselves, but they should still participate at a minimum. For example, they can do this by introducing the training and explaining why it is important or running a section within a training module. The danger with this scenario is that it creates the impression that this training is really for everybody else but not the leader.

Time and again we have seen training fail to deliver capability because the leader does not truly value the application of that training. Problem-solving is a prime example of this because, paradoxically, nobody will deny that we need to solve problems. To do this we need people to learn to problem-solve, but when problems arise, the leader, who doesn't understand the problem-solving process, does not insist on following the prescribed methods.

It will take time to have a system in place that creates the environment where capability is nurtured to meet the needs of the vision. But it starts with training and developing people on the principles and tools that will be core to your company's improvement approach. As mentioned previously, the 70:20:10 model should be used as shown in Figure 5.2.

We would highly recommend John Shook's *Managing to Learn* (Shook, 2008) as a great example of how the capability and confidence of a learner can be increased through a practical application of the A3 Thinking approach. This book provides perspectives from both the mentor and the mentee. This is classic coaching territory, as opposed to classroom-only delivery. The modern leader should also be a great coach if they want to develop capability amongst colleagues and peers.

EXAMPLE: THE LEADERS WHO TRAINED THE NEXT LEVEL OF LEADERS

During a first participation in an attempt to change culture on a site, one of the first questions we asked ourselves was "how are we going to teach them the lean principles and tools?" Whilst we, the so-called Continuous Improvement coaches, had a good understanding of the tools and principles, we had little credibility at the start. Using a sheep-dip, classroom training approach had little chance to engage managers and teams. We understood quite rapidly that people would follow a number of leaders, either because they were their manager or they were opinion leaders in the Management / Leadership population. So with the support of the General Manager, we took these managers through the training modules. The General Manager informed them that they will have to give the training to the next level of the organization (with a degree of support depending on their individual CI maturity). Benefits of this approach are numerous:

It created more training capacity than if we had had to rely only on pairs of experts, thus accelerating deployment.

Employees received training from their boss, so engagement was much stronger than if training had been given only by the CI expert. Their manager does not have to build a rapport, as he has built it over time. He will also find the right words and examples that will resonate with his team, rather than having experts raving about the wonders of the Toyota Way.

And very cynically, there was an element of manipulation here (for the right reasons though). As Managers knew that they will have to run the training module, they were much more focused when they received the initial training than if it had been a "free" training. Moreover, the fact that they had had to explain the approach to others reinforced their own belief in the approach.

As a change agent, you will need to continuously develop your capabilities using the 70:20:10 model. Don't wait for the next training program to come along, as today we can learn almost anything through online channels. Some predict the wholescale demise of physical learning institutions such as universities when you can now enroll in courses at all levels in the prestigious university of your choice. Getting practical experience, however, must remain the largest component of the learning equation. From our experience, change agents will need to gain proficiency in the following areas:

- Coaching and mentoring
- Principles of Lean, TQM, and Six Sigma
- The DM cycle of SDCA (Standardize, Do, Check, Act)

- The problem-solving cycle of PDCA (Plan, Do, Check, Act) with specifics on A3 methodology
- Situation appraisal via diagnostics
- Data analysis and the effects of variability
- Storytelling, communication, and presentation
- The basics of behavioral theory
- Self-reflection

If this list seems a little daunting, then why not start with our favorite topic – problem-solving. After all, you will eventually find that all of the above will be needed if you are to solve problems effectively and efficiently. And Lean thinking will tell us we should concentrate our problem-solving efforts in the places where the value is added.

Ability to Change – Motivation

In Chapter 5, we looked at what drives behavior. Simple but realistic models suggest that it is consequences that drive behavior, or more correctly, the perceived consequences. The theory goes that we take action based on what we think the outcome will be, and we are more motivated when the outcome is positive and immediate. Hence the role of reward and recognition in trying to nudge people toward the desired behavior. We can all think of simple examples of why this might work. You don't put your hand in the fire because you are certain to get a very negative effect which is felt immediately. However, when we get to a more nuanced situation such as making a change in the way we work, the perceived consequences can be very subjective depending on the numerous factors influencing every individual.

Even when attempts have been made to use positive reinforcement to drive behavior, we have seen unintended consequences arising. In *Punished by Rewards*, Alfie Kohn (1993) shows time and again how well-meaning incentivization has gone awry. It would appear that when we try to apply inducements to behave in a certain way, these are more often than not counterproductive. As leaders, it is appealing to think we can use simple inducements to help drive behavior, but we are not simple creatures. We are not the laboratory rats, dogs, or pigeons that were the subject of early behavioral research. We are far better at strategizing in order to play the system to our own ends, often to the detriment of the intended purpose of those inducements.

CONTROVERSY CORNER: CAN EVERYONE BE MOTIVATED?

I am often told that good leaders and managers find ways to motivate everyone. So if an employee is cautious about adopting new approaches, it must then be because we have not sold it well. Reality is probably less black and white than this. In our experience, the same people will always be ready to change, while the same other people will resist change. This is a well-known phenomenon in marketing called the Rogers adoption curve (or diffusion process).

Whilst this theory was originally developed about farmers and extrapolated to consumers, we believe that similar principles apply to adoption of new ways of working during transformations within companies. So rather than hoping that 100% of people will be motivated, look for innovators and early adopters. Once these people have adopted the new ways of working, use gentle pressure to make the majority follow. A very common way to do this is to start monitoring and reporting progress of adoption. After a short time, early and late majority will realize that it is more risky to stall than to adopt. Laggards are probably not that numerous, but they can be dangerous if they are in key positions as they become blockers. The most common thought with hindsight is that "we should have removed blockers earlier."

Hervé

The question of whether leaders can motivate people is much discussed today. It is our, and I'm sure your, experience that leaders and the systems they create can easily demotivate people. Overzealous applications of rules and regulations, burdensome bureaucracy, micromanagement, excessive monitoring of performance (online snooping software), pointless reporting without action, explaining why plans continually fail, massaging of data, and annual appraisals (beauty parades) can all demotivate. Kurt (Lewin, 1951) proposed that when making a change, we need to address both the *driving* forces and the *restraining* forces that we bring to bear. Part of the Lean philosophy is to drive out these restraining forces that add no value to the customer. When coupled with the premise that we should always have *respect for people,* we can understand how such systems require fewer extraneous driving forces. Leaders must recognize if they are promoting de-motivational factors as well as what they think are motivational factors. When these are in conflict there is an obvious hysteresis in play.

In a large organization with many subcultures, how can we tell what the current level of employee motivation is? Some leaders will intuitively feel if the culture is "right" or "wrong," but not all leaders have the emotional intelligence to be able to do this. Cultural surveys are popular ways of trying to understand the situation. Some global organizations such as McKinsey have their own standard questions, which means comparators can be made across sectors and geographies. These can also be done locally on a smaller scale or by other means, but if they are done, then actions need to be taken or they can be easily seen as another management fad. There is a degree of cynicism in most employees and it is easy to play up to those cynicisms with the use of these techniques.

When people have a clear vision explained and are adequately rewarded for the work they do, then this is the basis of motivation. Being treated fairly and with respect goes a long way. If we can also give people some agency in their ability to own the work and make improvements, then all the better. Sometimes it can feel like the work situation is a kind of artificial environment where we need to adhere to behaviors that create a dissonance with our view of normal human relationships. If this is the case, then we are likely to be demotivated. The best leaders are those with genuine conviction for what they do and how they work, and they will be able to bring others along with them.

As discussed previously, Frederick Herzberg's model is a useful framework to explain motivational factors. It explains that a number of conditions such as job security, pay, or physical working conditions (that he calls "hygiene factors") must be met to avoid dissatisfaction. Motivation can only come from absence of dissatisfaction and the presence of motivators (Figure 9.4).

Hygiene factors satisfied.	**Sleeping beauty:** Whilst there is little/no source of dissatisfaction, motivation is low. Sense of purpose must be created.	**The ideal situation:** Little/no source of dissatisfaction and high motivation.
Hygiene factors not satisfied.	**The worst situation:** Low satisfaction and low motivation, likely to result in high attrition rate and low productivity.	**The wasteful situation:** Efforts have been made to create a sense of purpose, but very practical considerations ruin all efforts.
	Motivation factors not satisfied.	Motivation factors satisfied.

Figure 9.4 Combining hygiene and motivational factors.

EXAMPLE: COVER ALL THE BASES

One magnificent example of an attempt to motivate a group of individuals with different inner needs is Henry V's speech before the battle of Agincourt in Shakespeare's play. The king's army is thrice outnumbered by the French army that is blocking the road along the French coast. So the king's army has a burning platform: they will have to fight to go back home. In a few lines, Henry V manages to find words that correspond to the inner needs of most people in his army:

- *For challenge-oriented soldiers, he explains the difficulty of the task and the glory that they will obtain by succeeding (and if to live, the fewer men, the greater share of honor).*
- *Key nobles, who are probably recognition-seekers, are named and therefore flattered (Then shall our names, Familiar in his mouth as household words- Harry the King, Bedford and Exeter, Warwick and Talbot, Salisbury and Gloucester- Be in their flowing cups freshly rememb'red).*
- *Finally, Henry appeals to team players (We few, we happy few, we band of brothers; For he to-day that sheds his blood with me shall be my brother).*

Ability to Change – Resources

Leaders need to ask themselves if the organization has enough spare capacity to effectively manage a change. The answer to this question will depend on many factors contingent to the setting you find yourself in and the way you choose to manage the change. Big launch programs covering the entire organization will require a release of human capacity that may be 20–40% of a leader's time and 5–10% of everyone's time. Where we have seen 12 weeks fully immersive change programs in action, then capacity must be freed and additional full-time support must be secured. Ratios of 3–5% full-time coaching staff to employees have been successful in these situations, albeit 12 weeks is only a kick-start or accelerated change in order to start the momentum with a mass audience.

A mismatch between available capacity and the organization's ambition will lead to frustration. If you can't release or buy in the levels of capacity suggested here, then you will need to look at more focused activity. Creating capacity for problem-solving activities at all levels would be a good first start and require less of a big-bang launch, the dangers of which we have covered earlier.

What are the technical systems your organization has that will help to deliver operational excellence? Many organizations are now awash with IT systems, cloud applications, and on-premise bespoke systems and databases that store vast amounts of data, and this data mountain is growing exponentially. A subset of the Industry 4.0 movement could be described as the Quality 4.0 movement. From a strategic perspective, all this data can be invaluable in giving market and customer insights as demonstrated by the monetization of the social media ecosystems, but as problem-solving leaders, we must now look at this data and see if it actually helps to solve the root cause of problems as they arise. In the Quality 4.0 world, the ability to link data easily and quickly to a deviation or defect would be a huge advantage in the problem-solving process.

The lure of technology could also be a hinderance in transformation efforts. Getting distracted by IT applications is easy to do and even within the confines of the general office software available today, there are now multiple applications awaiting to be discovered. These applications can be used very much as "lo-code" platforms with no additional costs. Don't let the use of technology be an excuse for lack of progress. Big data can solve many problems, but small facts are just as powerful in most cases. Make a start with what you have.

Implement

We mentioned earlier the "happy mappers" of the early Lean movement. The push to apply value stream mapping came about with the publication of the seminal *Learning to See* workbook (Rother & Shook 1999), which took us through the steps needed to analyze the current state of flow of value in a supply chain and the basic techniques to improve that flow. What many failed to do was the next stage of creating the *ideal state* map and then the incremental *future state* map along with its attendant transition plan of concrete actions at the 30-, 60-, and 90-day increments.

At some point, the change agent must make changes and those changes, if positive, will lead to an improvement in one of the SQCD metrics. These will be linked to making money, now and in the future. Another trap that the Lean movement fell into was a focus on 5S as a basic requirement and the obligatory kaizen blitz approach. If these worked at all, they often had no bearing on the flow of value because they were not conducted specifically to improve the flow. Sometimes we used these approaches in the misguided assumption that we were encouraging "engagement" in Lean.

We have consciously avoided tackling how strategy is created in this book, but it must be said at this stage, that whatever we implement must of course drive us closer to that strategy or keep us on the right side of legislation and regulations. So, leaders must first prioritize *what* we need to implement against strategy and "licenses to operate" in their geographies and sectors, then they must be able to prioritize *where* to deploy resources, tools, and techniques. In Chapter 3, we saw a way of prioritizing based on a diagnostic approach which helps to focus on key metrics but also on how to improve the flow of value. Leaders must also consider how much of a focus to put on results and how much on longer-term culture change activities.

Once again, if you are in any doubt about how to start the implementation, start with a pain-point. This could be a hygiene factor, a key metric, or an improvement in flow dependent on the level of operational excellence already in place. Building long-term problem-solving capability gives both results and the culture change foundations. Leaders must request and require problems to be identified and worked on using systematic methods. They should have a good working knowledge of those methods from personal practice. Only when it becomes the expected norm will you embed this way of working.

As we discussed in Chapters 7 and 8, once improvements have been made, we must sustain these gains, and the leader has a vital role to play in this. Leaders can check the effectiveness of the root cause analysis and the robustness of the countermeasures by a review of problem-solving activities. Countermeasures should be built into existing systems such as the DM system discussed earlier. We would expect leaders to be conducting regular process confirmation checks at the shop floor level. These could be random or scheduled, but they are more than just a chance to have a chat, as important as that is. Say we have had a problem with a particular product and we have identified that a new control is in place that the operators must comply with. Assuming we have eliminated the possibility of applying more effective control measures such as error proofing, automation, or SPC, then we will need to ensure that manual operations are done correctly. We do this through observation and open dialog with the operator to ensure the approved procedure is followed. As leaders, we also have an opportunity to ask about the next level of performance to be reached or what problems exist that we can help with.

All levels of management should be involved in this confirmation activity. Even non-production leaders can conduct confirmation checks with their people or indeed at the shop floor. This reminds us where the value-added activity occurs and the environment we are expecting our people to work in.

Leaders must avoid the trap of thinking we are implementing change because we have measured the amount of training we've done or how many 5S projects we have initiated.

HERVÉ SAYS: IS THE LEADER SIMPLY THE ONE WHO DECIDES TO LEAD?

After 24 months of (trying to) deploy operational excellence in a portfolio of 15 sites, I took time to reflect on progress so far, success factors, and impediments determining progress rate. Progress was quite uneven across the portfolio. Some areas were about to reach level 2 on our maturity assessment scale while others had hardly started preparations for level 1. Discrepancies were even noticeable within sites, as some lines were much more advanced than others even though the local managers were reporting to the same site lead.

The first conclusion was that one should not wait that long to reflect on success factors. The second conclusion is as important but also relevant to this leadership chapter. I looked for the presence or absence of a number of factors usually associated with success of improvement programs, such as engagement of site lead, level of resource, position of local owner (i.e., is he an outsider or is he part of local management), prior history of improvement programs, and experience of local owner. Neither of these characteristics turned out to be a predictor of successful deployment of our operational excellence program. Nor was any combination of these factors. The only factor 100% correlated with success was how self-driven was the local program owner. Obviously, a supportive site lead, access to resources, and a background in operational excellence helped. But the most self-driven local owners managed to make significant progress even though in some cases they had little experience with operational excellence, no resource other than themselves, and/or limited support from a site lead. This is no miracle. They just looked for solutions, motivated others around them, and focused their environment on deliverables. In other words, even though the organization had not given them a leadership title, they made themselves leaders.

Leadership Implements the "production system"

If we want to have an on-going legacy of continuous improvement, should we create our own version of the Toyota Production System? This is a question much debated in operational excellence circles, and the idea has some merit in that a system attempts to bring together many processes and make sense of how they interact and complement each other (or not, in many cases). The downside is that it's tempting to try to shortcut to a clone of the TPS because it works for Toyota. By this stage, you should already know that we don't recommend an attempt to simply replicate any system in your own setting as there are too many contingent factors to consider as discussed in Chapter 5.

Developing your own system, however, will be a drawn-out affair and require much in the way of the leadership understanding the purpose of the system and the elements within it first, but it should give you a better chance of sustainability if it fits with the existing culture and maturity levels in the organization. We must also remember that the TPS is only the Production part of the overall system. We have struggled to define operational excellence in many situations as it can often stray into strategy, marketing, product development, etc., and this should be borne in mind when attempting such an exercise. Leaders must not let this exercise be driven by the improvement team. A production system must be led by the production staff under the facilitation of a Sensei.

> There is a misperception that everyone at Toyota "gets it," that we walked into our roles, front-line assembly worker or vice president, and were automatically assimilated into the Toyota culture and able to grasp Toyota philosophies, concepts, tools, and techniques. Nothing could be further from the truth. Everyone within Toyota had to work to develop and sustain a problem-finding/kaizen mind, and it was management's role to make that happen and provide the coaching, mentoring, motivation, and systems to further that development.
>
> **Nate Futura**, Toyota HR executive of 37 years and author of *Welcome Problems, Find Success: Building Toyota Cultures Around the World* (Nomura, 2021)

When designing any organizational framework such as a production system, one of the best models to use is that described by Scholtes (Scholtes, 1998). In this model, we can clearly see the organizational design principles and where a production system fits into the overall scope of classic organizational design features and the priority of the thinking required.

We can see from Figure 9.5 that any lower-level design element must serve the higher elements. We should therefore be very clear about the purpose of the production system in order to design it correctly. This is where we have experienced some difficulty with getting an agreement on the purpose, since scope creep tends to come into play. In this very logical framework, everything else we need to run the systems should flow down to shape the lower level and

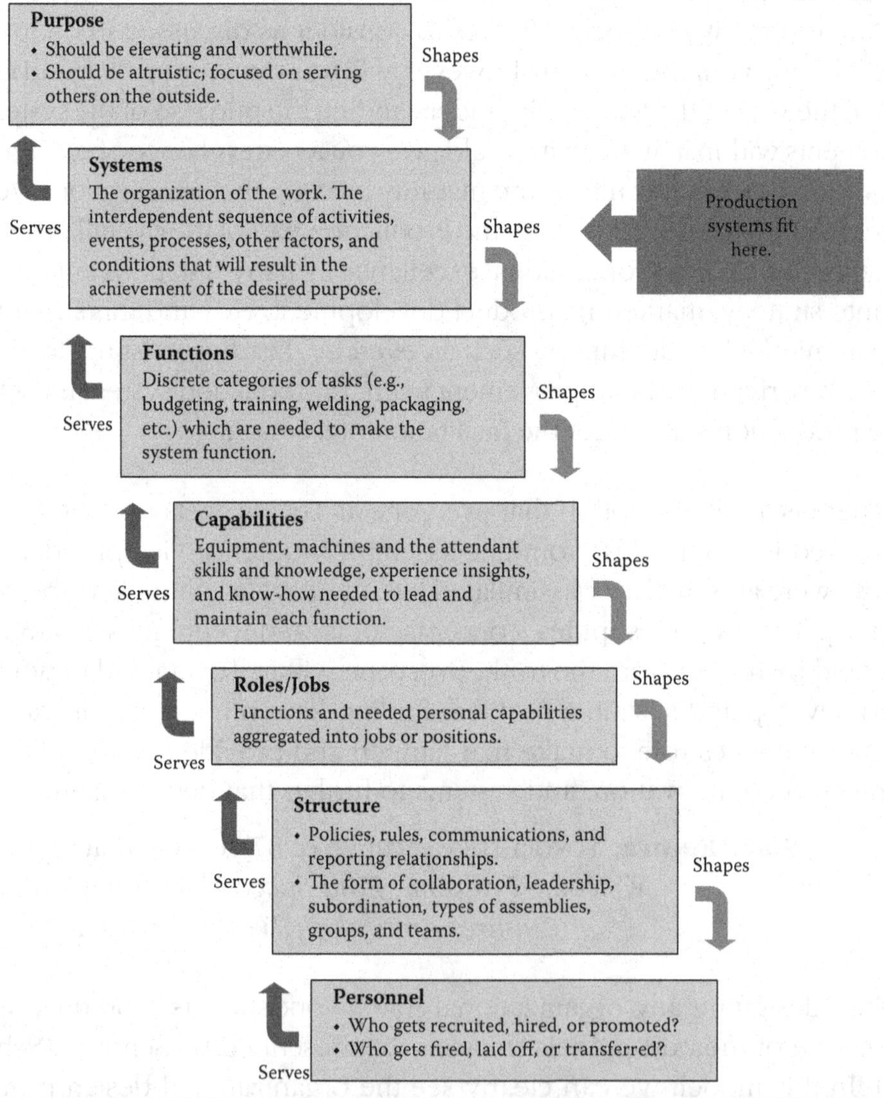

Figure 9.5 From purpose to personnel: a model for organizational design (see Scholtes, 1998).

hence serve the higher level. It is a very elegant model when designing a whole new organization, but also harder to apply in an existing situation.

From a diagnostic perspective, it can also be used when we see that systems are not working as we expected. Do all the lower levels align, are they fully realized, and do all the elements have the right measures to drive the expected behaviors?

How to Influence Leaders

The first step in influencing leaders is to be as honest as you can about your own leadership abilities. Get some good feedback from people you consider good leaders. Ask yourself how far up the leadership chain you need to influence, and how far up you *can* influence. Be realistic about this and set yourself some appropriate challenges. Maybe you are at a level where you can walk into the CEO's office and through sheer charisma, charm, and acumen, you will convert them to all that you hold dear. On the other hand, you may want to concentrate on your most immediate boss, manager, or sponsor and be satisfied with smaller changes.

It is often said that it is not the leader who makes the movement but the followers. You must have enough of all the attributes we have already discussed to be able to attract followers. So, occasionally turn around and go and help those followers to keep up or even to overtake you whilst you help the others coming along behind.

You must also ask yourself what exactly you want your leaders to do differently and how it fits in with your overall strategy. Once you understand what different behaviors you would like to see, then you can use a form of stakeholder management to assess where a leader or group of leaders are now and how much they need to move to get to the new situation. This is rather Machiavellian, but you can also look at how difficult it will be to move each individual to the desired position. There are all sorts of ways people can be influenced. Some are more sinister than others, and it would be easy to suggest we use all of these to achieve our goals like a crazed puppet master pulling the strings. Think PsyOps, propaganda, and Orwellian double-speak. Before you get too carried away, however, just imagine if some other group were plotting how to influence you, and how you would feel about that. So we should probably stick to more acceptable methods such as direct communication, storytelling, emotional hooks, repeating messages, reinforcing mechanisms, and all of the more honest theories of persuasion.

Stakeholder Analysis

Leaders are a key target audience to influence, but there are always many more players to consider when we embark on any change. Forgetting or ignoring any of these could severely disrupt the implementation phase, as the best-laid plans could hit the rocks if we fail to identify who is involved and what actions we need to take with each group. The concept of stakeholder analysis can be applied to try to give some structure to this approach. You can use a Supplier-Input-Process-Output-Customer (SIPOC) model to initially identify who may be affected if we change the process. Suppliers, Customers, and those who action the process are likely to be the key stakeholders. From this, we can map the stakeholders onto the grid shown in Figure 9.6, and then devise the stakeholder engagement plan based on these quadrants.

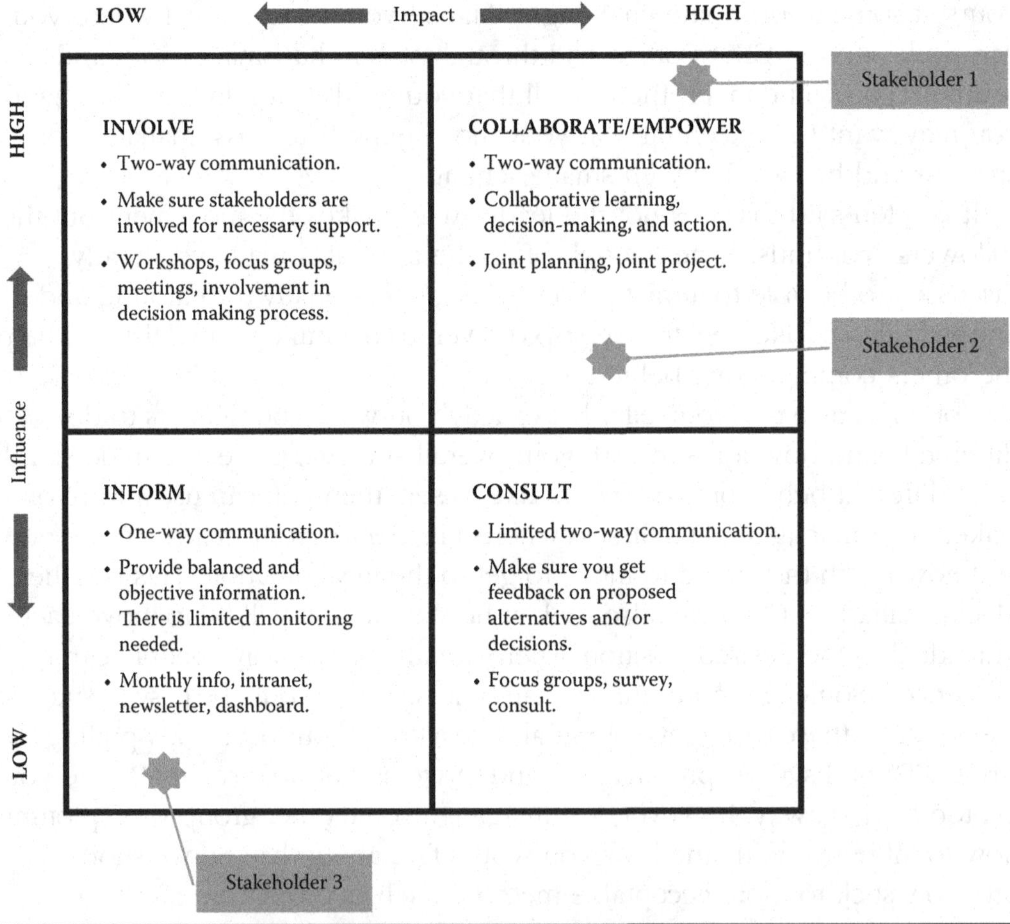

Figure 9.6 Example of a simple stakeholder matrix.

What happens when you come up against such resistance to your ideas that you fear no amount of persuasion will help? Does your leader have a "we are not doing Lean here" attitude? In the example earlier, that leader was probably right to make that call, so be open to the fact that some leaders do actually know how to lead. They just may disagree with your approach or have different drivers to you. In another example, we saw that letting leaders define their own approach had massive benefits. You will need to be adaptable to the fact that you can't always move things in the direction you want, so work with your leaders to deliver what they want. That way you will gain more capital for your own ideas.

Sometimes it can help to visit best practice sites with leaders in order to show how other organizations have promoted operational excellence. We can all enjoy and be inspired by the story of others, but in practice it proves difficult to get any real change from these visits. Just ask Toyota, who continue to host such visits.

If you really can't see a way forward for the changes you are passionate about and that have worked in the past, then it may be time to move on. Many of the best consultants simply refuse to work with organizations if they don't think the senior management team are committed to changing themselves. They know how futile and frustrating it is in those situations, and they have the option to walk away, reputations intact. It's a tough choice, but sometimes the right one. As Jim Collins says in Good to Great (Collins, 2001), you first need to get the right people on the bus and the wrong people off it.

Most of the ideas we discuss in this book take a long time to embed. Of course, we should push for pace, but sometimes change can take place over years or even decades. If you stick it out long enough, leaders will inevitably come and go, and dependant on your age and experience, you will see that you naturally have more and more influence over time. Your contemporaries start to get in positions of authority, and the relationships you have forged start to pay dividends. New managers look up to you for advice. If you are at the younger end, then don't despair, just be as good as you can and people will start to respect that.

So let's be positive and assume that you have leaders you can work productively with. We've set out in this chapter some of the attributes we would expect leaders to display in an organization that aspires to operational excellence. As a change agent, you will need to demonstrate these as well as influence other leaders to show those same attributes.

A Note on Personal Effectiveness

In our experience, getting help with developing your personal effectiveness is always very beneficial. The type of training on offer on this subject will vary as will the particular tools and techniques taught, so if you are, at first, unimpressed, then try a different course. We have already mentioned the Myers-Briggs type indicators, but there are many such methods designed to help you deal better with the numerous personal relationships you will need to develop. Coaching skills must also be well honed, so we recommend some formal training in that area. You may also have formal training programs to tap into if you are part of a large organization. Some of the best training we have received has been from the top consultancies we have worked with. They have excellent in-house change agent training and development programs for high-level, high-impact assignments.

Effective communication skills are always near the top of the list of influencing skills. The Boston Consulting Group provided us internal change agents with a simple set of templates and structures to help with influencing the senior levels in a business that they termed "delivering powerful presentations to senior management." The aim is to develop a compelling storyline for the change and present it in a way that clearly sets out the results of your work in a form that engages the audience. We have all endured presentations that have failed to do so. Below are the 5 cardinal sins of presentations to be aware of.

1. No clear message (slide title; subject + deviation).
2. No benefit to the recipient of the presentation.
3. No logical sequence of content.
4. Content is too detailed.
5. Presentation is too long.

Effective presentations, like effective written communications, require applying a strict editorial discipline followed by a delivery that is clear and to the point. Senior managers will have limited patience with hearing about problems and proposals that they can't relate to quickly. You may be the most passionate person on the subject at hand, but if you can't get the backing of management to take the work forward, then either you have failed to convince or the subject is deemed not to be a priority. The A3 Thinking process as described earlier will help you to describe the problem, the effects (realized or potential), and how you have analyzed the situation to arrive at the proposed countermeasures. Presenting those findings in a convincing way is the next step. You can use the below COAST framework to help self-edit your presentations, and then practice your verbal presentation and get feedback from a trusted source. Remember that less-is-more when it comes to effective presentations.

Core message	Which question should be answered?
Objective	Why do you want to deliver this message?
Audience	Who is your audience and how will they perceive your message?
Simple and short	Are there any more dispensable slides that can be removed without losing key messages?
Touch and engage	Are the messages framed to the audiences' needs and perspectives?

Once you have polished your presentation by using the above frameworks, the last piece of advice is to add a simple starting slide that succinctly sums up the presentation in an "executive summary" style (Figure 9.7). This is the hook that will get the attention of the audience and signposts what they will be hearing about. They may have asked the Key question of you themselves, or you may be introducing this question for the first time to pique the interest of those leaders in attendance.

You can see from the below example that we are left with a Key question that needs answering. The rest of the slide pack must address this question

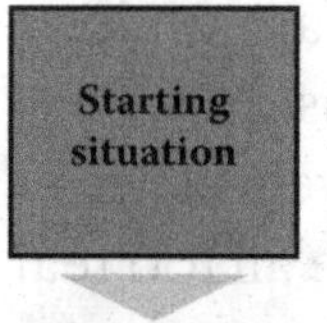

- The time to deliver a presentation to senior management is very limited.
- Managers have to make decisions based on the available information.
- Every presentation is expected to end with a clear recommendation.

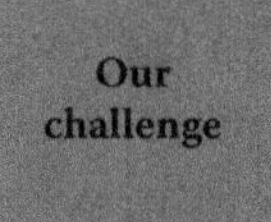

- All key messages need to be clearly presented to tell a compelling story.
- The selected content has to be in line with the expectations of the audience.
- The current context of the audience needs to be taken into account beforehand.

Key question

- What principles do you need to understand to deliver a powerful presentation?

Figure 9.7 Starting slide example for effective presentation of ideas.

succinctly. For example, if we need to grow sales, we would need to see a breakdown of where sales may come from and why we think additional sales would be achievable. This is where a "lever tree," "KPI tree," or cause and effect map can be most effective, as they all attempt to breakdown the question (or problem) into constituent parts and to show the relationships. By working on the lower levels, we can influence the highest level just like when we work on the inputs to a process as the only means of altering the outputs. When dealing with a lot of independent branches to a tree of this kind, it can also be useful to categorize the lowest levels in terms of what is in our control, in our influence, or outside of our control entirely. You can do this with colors for example. It is a way of recognizing concerns raised but focusing attention on the control and influence items.

Written communication of this type is essential and will be a permanent record of the thought processes you have been through. With the right delivery, you will have done your best to influence the senior leaders in this formal way. Just as important, if not more, can be the informal cup-of-coffee approach if you have that opportunity. Either way, you should reflect on the end result, be it in your favor or not, and see if you can improve the approach for the next time. After all, change agents are not Svengalis, able to mind bend their audience into submission.

A Leader's Perspective

If we are to influence leaders, then we should also be able to put ourselves in their shoes from time to time and consider what pressures they are under. You will find, as you move up in any organization, that you must now consider a much wider range of topics, and that is true at all levels. The frustrations and challenges faced by the average team member are all too real, but the change agent must be a bridge across the organizational levels, seeing the challenges at each level. You will gain a much greater standing in the eyes of the senior team if you can articulate challenges in their own language. Take every opportunity to spend time with senior leaders and engage them in what challenges you face, and they will usually be more than willing to tell you about their challenges. Where you have common ground, and where you believe your skills can help, then you have areas of influence to exploit. Sometimes a 6-hr drive each way to visit a site with the managing director can go a long way to mutual understanding. That's a lot of one-to-one time, and if you are ever in that position, we advise having some well-planned out topics of conversation, including how you are viewed by the senior team. Get some personal feedback, even if it's just over a cup of coffee at the service station. You should, of course, also offer to do the driving!

We've asked a respected and successful senior leader to give us his perspective on many of the subjects we've touched upon in this book. In this more formal approach, we get an insight into how this leader thought about the pursuit of excellence. Informal discussions are just as effective in understanding the perspective of key stakeholders.

A VIEW FROM THE TOP

My name is ernst hoogenes, 59 years old, I studied mechanical engineering and mastered in simulation modeling of the product streams in big warehouse operations of major retailers. During my study I was very interested in industrial organization, systems design, business administration, economics, and logic. I worked at the retailer for 6 months to translate the model from main frame to the PC (IBM AT (1986)!), and then joined the management development program of Hoogovens (later Corus and Tata Steel in Europe).

During my career I had 15 different positions, from supply chain management, to project management leading the construction of a new galvanizing line, to plant manager, manufacturing director, managing director of an international business unit of Tata Steel, director of Business Excellence of Tata Steel in Europe, director of R&D Europe, and finally Chief Technical Officer of Tata Steel in Europe, responsible for group quality and compliance.

For me, excellence is designing what you do (not just at work!) through systematic processes in order to achieve the desired outcome in a predictable way and continuously improve both the processes and their outcomes. A process in its most simplistic way is a sequence of activities/actions/events.

My definition of excellence has a number of aspects to it. First of all, the desired outcome has to be determined. Start with your goal in mind (Stephen Covey). The outcome has to predictable and the process systematic. Then you can compare the outcome to what you desire it to be and analyze where deviations take place because you have defined the systematic or structured process. In defining the desired outcome you have to look at how good looks like through benchmarking. The Baldridge Model for Business Excellence, used by the Tata Group as the Tata Business Excellence Model thus strives for continuous improvement of all you do in your business. It looks at the

Systematic Approach (A), the Deployment of that approach (D), execute it, Learn from it (L) and integrate the processes (and understand their interdependencies), and look at the outcomes in an integrated manner (I). Without this ADLI framework, you basically work too much with trial and error and cannot understand why your results or outcomes are not what you expect them to be, let alone continuously improve the outcomes. In today's fast moving business environment, you need to be better than others through innovation and operational and business excellence!

In order to achieve operational excellence, the vast majority in your company needs to understand the need for excellence, the principles of it, and their role in it and become willing to deploy excellence in a systematic way. That is the culture that needs to be established in that company. And as we know, "Culture eats strategy for breakfast." In other words, as a senior manager, you must practice what you preach, show the right behavior, continuously interact with all levels, show interest in what they do, get to know them and what their abilities are, and trust they will use those abilities to their maximum because they are trusted, taken seriously, and complimented for their contributions. Try to constructively work towards improvements, not by criticizing, but by recognizing, supporting, and celebrating success!

We all know intuitively that what we say is only 5–15% of what people really observe. How we say it, if we are consistent, but most importantly what we do ourselves, is far more important. So senior leaders should be consistent - which is not inflexible but if you change your mind due to new insights - share and show why you changed your mind. This also shows you are open for suggestions and helps create an environment of openness, willingness to listen, and honesty!

As mentioned before, the senior leaders need to show by doing, get involved themselves, and not "manage it away" by letting experts do it for them. Yes, you need experts both to train yourself and the people that you work with, and to help gain insights that go further than what (most) leaders and managers can develop themselves. If you define three levels of skill, I would say that everyone needs to understand the basics through a general induction. Then the majority needs to get to work on their own processes by training "on the job with some class room support": the practitioner level. Then there is the Experienced Organizer and Integrator of Excellence. They typically are also involved in local assessments (NOT audits! An audit looks for compliance, right or wrong; an assessment looks at the level that shows proper implementation and gives opportunities for further growth). Finally, there will be some real experts who live and breathe excellence as a full-time job. This can be a career development role or a few years after which the experts move into managerial or leadership roles. This way the organization also sees that excellence is valued as part of a career path!

In the Tata Group (more than 100 companies and some 700,000 employees world-wide), it's an honor to be selected as a Business Excellence assessor and it is seen as an important part of your career. Within one company you can do the same with operational excellence, innovation, etc. Celebrate, recognize, and make it a part of career development.

What is very important in all of this is that the whole executive committee, management team, etc., should agree beforehand that this is the way to go! If one or a few of the members don't show the same behavior and interest or even actively say or do different things, then it will be hard to create the desired culture. I think, looking back, that's the most difficult part and that's our major opportunity for improvement.

Summary

Most books on leadership are designed to help leaders become more effective in their roles. In this chapter, we have looked at leadership from the perspective of the change agent, who is both a leader and a developer of leaders. The ideal situation is that of the leader embodying both of these roles, which is the case in rare instances such as that in Toyota. Comparing our situation to the Toyotas of the world can be a de-motivating exercise at worst, as we begin to understand the gap we have in our own organizations. That's why we always recommend you start at your current state, set a realistic vision of where you want your organization to be, then design the stepping stones to achieve that state. There are lots of areas for improvement in any situation.

If you and your leaders are struggling with how to start, then we will always recommend you start with a pain-point. Maybe at the hygiene level if that's appropriate for your maturity level, or at a more concrete, customer-facing issue. Choose a method(s) and get started. There can be no substitute for practicing problem-solving using a scientific method at the lowest level in the organization. Add in the priority of improving the flow of value, and you have the basis of a production system. If you can take your leaders on that journey of discovery with you, then congratulations – you've become a change agent.

Get started on your Chapter 9 learnings – reflecting on the impact of leadership on change efforts

I. *Using Knoster's model to assess past and/or current change efforts*
   a. *Looking at past change efforts, what elements of the model were weak or absent?*
   b. *Looking at current change efforts, what elements of the model need attention?*
   c. *What actions will I take to influence leadership to address any shortfalls in the model?*

II. *Using the Stakeholder matrix to define/strengthen my engagement plan*
   a. *Who are the stakeholders in this change effort?*
   b. *Where does each stakeholder sit on the matrix?*
   c. *What does the matrix tell you about prioritizing stakeholders and what changes to make to the engagement plan?*

III. *Practicing the three key elements of persuasion*
   a. *Which of the three elements of persuasion am I least comfortable with?*
   b. *What event or presentation will you use to practice this element and ensure you cover all the elements?*
   c. *Reflecting (or getting feedback) on that event, what went well, and what could be done better next time?*

Chapter 10

Conclusions

Hervé Duval and Fraser Wilkinson

> It is quite amazing how two people can read the same book and yet reach different conclusions.
>
> **Nitya Prakash**

The premise of this book was that we reach back in time and offer our younger selves some sage advice on how to navigate the tricky waters of being a change agent. To do just that, we have shared what has worked for us and what has tripped us up along the way, as well as some examples and case studies to provide some color. We've distilled much of our experience into some short learning opportunities, but also some pointers to further study areas that have helped us form useful thought processes and patterns that can be universally applied.

We started with some basic theories and the predominant practices that have shaped the operational excellence arena. These will become the foundations for anyone in the improvement profession. Next, we covered a way of diagnosing and prioritizing improvement efforts around the key business metrics of Safety, Quality, Delivery, and Cost and the importance of understanding the flow of value. Once we were clear on what we needed to work on, we then offered a number of options to organize and resource the improvement efforts internally and externally. A number of industry-standard deployment methods were then discussed along with suggestions on the situations these are best suited to. This led us onto our favorite subject, which is the improvement effort itself and the central role of problem-solving in any

DOI: 10.4324/9781003486022-10

organization. After we have made improvements, it is vital that we maintain the gains. We looked at the Golden Triangle and the full DM system as a means of maintaining and improving process stability and capability. Wrapping up our journey, we delved a bit deeper into the role of leaders in bringing together all the above subjects.

We have given many examples and held up many organizations as being role models in certain elements of operational excellence. Let's remind ourselves that we set out to help those change agents who focus on creating the operating systems that improve the effectiveness and efficiency of delivering the product or service to the customer. Even the best operational systems cannot, however, guarantee success if the strategic direction of the organization is in doubt. The life expectancy of organizations is ever decreasing, and even the likes of Toyota have stumbled along the way. The one-time darling of the stock market, General Electric, has seen a dramatic decline in share price and revenues since 2000, but can this be blamed on any failure of Six Sigma or the Work-Out programs? Many organizations are kept afloat by financial engineering alone. We can't all work for truly excellent organizations, but we can contribute to the journey toward excellence wherever we find ourselves working.

Finally, let's remind ourselves of the questions we set out to answer at the beginning of this book. These were the questions we've had to ask ourselves in our careers, and we're sure you will be asking the same as well as many, many more.

- *How can I add value as a change agent?*
  Open the leadership team's eyes, solve big issues to generate benefits (but above all to demonstrate that the approach works), and become a multiplier by inspiring and coaching disciples who will in turn generate more value than you would on your own. Follow the "I will, if you will" principle. Do some and teach some.

- *How do I get started?*
  Prepare to engage with leaders, then obtain their real commitment, not lip service. Get yourself a mentor, sensei, or just someone to debate things with. If in doubt, start with practicing problem-solving. Avoid creating a comprehensive set of standards or a production system, but do some thorough background reading on the theory and principles outlined in Chapter 2.

- *How do I influence the key stakeholders?*
First, identify and categorize key stakeholders via a stakeholder matrix approach. Appendix 6 details engagement questions for dealing with leaders. How you influence key stakeholders depends on their position on the adoption curve (see Chapter 9's controversy corner: "can everyone be motivated"). They can be convinced through a variety of approaches, combining carrots (everyone needs something, whether it is recognition, challenges, or being part of a group) and sticks.

- *How can I gain the trust of the organization?*
Trust is about doing what you say you will do, being dependable, capable, and collaborative. If you don't have any past track record of delivery, then that's what you need to demonstrate. Be a proactive problem solver and don't wait to be told what to action.

- *How can I overcome skepticism about the latest fad?*
This is a common issue many organizations have experienced with Continuous Improvement programs that have not been sustained. Why would your approach be different? There is no magic wand here. You cannot convince with slides and speeches people who have witnessed failure in the past. Only actions will convince them. Get quick wins, ideally with one opinion leader in the team (someone genuinely interested in improvement, not a blocker/late adopter as per the adoption curve – see Chapter 9's controversy corner). A converted former opponent can work wonders.

- *How do I know what tools and techniques to apply?*
You will only need one problem-solving approach and one DM system. We have established in Chapter 6 that the main problem-solving tools all follow a similar structure, so there is no bad choice. Choose the problem-solving approach that you and your organization are comfortable with (it is often only a matter of refining the existing one rather than importing something alien). The DM approach includes a toolset that is more prescriptive, so there is no doubt about what to choose (see Chapter 8).

- *How much standardization of improvement methods should we have?* It is important to standardize improvement methods, as it provides the organization with a common language on which the new culture can be built. Training is easier, and so is cross-functional problem-solving. Finally, transferring people across departments is also easier. The downside of trying to standardize in an existing setting with multiple locations and cultures is that you may have to wait a long time for this. Only standardize the important things, and even then give some leeway on when the standards must be adopted. Central committees, however well populated and managed, can still be seen as ivory towers.

- *How can I be a multiplier?* We often heard that the critical mass of change agents required to make a transformation successful is at least 0.5% (i.e., one person for two hundred employees). But it will take ages for each agent to transform two hundred people. So, the aim of the change agent must be to become a multiplier, i.e., to turn others into change agents. This will happen by explaining the vision to make them want to join the cause and arming your followers with the tools described throughout this book.

- *How much should I be doing and how much should I be coaching?* The most crucial point is that the proportion of doing and coaching should vary as maturity of your audience increases. Also, the urgency of change required will guide this. The "results verses culture" model in Chapter 5 will help us think about what balance is needed.

- *How do I know if we are making progress?* A few quick wins are necessary but are no guarantee of success. Progress on completing the deployment plan is also good. But, sadly, true progress can only be judged in the long term. The two most important benefits that must be observed are financial (especially cash flow improvement) and organizational maturity (to be evidenced by improving maturity assessment results). A simple indicator could also be the amount of doing you are asked to do verses the amount being done by others.

- *How can I tell if what we are doing will be sustained?*
  Results without improving maturity are at best a good start that you are going to struggle to maintain, and at worst a bit of luck. Equally, glowing maturity results without financial impact just demonstrate that your assessment process is too lenient. Progress in both areas should give you a warm feeling. Sustainment is an open-ended concept, but if your systems and processes change as personnel and management changes, then this would indicate that individual preferences are stronger than the system.

- *How do I improve my own improvement skills?*
  Stay humble (see the false learning curve in Chapter 2). Read widely. Join the Lean Institute and other online forums. Meet similar-minded people. Go to Japan (or a Toyota, Nissan, or Honda plant) to get a feel for what excellence means. Many locations have organizations run by local or state institutions that can offer sharing and learning experiences. Self-reflection and feedback are the nutrients of the change agent's growth.

Some of the questions we have tackled in more detail than others and much will remain for you to ponder on. Maybe you now have some additional knowledge or areas for further research. We hope you have agreed and disagreed with our arguments and points of view. We all continue to read, share, learn, and visit others to expand our knowledge; it's a continual improvement journey after all.

That younger self we met at the start of this book may not have taken the sartorial advice we gave, but we'd like to think he would have enjoyed an honest view of what his future career may have in store. And if any time travelers would like to do the same for us, we'd very much appreciate it.

We'll leave you with a final saying that is much repeated by those who really understand where excellence comes from.

Before we build cars, we build people

Fujio Cho, honorary chairman of the
Toyota Motor Corporation

Checking what conclusions you have drawn from Chapter 10 – reflecting on your personal and organizational aspirations.

a. *How did your expectations change after reading this book and why?*
b. *What sort of help did you get with applying and learning the concepts, methods, and tools?*
c. *What resources of time, money, and opportunity did you get or not get from your organization?*

Chapter 11

Case Studies

Hervé Duval and Fraser Wilkinson

- **Case Study 1:** Our problem-solving is a problem
- **Case Study 2:** Changing the way we manage stock for a performance step change
- **Case Study 3:** Implementing 5S: a top-down, bottom-up approach
- **Case Study 4:** Diagnosing to determine improvement priorities
- **Case Study 5:** What if Toyota ran your house?

Case Study 1: Our Problem-Solving Is a Problem – Fraser Wilkinson

Case studies are a great way of bringing theory into the real world. In the example that follows, we shall see how the ideas discussed in this book can be related to a very real and physical problem on one of the production lines we have encountered. This is not an opportunity to apportion blame or point out individual failings because, as we shall see, all of the opportunities for improvement can be related back to a systemic issue. Without systems in place and operating effectively, we are reliant on the brilliant, creative but often fallible human being to remember to do the things we should be doing.

The Problem

Customers are complaining about contaminants on the surface of a product. Complaints are coming in from a number of customers who use this particular

DOI: 10.4324/9781003486022-11

product type to manufacture a finished good that can be sensitive to contamination of this type. It's not the first time they have complained about this contaminant, and a previous root cause analysis was supposed to have eliminated it the previous year. This type of contamination always seems to get worse during the winter months, so it could be seasonal or weather related. It is now the biggest source of customer complaints for this production site, and costs for remediation and claims for production losses are rising rapidly. The pressure is really on the production unit to, "sort it out, now."

The production units have a number of people responsible for problem-solving. They have checked all of the usual sources of contamination they can think of, but they can't get to the bottom of the problem. Some of them have been trained in Kepner-Tregoe© (KT) problem analysis tool and the A3 Thinking approach, and they've made a start on using the IS, IS-NOT question set, but they say this technique does not work for them because they don't have any IS-NOT conditions!

Eventually, with a push from senior managers, they reach out to the Quality Assurance (QA) group for help. The QA specialists agree to facilitate, but on the proviso that they follow the A3 Thinking approach and apply the KT tools of Event Mapping (a type of 5 whys) and the IS, IS-NOT Problem Analysis as part of the seven-step A3 methodology. Stakeholders are identified, an owner is assigned, and the workshops begin. From the trend data of complaints, this looks like we have a performance gap or deviation starting from a specific point in time and the contamination is becoming more prevalent. Something looks to have happened that has caused this upswing from the base level of contamination we observe over time. This leads the facilitators to suspect there is a "special cause" at play, and so an investigative approach is followed.

The first stage is to look at what is already known about how this contaminant can get on the surface of the product. An interrogation of the Failure Mode and Effect Analysis (FMEA) showed only one possible failure cause for this deviation. When the detection and prevention measures recorded against that failure mode were checked, these were deemed to be still working.

After defining the problem in terms of the *subject and deviation* and what the *effects* are for the business, the team identified the *containment actions* needed to protect the customers from further disruption. Once these were in place, they moved onto conducting the Event Mapping. This starts with the event (subject and deviation again) and maps the effects first, then moves onto defining the chain of cause and effect based only on known facts and at each stage describing a subject and deviation. They are only interested in what went wrong, not all of the things that went right as well, so it's different from process mapping. There may come a point where the root cause is unknown from the facts at hand. At that point, the team needs to start on the IS, IS-NOT analysis. This tool is a way of helping to gather relevant facts relating to the problem (defined by the subject and deviation). A series of open questions is used to help define in detail the problem specification (not the problem statement, which is too vague to be of use for this tool). Questions are based on What? Where? When? How many/much?, and What trends? we observe in relation to this problem statement. For each question, we require an IS statement and an IS-NOT statement. For example, what product type IS affected, and what product type could be affected but IS-NOT, such as other product types being processed on this unit (not all other products made by this organization). This questioning continued for a number of sessions with the team, each time highlighting gaps in the team's knowledge or flushing out where assumptions were being made. The local team was forced to get ever more detailed facts about the contamination, such as a detailed description of the contaminant from spectrometric laboratory analysis and a scanning electron microscope. Exactly where did we see the contamination and where did we not see it? What was the size of individual contamination incidents? How many unique incidents on a product?

The local team was getting very frustrated at this level of detailed questioning, and some of the senior management team just wanted them to "do something" to tell the customer. That's what had happened the previous year, and the problem had "gone away." With the help of a sympathetic senior manager, the facilitators insisted on more Go-sees for any missing facts and for customer representatives to get as much information from customers as possible.

After three sessions together, and with the facts emerging, the facilitators realized that they were dealing with two distinctly different manifestations of the same contaminant. One was as if an aerosol had been spraying over a large surface area, and the other was in discrete spots of 2–5 mm diameter. These phenomena were also seen together and on different parts of the same product. This led the team to conclude they may have two separate root causes at play. It was decided to split the root cause investigation into two event maps and two IS and IS-NOT analyses. We follow the spotted contaminant investigation below.

After many hours of painstaking inspections of the product and workplace, the team now had a very detailed problem definition consisting of the IS and corresponding IS-NOT statements. After one session of observation at the line, it became apparent where on the line the contaminant must be generated, from an index point on the product. By its nature, the contaminant did not show up immediately but required some time to develop so it was not immediately obvious and access to the line was restricted when it was running. At this point then, the team could eliminate everything prior to that point as a source of contamination.

Next, the team compiled a list of all *possible causes* from the local workforce. These were numerous and diverse and reflected a wide range of opinions on what was causing the contamination. Each possible cause was then run through the problem definition to see if it could fully, or with some other defined condition, explain all of the IS and the IS-NOT statements. This made it easy to eliminate the majority of possible causes by logic. The most likely cause remaining was a contaminated air supply from a particular compressor that fed the part of the line that was suspected of depositing the contaminant. The local team was adamant that the air was dry and clean and that filters and dew point meters were all effective. An external specialist also inspected the air system regularly without reporting any anomalies. The team was again dispatched to keep looking and keep monitoring the dew points. When the line was briefly down for maintenance, it was inspected visually for signs of leakage and tested for leaks under pressure. Air vents were a normal part of the system, but the air was considered to be clean and dry.

All the facts on paper, however, still pointed to this air supply, so the facilitators were insistent on further and more thorough Go-sees. Eventually, an engineer decided to trace the whole air supply again (it is a big and old plant with many modifications) to look for anything unusual, until at one end of the pipework he discovered this system was connected via isolation valves to another air system for a separate part of the line. After much deliberation, he decided to switch off the compressors and check the isolation valve. Brown sludgy water was found in the "clean" air system. The isolation valve had rusted through in places. Normal pressure differentials meant that for most of the year, the clean air system would leak into the other system, but on plant shutdowns for extended maintenance once a year, the pressure differential would force contaminated water into the clean air supply. It would then take time to work its way down to the lowest points and lead to occasional contamination.

The engineers then opened all of the air filter bowls on the end of the line and 20 of the 26 were contaminated with water and oil. The dew point meter was located right next to the compressor in a section of new pipework, and would never have picked up the water at the line end. Back to the IS, IS-NOT and this possible root cause was seen to fit the facts on paper as well as the facts on the ground.

So now the team had discovered the root cause, but I hope you have lots more questions to ask about this case. If not, then please spend a little time to think about them or go back and read the main body of our book for some prompts.

In the full investigation, there were a number of legs to the event maps, meaning not just one direct root cause was established. Event mapping also asks about any *broken barriers* that were in place that could have prevented the chain of cause and effect, and these were also numerous. In addition, there are *contributing circumstances* that don't directly cause the event, but they will make the event more or less likely, or the event to have a greater or lesser effect (bigger deviation) than otherwise.

The obvious barrier that should have detected this issue was the dew point meter. The other barrier was the routine inspection of the filter bowls. When the maintenance schedule was checked, it was found that these inspections had been stopped 4 years previously to save money. The piping and installation diagrams were not kept current and did not show the isolated connection, which was put in place to act as an emergency supply. Nobody could remember when it was done.

Countermeasures

Countermeasures were identified by the team:

- **Eliminate root cause:** isolate the two air systems and install a backup compressor.
- **Eliminate root cause:** open and drain all legs of the pipework.
- **Eliminate root cause (longer term):** install stainless steel pipework.
- **Effective barrier:** move the dew point meter.
- **Effective barrier:** reinstate the routine maintenance check of filters.
- **New barrier:** automated email notification from statistical process control (SPC) software on dew point readings. Regular review of SPC readouts.
- **New barrier:** change all filter bowls for transparent versions to enable a visual factory check.

The aerosol type of contaminant was the same as was seen the previous year and was traced to a dosing system and incorrect mixing and application of a protective substance onto the product surface. Initially, it was thought a change of supplier for the protective substance was to blame. The pressure came on to change back to the original supplier although this would have made no difference.

A "lessons-learned" session and a formal, independent sign-off of the Corrective and Preventative Actions (CAPA) were discussed but not enacted. Eighteen months after the root cause investigation, customers once again were complaining of this same type of spotted contamination. This time it was traced to a different part of the same production line. The source of the air supply in this case was the one that was passing water into the "clean air" system previously.

Systemic Failures

I ask myself what should have happened in this case? If I were able to recreate an alternative future of operational excellence in this organization, what would we see? The first and simplest answer is – nothing unusual. Move along, nothing to see here. The DM system would have prevented the contaminant problem from occurring. As this problem had occurred in the past or could even have been anticipated by a thorough risk assessment via the FMEA process, the organization would have put in place control mechanisms that would have been enacted as part of the routine management of the line. A management of change (when a deviation from existing process conditions occurs) would have been conducted when the lines were first connected and isolated, and a check of isolation valves would have been a regular maintenance activity.

A review of temporary cost-saving activities would have re-instigated the filter bowl checks before they became ineffective. The filter bowls would have been checked, and they would have indicated a problem was likely. By more thoughtful design, the dew point meters would have been in a place that could detect moisture where it is most likely to cause contamination – at the outlet end of the air system in the vicinity of the product. Failure to carry out routine maintenance checks would have been highlighted via daily review meetings and remediation actions put in place.

Layered process audits and a series of quality-focused discussions by the senior management team would likely have uncovered gaps in the FMEA and Control Plan on this well-known potential contaminant.

More Systemic Failures

Let's take a scenario where we are in the early stages of operational excellence deployment and see how the future might look in the above case. Assuming the contamination has occurred, what would we like to have happened? A detailed problem specification would have been started as part of a defined customer complaints procedure (based on the 8 Disciplines – 8D* or the A3 Thinking process). The FMEA and Control Plan would be consulted and a review of existing control mechanisms conducted. This would include confirmation checks that any relevant Standard Work (or Standard Operating Procedures) are being undertaken in the prescribed way and by all who are signed off as competent to conduct these SOPs. This is the Standardize-Do-Check-Act (SDCA) stability cycle in action as the first response. Only when this has been checked can we move onto the full Plan-Do-Check-Act problem-solving cycle.

The senior managers who demanded, "do something" are now ensuring that the problem-solving process is followed correctly and thoroughly. They assure the customers that sufficient time and resources is being allocated. They do not jump to conclusions based on incomplete facts and general assumptions. They exhibit leadership behaviors that are aligned with the goal of creating a problem-solving culture.

The local teams are able to facilitate the problem-solving process themselves without external help because they have done so many times after being trained and mentored through their defined competencies. Training is only 10% of the activity to reach a competency level; 20% is on the job learning-by-doing and 70% is self-study. There are recognized and respected problem-solving practitioners who are becoming experts themselves. They are tenacious at gathering relevant facts and challenging assumptions. They avoid putting *possible causes* into the event map but they work with respect to gather everyone's ideas on possible causes. Only when they have enough facts do they test possible causes through the IS and IS-NOT statements. They verify possible causes with data.

The team would link all countermeasures to the causes in the event map (or why would you do them?). They build sustainable Corrective and Preventative Actions into the DM system tools such as FMEA, Control Plan, and Standard Work. New standard work is added to the confirmation schedule for Team Leaders to verify they are being adhered to. Management ensures that lessons learned are conducted, and if required, communicate actions to the wider organization. For example, they ask everyone to check what other maintenance checks were canceled for cost savings. They suggest air, water, and oil systems are all surveyed to check for isolations that could add contamination. Senior managers ensure other parts of the organization do these recommendations as part of the senior managers' DM routines.

*8D is a team-based corrective and preventative action methodology promoted by Ford Motor Company and is widely used in industry for customer complaints resolution.

Key Learnings from Hervé

The need to be seen to be doing something (or sometimes even simply the urge to do something that is present with some personality types frequently encountered in manufacturing) is a bane for the rigorous problem-solver. Our democracies are also burdened by the same issue. In France (and probably in many other countries), politicians immediately react to events by proposing a new law. Journalists will ask them within 2 hours what should be done. No one will give enough time for a proper investigation for fear of being seen as indecisive. This type of approach will usually result in more waste. Acting without having understood the cause is just like throwing darts in the dark. You will add more work, spend more money, and usually waste time. Moreover, if the problem disappears, you will never know whether you actually hit the right cause (until the defect reappears in which case you will know you have failed). Being able to resist this pressure and sticking to rigorous problem definition as mentioned at the beginning of the case is a great achievement.

This case study also illustrates the importance of going beyond a superficial analysis. Everything looking normal does not mean that everything is normal. In particular:

1. Everything often looks normal from a distance. Go see! Without the doggedness of the engineer who traced the whole air supply and his go see approach, the team would not have uncovered the contamination of air filter bowls.
2. Having access to measurements can be a trap if one does not understand what these measurements can and cannot tell us. In this case, having dew point measurement in place led the team to believe that everything was in order in the whole circuit. Once you understand the limitation of the measurement because of its location, you can accept that contaminant could go undetected.

Case Study 2: Changing the Way We Manage Stock for a Performance Step Change – Hervé Duval

Problem Description

In this steel processing plant, finished products stock was traditionally varying between 20 and 30 kT (kilotonnes). The direct consequences of having so much stock (and therefore saturating storage space) were huge:

- **Safety:** There is no need to explain that a saturated storage space is a more dangerous environment than one with a normal stock level.
- **Quality:** As steel coils had to be sometimes stacked and constantly moved to optimize storage space, they would often be struck by handling equipment. Damaged outer laps were triggering multiple customer complaints.
- **Cost:** As the initial storage space was saturated, finished goods often had to be stored in another warehouse owned by the company but located 800 m away from the site. This warehouse had to be heated and monitored. Finished goods had to be transported back and forth. All in all, this external storage cost the site c. $1 M per annum.
- **Working capital:** This finished good stock tied in $15 M to $25 M worth of cash (depending on steel price evolution and stock level).

Interestingly, this situation had also less measurable but important consequences. Stock levels had been a cause of disagreement for years for all the reasons listed above. Some aspects of performance can easily be attributed to certain teams, but stock performance is not one of them. The consequence was a constant blame game between departments. Sales, Manufacturing, and Supply Chain were all blaming each other. "We have to keep stocks of finished goods because of Manufacturing's quality problems." "Customers have asked us to dispatch this coil but the Transport team cannot find a truck." "Sales put pressure on us to manufacture on time, but finished products remain in stock for weeks once we have worked hard to adhere to the requested schedule!"

This stock level corresponds to about 3 weeks of stock given an average weekly production of about 8 kT, yet the best possible lead time on most products is 3 days! So there was clearly an opportunity to improve.

The Selected Problem-Solving Approach

This situation had been the same for years. Pressure to release working capital was getting more and more intense. Seemingly random targets set from the corporate center were continuously lowered. At some point, the Sales Director turned to me for an unbiased analysis of the situation.

The usual old remedies had been used with limited success and certainly no lasting impact. I decided to apply structured problem-solving "by the book" as I knew that this would tackle the main obstacles (lack of understanding of the causes, lack of trust in the stock reports in the IT system, lack of ownership, no commitment to targets). I started with an A3 report. The key elements of this A3 were a comprehensive Root Cause Analysis and a Pareto analysis of stock levels by problem cause.

The A3 was built during a series of iterative interviews, continuously enriched with new data analysis to put numbers on statements made during previous conversations. This transversal, non-threatening, data-based approach helped to build consensus around the relative contribution of each issue. This deescalation helped focus the organization's energy on countermeasures rather than culprits and excuses. And most importantly, this form of engagement slowly changed some of the fundamental underlying beliefs that could explain some of the behaviors we observed (Table 11.1).

Table 11.1 A comparison of "old" verses "new" beliefs in a case study

Old belief	*New belief*
In our industry, it is normal to have high finished product stocks.	Stocks are a consequence of poor flow. If we solve issues that hinder flow, stocks will decrease.
We never seem to have the right reference in stock. We are unlucky (salesperson belief). We need to have better forecasts from sales (manufacturing belief).	Trying to foresee reference-by-reference customer consumption is a waste of time. We will never get it right, so the best way to delight customers is to ensure that internal lead times are much shorter than lead times required by customers.
If I lower my stocks, service to customers will worsen.	We can reduce stock and improve service at the same time by removing obstacles to flow.
Targets set by the company will always be too high because the center is disconnected from our reality.	We can easily beat these targets because the center is disconnected from our reality (they are used to poor overall industry performance).

Once we had all verified and agreed the causes, achievable stock levels, and priorities, things became much easier. A few process issues got rapidly fixed.

We gave visibility on performance by introducing a daily monitoring system where stock was split between owners. The old report assigned all stocks to the Sales team. The new one assigned each coil precisely to the people who needed to do something to make this product move (e.g., products blocked for quality reasons and awaiting inspection were assigned to Operations in the new report and no longer to Sales). This clarity had a number of consequences:

1. Operations started to process "abnormal" situations much more rapidly as these coils had become more visible.
2. Clarity removed excuses. Some 90% of the stock was still the responsibility of Sales, but coils from the 10% owned by Operations had always been used by some salespeople as an excuse to explain that their stock KPIs were "polluted" by others.
3. The difference between sales teams that had too much buffer and the others became very visible. This created peer pressure to stop "hoarding."

Looking at the DM cycle and in particular at the Golden Triangle, we can see that we had defined standards (mutually agreed levels and practices) and created some visual management through this new report. The last element of the triangle that was missing was standard management, so we created a weekly stock review. The first ones took more than an hour, but as stock management improved, average duration dropped below 30 min. In fact, current maturity is such that we have stopped this weekly meeting and standard management is now ensured by Sandra, the customer service manager. In a good application of the subsidiarity principle, the Management Team no longer needs a weekly meeting.

Results

Finished products stock has been halved. It now fluctuates between 10 and 14kT. We have therefore released approximately $10 M of working capital. At the same time, service levels improved. And we closed the external warehouse, yielding an annual saving of $1 M pa. These results have been sustained over time. For the 4th consecutive year, the end-of-year stock level is lower than the previous year.

Key Learnings from Fraser

Structured problem-solving is a powerful consensus-building tool that can help change underlying beliefs. In this example, we see that as a result of applying a facts driven and no-blame approach to a critical business problem, we start to develop a high-performance, cross-functional team.

Tools and techniques are often just a means to highlight that it is sometimes the mindset of the people involved in a process that determines speed of transformation. That's why any analysis must consider the human performance drivers. We see that underlying beliefs resulted in behaviors that seemed rational to each player, but the overall process suffered. In fact, there was no standard process until this intervention. One key stakeholder with the wrong mindset is sometimes enough to block progress. In this example, the arrival of Sandra, an enthusiastic customer service manager, tremendously accelerated pace of change. She drove the process with the same tools as her predecessor but with a deeper belief that having old stocks was not acceptable.

Sometimes we can make rapid progress just by effective monitoring and review with the right team members. Departments create silos. Change agents can often find success by bringing the right people together with simple tools and techniques and a common goal. Don't get hung up on complex methods when simple ones will do the job.

Case Study 3: Implementing 5S; A Bottom-Up, Top-Down Deployment – Fraser Wilkinson

This is the story of how a largely bottom-up initiative gained the serious attention of management at a medium-sized medical devices manufacturing site. 5S workplace organization can have a dramatic effect on the attitudes of many of those involved. We'll see how 5S has helped in an industry that is so reliant on demonstrating control of processes and workplaces. In a company that would have prided itself on its working conditions prior to 5S, the results were impressive.

When I was inducted into the embryonic 5S team I suppose I was like most people who don't really understand 5S - they always ask what all the fuss is about. Why on earth did we need five people full time to simply organize the workplace, and why did it need a budget of $150,000 for a site of 400 people? We actually achieved what we did with far less than that, but I know now why it was thought to require those resources.

In June 2000, the company was going through a tough financial time with a wide range of products stocked out due to in-process failures and the customer base was desperate for more. Six Sigma was being implemented with 8 trained Black Belts and 16 trained Green Belts, and some value stream mapping had shown some good results with cell design in the final packing area. The company is part of a major health care provider with a corporate mandate to use Six Sigma and Lean Manufacturing tools to world-class performance levels. It's what they call Process Excellence, which is the group of two that I worked for at the time under the management of Andy, a scientist with excellent product knowledge but no real experience of Lean.

The other player in the push for Lean is the then Process Engineering Manager, who is a keen disciple of Lean Thinking and Six Sigma. He sets up the first incarnation of the 5S team under what is called the "recovery program" and we engaged the help of a Lean consultant, Alan. At this point, these were the only members of the team with a real idea of how important 5S is.

Alan ran the first workshop in mid-June to kick start one of the blending operations, which is basically a corridor from which separate work bays emanate. The workshop is a full 2 days where no production is allowed. Although not part of the team at this stage, I hear that it is a great success and the corridor is now clear of all obstructions. There was an initial 5S audit done by the team before the event, but overcomplication means it was no less than 100 questions. It was of little wonder then that audits were not maintained after the initial event, although the 5S team was guilty of underestimating the ongoing support required. In the early stages and dependent upon the characters involved, a high level of support is essential for as long as it takes to become self-sustaining. We had found that some work areas are up and running in weeks, others 6–8 months.

The second workshop is in our testing lab that runs all the release for sale quality checks. Alan also ran this one and I was part of the event as a trainee and participator. Alan confesses to have been a little concerned that on first appearances there's not much wrong with the work areas on the site. This was the smoke and mirrors effect of a medical device company that likes to keep things clean, even if we no longer needed them. This event unearthed 2 years' worth of pipette tips and other consumables as well as a vintage laptop, not to mention skips worth of unneeded furniture and equipment. The event was a revelation to me, as we began to ask questions on the seven wastes, conducted some process activity mapping, and looked at layout and inventory. Everyone agreed the event was a success and the people were enthused with the approach, yet again we let them down by not returning with enough gusto to push forward on the actions and keep the audits going.

At that point in the story, we had a full-time 5S leader in Ali who worked as a Process Engineer for the engineering team, with myself and three others, devoting at least half our time to establishing the 5S team. We were soon bogged down in doing all those wonderful sounding things like writing a team charter, scope statement, budget request, and forms and templates for everything. We had the best and most comprehensive audit sheet ever conceived and we actually devoted considerable time to design the 5S logo. What we hadn't done was start a 5S program. Because of the 2 days, we ask out of production there are no more immediate takers for the workshops and there is no mandate from Senior Management to put 5S in place.

And so ended the first attempt at a 5S program and the team disbanded without securing a budget or any real commitment from management to continue the roll out. With delivery problems still at the fore 5S was probably seen as a nice to have and as no more than a housekeeping exercise. We had failed to convince senior management of the benefits in terms of quality and productivity improvements that experience suggested were possible.

The Process Excellence group was then the Engineering Manager and myself and we continued to promote 5S as one of the foundations of Lean manufacturing but it's not until the beginning of March 2001 that we ran our next workshop. This time things are different in a number of respects. First, we are asked by the production department to conduct a workshop in one of our environmentally controlled areas or cleanrooms. So we have pull but not much to pull on. I took a day to put together the training package and the audit sheet that will become the standard set of questions. We had chosen to use the terms Sort, Set in Order, Shine, Standardize, and Sustain for our program and there's just five questions on each. We stuck to the same format as delivered by Alan but only over 1 day. There was an hour and a half in the classroom followed by a workplace scan to take photos and make notes and to get a segregation area in place. The rest of the day was given over to actually doing as much of the Sort and Set in Order as we could.

Like Alan, I wonder just what we were going to do in a "cleanroom" environment for the Sort stage. By the look on the faces of the team after the training, they were just wondering what they were going to be doing full stop. So the day progressed and by the end, they'd identified equipment, tools, and general clutter that really shouldn't be in the cleanroom. At the end of day review, we had an action list, an audit score, a pile of things to dispose of, and a lot of questions as to where 5S fits in the greater scheme of things. Being far from an expert on the mechanics of 5S and not really knowing how the program is to be run I was at a loss to answer them fully. The team knows how 5S went in the other two areas and I was secretly thinking this could easily go the same way. What I hadn't figured out was striking gold with the supervisor of the area, Max. Here was an individual with influence and respect way beyond his official position.

Max had seen many initiatives come and go from attending a Goldratt seminar to any number of attempts to make a manufacturing plant out of what was in effect still a laboratory environment. What Max begins to see in 5S though is a way of thinking about workplace organization that if applied with conviction could have long-lasting effects. We tried to make the 5S activities directly concerned with attacking the seven wastes of the Toyota Production System and that gives a much more powerful slant than just housekeeping.

So now we had a true convert in a position to drive through the 5S in one of our work areas. Max also brought along the Team Leader, Chris, and together they really took on the 5S and before long we had a success story. This time we also made an agreement to meet with Max for half an hour a week to review progress and provide direction and this date was kept faithfully for over a year since the first workshop. This demonstrable commitment was certainly a big factor in keeping the momentum going.

The only trouble was we had a success story in a restricted access room with no real opportunity to view from the outside. So Max set up the 5S board in the corridor outside the cleanroom and this is where we showed the progress with before and after photographs, audit scores, and action lists.

Soon after this, Total Productive Maintenance (TPM) becomes a hot topic again and the Engineering Department became interested in rolling out 5S but they don't really know how to make the transition between what we're doing and TPM. As it happens, they needed to get the scheduled maintenance plan, machine capability index, and spares policy in place and so they headed off to do that and we continued rolling out 5S in the production areas.

The next two work areas we hit were also a success and the Team Leaders, Gill and Tyrone, were soon both converts to the cause and they start to see benefits in terms of never running out of consumables and an improvement in organization. A major benefit for the groups doing 5S was that when internal or external audits were scheduled there was no need to conduct a major clean-up exercise, since the work areas are always well organized and there is nothing in them that is not required for production. This is a big deal for a Food and Drug Administration (FDA) audit where poor performance can severely restrict your ability to sell product. Significant audits occurred almost monthly from bodies such as Lloyds for ISO9000 and ISO14001, GMED, and numerous corporate functions. Each of them was very impressed with the workplace organization and the word started to spread to Senior Management that we really had something to be proud of here. As Max said, "I used to dread a visit from the auditors but now I'll invite them in anytime."

It's now September 2001 and the Engineering Department employs two "industrial engineers" who in effect joined the Process Excellence group on our first Kaizen Blitz event on one of our packing cells. Leigh came from Toyota and Ian from a tier-one automotive supplier. They both had far more practical experience of Lean implementation than anyone else on the site. It soon becomes clear that they didn't think that much of our 5S approach. For Leigh 5S is something that Toyota (4S as they call it) do only after they have done all the pre-production runs for a new line and Ian thought we have gone too far with including Standardize and Sustain in the audit questions at this stage.

They both made the point that we had actually baked in a lot of the waste by not doing the waste analysis, cell layouts, and cycle time analysis first. Our sister sites also employ a Lean consultant who favors the redesign approach first and just used 5S to put the new standards in place. I thought there was room for each approach since if you have the right people and support 5S can be a very good continuous improvement engine fulfilling part of the incremental improvement function. Our General Manager tended to agree with the consultant's approach but was still quick to invite dignitaries to meet Max and show them how organized we were.

Ian and Leigh gave us two more 5S trainers and we continued to schedule work areas for training. After the success of our last three areas, however, we hit a number of work areas where they didn't take it to heart and it was a real struggle to get things moving. It really is so dependent on the characters that are in charge since there was still no formal stated requirement to get 5S in place across the site. But this was soon to change when the manufacturing manager Ian decided that 5S is the only thing that seemed to make a difference in people's attitudes. He put it in all his Managers goals to get a consistent score of 90% plus in audits and they in turn put it in their people's goals. This had a very positive effect on some, but others were still not taking it up.

By July 2002, we had 6 of the 18 work areas trained in 5S and so it became obvious we needed to have a forum for practitioners to get together and this became the 5S Monthly Support Group that met on the first Monday of every month. It was at this meeting I introduced the 5S model which states the five elements I believed were the minimum needed to be in place for success. These were the weekly audits, the weekly review with the trainers, a work center meeting (or agenda items at the weekly meeting), a board with photos, and attendance at the monthly support group. If these are in place the work area goes green on the training matrix and there is definitely a correlation between those who have these and the level of success we see. We used one of the meetings to conduct a cross-audit where practitioners got together to audit a work area as pairs and then compared the scores. The consensus is that this was a very useful exercise and it highlighted a few interesting aspects. The scores were inconsistent showing that standards are required for each question and this is where operational definitions would be useful. What's also interesting is the number of people who have not been around the whole factory for an awful long time. In fact the exercise is so beneficial we decided to formalize it later as the X-audit fixtures list to complement the 5S Champions League. The Champions League came out of a visit to a contact lens manufacturer where we saw a league table of 5S scores. The football connotations are apt enough since the League engendered a fair amount of pride, passion, controversy, foul play, tactics, and even some tears.

The League scores were rolled up into an average of a Work Centre Manager's work area audit scores, varying from one to five work areas, and reported monthly. The X-audit rates declined rapidly with only three or four performed each month so we agreed to make this a penalty offence and we deducted the highest weekly score from those areas not doing their monthly X-audit. It was only an hour a month after all. There was a prize of chocolates for the League leader and the most improved and there was usually a good response from the teams who did well. But for some the scores proved to be too rigidly applied and all sorts of issues were put forward, like groups who weren't allowed in to X-audit and some said they did it but didn't sign the sheet and there are mutterings of not participating anymore. And I suppose here lies the predicament of how performance measurement could go wrong.

Eventually, all 18 work areas were trained and conducting audits. We struck gold along the way with certain individuals really taking to it and even requesting to get more involved with Lean and kaizen. These were the people we identified to nurture and support as they displayed all the right behaviors toward improvements. After all, leaders can come from anywhere. Max won the Lean Practitioner of the Year Award and got a trip to the States out of it to the Process Excellence Conference. I overheard our General Manager telling Max he was a "spiritual leader" for the site!

Middle management was all on board but the degree of demonstrated commitment varied from compliance to active involvement in 5S activities. The Senior Management Team all declared support yet most were not actively involved. We had a good, though controversial, and one-dimensional, measurement system that gave ample opportunity to put a sporting slant on things and have some fun in the Newsletter. It turned out that we didn't need four people full time and $150,000 budget and the success was achieved largely without the active involvement of Senior Management, with notable exceptions.

I left the business shortly after this time but my contacts assured me the 5S program went from strength to strength. The site Production Manager took the learnings and applied them in his next site management position. My key learnings from the experience were that 5S is one of the best countermeasures to the seven wastes but it needs to be applied after initial exercises to reduce these wastes. It's part of the unfreeze>change>freeze cycle or more technically the SDCA and PDCA cycles in play. The seven wastes can all be reduced by 5S activities.

1. Transport
2. Excess inventory
3. Excess movement
4. Waiting
5. Overprocessing
6. Overproduction
7. Delays

Key Learnings from Hervé

This case study illustrates how young and enthusiastic practitioners could easily be fascinated by the tools and miss the point (do not worry young Fraser, the young me made similar mistakes). One of the key missing elements was understanding why we want to roll out 5S. There are deep, fundamental reasons to deploy 5S that have been briefly touched upon in this book. On a more tangible level, one does not want to spend energy on fixing things that are not broken. Will the business results improve if area X reaches a high level of 5S maturity? Therefore, more experienced change agents mentioned in the case use 5S in conjunction with process improvement. Do not bake in the existing waste.

Most improvement tools must be learned and mastered by doing. 5S is no exception. There is no need to spend days in a classroom. Teams are usually suspicious at the start and classroom training will not convince them. I remember my first Single Minute Exchange of Dies (SMED workshop) with a team of operators. I opened the initial training by asking each of them why they were present today. All of them were quite negative. Answers ranged from "my boss forced me to be here" to "I was told that there will be free sandwiches." A long classroom session would have been horrible. Fortunately, it was planned to be short. We rapidly moved to the shop floor and started to do things. When they realized that they could have an impact on their environment, their mood changed completely.

The 100-question audit is a great example of hell paved with good intentions. Change agents must stand in their client's shoes. Quite clearly, if you expect people to answer 100 questions, you are very naïve. Whether you have chosen the carrot or the stick approach, you must make the user's life as simple as possible to maximize chances of sustaining a process.

Finally, and most importantly, the case illustrates the importance of the line showing interest. The situation changed drastically once Ian added a 90% 5S performance to the list of targets.

Case Study 4: An Example of Stakeholder Value Flow Analysis – Hervé Duval

The diagnosis outcome (Table 11.2) summarizes findings of a full diagnosis carried out in a European plant. It illustrates several important points:

- This Diagnosis provides a simple, yet comprehensive overview of a business. It focuses on the business performance rather than its financial performance (our CFO kept on repeating "profit is an opinion"). It looks at all the other stakeholders' needs (customers, employees, and society) rather than just the shareholders'.
- It also highlights information gaps. For example, there is not enough recent information available on customer perception or on employee morale and engagement.
- The diagnosis determines areas of focus for problem-solving (in this case on time delivery, quality, and water management).
- Finally, it highlights discrepancies between priorities and current initiatives and projects. In this example, the diagnosis shows that line speed increase investment projects should be put on hold as long as the lines are not always running at full speed. This conclusion helps saving cash that could be better spent on, e.g., quality improvement equipment (Table 11.2).

Table 11.2 An example output of a diagnostic as outlined in Chapter 3

Diagnosis	*Actual data required*	*Current situation Symptom and observed effect*	*Benchmark data (other sites, competition, customer requirements)*	*Running projects What are the main Annual Plan strategies attached to each performance objective and their expected impact? Strategy status (at risk?)*	*Proposed Priorities*
Safety	LTIF AKIF Process safety (nr of fires, nr of environmental incidents)	People Safety After continuous improvement for 10 years (number of accidents divided by 5), LTIF, and RECF have been stable/slightly on the increase for five years now	People safety performance is worse than the average of the group (see group league table)	New safety initiative to start (based on behavioral safety)	Continue with new safety initiative
		Process Safety No major incident in the last three years. Number of fires have been steadily reducing over the years	Difficult to find a relevant benchmark for process safety as there is no comparable site within the group		
Quality	Customer claims Non-prime rate Rework In % and in Cost/T and or% of turnover	Customer claims: Excellent progress. Both number and cost of claims have reduced every year for the last 6 years	Latest customer survey available is already 3-year-old. It showed at the time that quality performance was considered to be on a par with competition.	Operational Excellence program underway for 7 years	Relaunch customer survey to check customer perception of quality
	Cost of Poor Quality	Overall CoPQ per ton produced has been decreasing year on year for the last 6 years, but still have a significant impact on business result (total	Difficult to find a relevant benchmark for quality as there is no comparable site within the group. However, non-prime		Review Operational Excellence program to understand how improvements could be

(continued)

Table 11.2 *(Continued)* An example output of a diagnostic as outlined in Chapter 3

Diagnosis	*Actual data required*	*Current situation Symptom and observed effect*	*Benchmark data (other sites, competition, customer requirements)*	*Running projects What are the main Annual Plan strategies attached to each performance objective and their expected impact? Strategy status (at risk?)*	*Proposed Priorities*
		CoPQ is c.$18 M pa, down from $25 M 5 years ago)	rate is similar to the business unit's other site's performance for common products		accelerated as the size of the prize is big
Service	OTIF	1. OTIF (% On Time In Full) • 85% orders delivered on time	Latest customer survey available is already 3-year-old. It showed at the time that delivery performance was considered to be on a par with competition, but below market requirement	None	Priority is to improve delivery performance reliability to meet market requirements
	Leadtime	2. Lead time • Time to deliver from order placement to customer depends on product specifications. Ranges from 2 weeks (20%) to 6 weeks (80%)	Best lead time offered is the best on the European market		Whilst it would be useful to expand short lead time offering, the priority is to deliver on time. Missed deliveries must be analyzed and a problem-solving approach must be deployed

(continued)

Table 11.2 *(Continued)* An example output of a diagnostic as outlined in Chapter 3

Diagnosis	*Actual data required*	*Current situation Symptom and observed effect*	*Benchmark data (other sites, competition, customer requirements)*	*Running projects What are the main Annual Plan strategies attached to each performance objective and their expected impact? Strategy status (at risk?)*	*Proposed Priorities*
Volume	Asset Utilization rate. Is the operation a local bottleneck? A TSE bottleneck (i.e., would we immediately sell more or would we just create additional idle capacity?)? OEE	Sales volume is limited by produced volume. Market share is only 6% so market is not a constraint. production step		Investment projects are currently being reviewed to increase maximum line speed	Before spending cash to increase line speed, quality issues should be solved to ensure that all products can be processed at maximum line speed. This would lead to an increase of output of c.12%
		Initial production step has less capacity than finishing lines but additional volume to feed finishing lines can be purchased on the market. So constraint is the output of both finishing lines, rather than initial production step			
Cost	Cost breakdown (raw material, people, energy, etc.)	Cost breakdown (raw material, salary, energy, etc.): Raw material 80% Labor 10%	Difficult to find a relevant benchmark for as there is no comparable site within the group.	Further energy consumption reduction project Digitalization approach to reduce costs	See proposed priority for Quality: higher right first-time rate will reduce

(*continued*)

Table 11.2 *(Continued)* An example output of a diagnostic as outlined in Chapter 3

Diagnosis	*Actual data required*	*Current situation Symptom and observed effect*	*Benchmark data (other sites, competition, customer requirements)*	*Running projects What are the main Annual Plan strategies attached to each performance objective and their expected impact? Strategy status (at risk?)*	*Proposed Priorities*
		Energy 5% Others 5% This cost structure reinforces the importance of achievement high raw material yield ratios	However, benchmark carried out by trade association demonstrates that the site is one of the best in Europe in terms of energy efficiency		raw material consumption
Morale	Cost breakdown (raw material, people, energy, etc.)	Employee morale Attrition rate is low but has slightly increased in the last two years. There has not been any employee survey done in the last four years, so there is no indication on morale level nor issues	Attrition rate is lower than national average and sector average		Relaunch employee survey Drill down attrition rates (rate by employment category, i.e., managers vs shop floor worker)
Environment	Various Environmental KPIs	Environmental compliance (air, noise, water, wastes) Water management: one incident last year and a number of "near misses" (unplanned discharge of process water into the river)	No benchmark	CO_2 reduction (see cost column)	Apply problem-solving and Daily Management to water management to eliminate risk of river pollution
		Wastes generated by the sites have been steadily decreasing over the last three years		Waste reduction	

Case Study 5: What If Toyota Ran Your House?

This is a fun look at some of the everyday, domestic issues that we may all face at one time or another. If you live alone or are part of a big family household, you will be confronted by what we may call "domestic failures." Defects in the expected outcomes of domestic processes come in many different forms, from lost socks to dirty dishes from the dishwasher. When you are in the business of operational excellence, you will soon start thinking about how you can apply what you've learned to the more effective and efficient running of the household. After all, there are striking similarities in running a house to running a business. Command and control bosses, a rebellious workforce, power struggles, lack of a clear vision, and budget constraints can all add up to a less than optimal performance. And so we should ask ourselves - what if Toyota ran the laundry process? Or ran the competence development program? You get the picture. Have fun thinking about how Toyota could improve your domestic processes but even more importantly if any of the relationships would survive if they did!

Hervé, How Would Toyota Approach a Messy Wardrobe Situation?

Once you have understood 5S at work, it is likely that you will want to apply it at home. Wardrobes can sometimes be a messy place. My wife and I used 5S to improve ours and deployed the same process with our then 4-year-old daughter.

First, we got rid of anything that did not belong to the area. This included clothing items that we knew we would never wear again and interesting items that did not belong to our wardrobes (such as tennis rackets!). I would like to share a tip here: put a sticker or sticky-note on each piece of clothing that you are undecided about. Remove the sticker when you decide to wear the item. At the end of the season, you can get rid of any item that still has a sticker on it.

In a second stage, we set everything in order. We introduced boxes as the standard location for socks, T-shirts, and polo shirts. Our daughter was too young to be able to read at that time, so she drew socks and other pieces of clothing on labels to identify which box corresponded to which item.

Step three, shine, was fortunately short as the wardrobes were in good condition. All we had to do was fix a door that was not sliding properly (which had encouraged us to overstock the other half of the wardrobe in the past). At that stage, our wardrobes looked great, and we saved a lot of time in the morning. But how long were they going to remain like that?

We did not apply the last two "S" to our bedroom, which ultimately led to the mess coming back. However, we managed to continue the process with our daughter. A simple inspection in the evening before going to bed ensured that we maintained the standards. And through discussions, our 4-year-old found solutions to further improve her wardrobe. The added benefit was that she was even able to take care of her clothes once they had been washed and ironed, which freed up some of our time and made her more responsible.

Fraser, How Would Toyota Ensure That the Dishwasher Cleaned All the Dishes?

Do you notice an unacceptable level of variability in the performance of the dishwasher? I know I should talk with data, so the first thing Toyota would do is categorize and quantify the defects. Where in the dishwasher, on what dishes or cutlery do we see the defects? What is the nature and size of the defect (usually food residue). When do we see a rise in defects? Ah, but be careful because we also need to look at what conditions were in place when excessive defects occurred. By the way, what is the "normal" defect level of the dishwasher? Does it ever reach 100% (spoiler alert – yes it does from a customer point of view). What are the conditions when we get the best performance (spoiler alert – it's when one of us in particular loads the dishwasher) and the worst performance (spoiler alert – it's when one of us in particular loads the dishwasher!).

We have many small group activities around this problem (read arguments) where we brainstorm potential causes (blame each other) and look at countermeasures (tell other people what to do). Okay, so Toyota would say we need to suggest potential causes such as the way we stack dishes, the gap between dishes, the amount of food that goes into the dishwasher (please don't feed the dishwasher, it does not eat baked beans), or if something is preventing the spinner from turning. Basically, we should prove the best way with data, create a standard operating manual, and then train everyone and do regular but random confirmation checks. We should monitor the defect rate and look at human performance issues (no blame) if we see a deterioration. Praise the operator for the right behavior, although sometimes many different operators work on a single load. If things don't improve, then use performance management and move the operator out of the business (okay, not an option unless they leave home). Sound familiar?

So For a Bit of a Challenge, Why Not Think About the Following

- How would Toyota ensure all socks end up in pairs?
- How would Toyota ensure oldest items in the fridge are used first?
- How would Toyota reward good performance?
- How would Toyota ensure fair distribution of the chores?
- How would Toyota ensure bedrooms are kept tidy?
- How would Toyota make sure the lights are switched off when not needed?
- How would Toyota keep shower time below 60 min?
- How would Toyota make the perfect cup of coffee?
- How would Toyota ensure little boys aim straight?
- How would Toyota get to the cause of the ever-diminishing teaspoon availability?

Appendices

- **Appendix 1:** Glossary/Jargon Buster
- **Appendix 2:** Common Key Performance Indicators
- **Appendix 3:** Tools Used in A3 and DMAIC Steps
- **Appendix 4:** Hierarchy of Root Cause Analysis Effect
- **Appendix 5:** Assessment of Control Mechanisms
- **Appendix 6:** Where to Start?: Key Questions I Need to Discuss with Leaders
- **Appendix 7:** Speaking Like a Broken Record: Our Main Aphorisms
- **Appendix 8:** The 7 Quality Tools

Appendix 1: Glossary/Jargon Buster

Acronym	*What It Is*	*Purpose*
A3	Short for A3 Thinking	A problem-solving methodology based on the scientific method and attributed to Toyota Motor Corporation
CAPA	Corrective and Preventative Action	The process that captures the non-conformance or repeat offending defect, ownership, Root Cause Analysis, conclusion, action, and reporting process
CoPQ	Cost of Poor Quality	A measure that takes account of the full cost of not-right-first-time outcomes. Includes the "hidden factory" of rework and discount sales

(*continued*)

Acronym	*What It Is*	*Purpose*
CP	Control Plan	Captures the process function, product, process, specification, evaluation, and control method
FMEA	Failure Mode Effects Analysis	Captures potential failure modes, their characteristic, and effect on output
KPI	Key Performance Indicator	The indicators that are key to objectives and vision of the business/ department that determine current performance
LeTCI	Levels, Trends, Comparators, Integration	A means of assessing the maturity of an organization in how it manages its measures of results
OFI	Opportunity for improvement	A gap, usually revealed by an assessment
OGSM	Objectives, Goals, Strategy, Measures	A Strategy Deployment Process
PFC	Process Flow Chart	Describes the process of focus, customer, function, sources of variation, input, and output characteristic
PMO	Project Management Office	A group of people in charge of defining and maintaining standards and centralizing reporting for a portfolio of project
R&O	Roles and Objectives	Capture responsibilities and objectives of each Dept or function
RCA	Root Cause Analysis	Identifying the root cause of a non-conformance
RPN	Risk Priority Number	Part of the FMEA ranking/prioritizing process, Severity of non-conformance, Likelihood of occurrence, and potential detection defect
SLA	Service Level Agreement	Identifies critical agreed output and performance indicators Vs actual performance
SOP	Standard Operating Procedure	The document that captures the task/ operation, elements of the work, the key points, purpose, and depiction of the criticalities of the task/job

(*continued*)

Acronym	*What It Is*	*Purpose*
SPC	Statistical Process Control	A visual and graphical process document/template that captures the critical process variation and control points/limits
SQDCME	Safety, Quality, Delivery, Cost, Morale, Environment	A common set of metrics (KPIs) used in many industries but most common in automotive settings
SVFD	Stakeholder Value Flow Diagnostic	A means of assessing an organization based on the SQDCEME metrics from a stakeholder perspective
SWP	Safe Working Procedure	A type of working procedure or standard operating procedure that includes a risk assessment and safety considerations
TPS	Toyota Production System	A system derived from the operating principles of the Toyota Motor Corporation
VSM	Value Stream Mapping	A method of mapping the physical value-adding activities and information flows that allow production to proceed from forecast, order entry, production, and supply chain
8D	The 8 Disciplines of problem-solving customer complaints	A team-based corrective and preventative action methodology promoted by Ford Motor Company and is widely used in industry for customer complaints resolution 1. Form team, 2. Describe problem, 3. Corrective action, 4. Root cause, 5. Verify corrective actions, 6. Permanent corrective actions, 7. Prevent recurrence, 8. Congratulate team

Appendix 2: Common Key Performance Indicators

Table 20 Examples common KPIs

Attribute	*KPIs*	*Comments*
Safety	Lost Time Injury Frequency (LTIF)	Number of accidents per million of hours worked
	All Known Injury Frequency (AKIF)	Number of accidents per million of hours worked
	Number of Process Safety incidents	
Quality	Complaints (incl. warrantee complaints)	Number of complaints as a % of total orders
	Right First Time (RFT)	% of parts/orders produced without a quality issue
	Non-prime	% of parts produced with a defect that can be sold in a downgraded category
	Retreatment	% of parts that had to be retreated before being sent to customer
	Scrap	% of parts that had to be scrapped
	Cost of Poor Quality (CoPQ)	Total cost of complaints, non-prime, treatments, and scrap
Delivery	Delivery performance/OTIF	% or orders delivered on time in full
	Days of stock	Quantity in stock divided by average consumption per day
Cost	Cost Pareto	
Morale	Attrition rate, employee survey results, vitality of suggestion scheme	% of employees leaving the business per year
Financials	EBIT, EBITDA %, Cash flow statement	Typical financial KPIs
Environment	Environmental compliance index, number of neighbors' complaints	

Appendix 3: Tools Used in A3 and DMAIC Steps

Table 21 Tools used in DMAIC and A3

Six Sigma tool name	*A3 Thinking step*	*Phases of DMAIC in which tool is most commonly used*				
		D	*M*	*A*	*I*	*C*
Affinity Diagram	1	X		X		
Brainstorming	4,5			X	X	
Business Case	1,2	X				
Cause-and-Effect Diagrams	4			X		
Charter	1	X				
Consensus	5				X	
Control Charts *For continuous data* Individuals (X-MR) X-Bar R Exponentially Waited Moving Average *For discrete data* p, np c, u	4,7		X	X	X	X
CtQ (Critical to Quality) tree	2	X				
Data Collection Forms Check Sheet Frequency Plot Check Sheet Confirmation Check Sheet Concentration Diagram	4		X	X	X	X
Data Collection Plan	4		X	X	X	X
Design of Experiments Full Factorial Reduced Factorial	4			X	X	
Flow Diagrams (Process Maps)	2,4	X	X	X	X	X
Frequency Plots (Histograms)	4		X	X	X	X
FMEA (Failure Mode and Effect Analysis)	4,5		X		X	
Gauge R & R (Measurement System Analysis)	4		X			

(*continued*)

Table 21 ***(Continued)*** **Tools used in DMAIC and A3**

Six Sigma tool name	*A3 Thinking step*	*Phases of DMAIC in which tool is most commonly used*				
		D	*M*	*A*	*I*	*C*
Hypothesis tests t-test Paired t-test ANOVA CH Square	7		X			
Kano Model	2		X			
Planning Tools – Gantt Chart	6	X			X	
Pareto Charts	2,4		X	X	X	
Prioritization Matrix	4,5		X		X	
Process Capability	2		X		X	
Process Sigma	2		X		X	
Regression	4			X		
Rolled Throughput Yield	2	X				
Sampling	4		X	X	X	X
Scatter Plots	4			X		
SIPOC (Supplier, Input, Process, Output, Customer)	2	X				
Stakeholder Analysis	2	X				
Standardization	5					X
Stratification	4		X	X	X	X
Stratified Frequency Plots	4			X		
Time Series Plots (Run Charts)	4		X			
VoC (Voice of the Customer)	2	X				
Other tools						
Value Stream Mapping	2	X		X		
Constraints Mapping (Theory of Constraints)	2	X		X		
Kepner-Tregoe© Situation Appraisal	2	X				

(continued)

Table 21 *(Continued)* Tools used in DMAIC and A3

Six Sigma tool name	*A3 Thinking step*	*Phases of DMAIC in which tool is most commonly used*				
		D	*M*	*A*	*I*	*C*
Kepner-Tregoe© Problem Analysis	4			X		
Statistical Process Control	4,7		X			X
Control Plans	7					X
Standardized Work	5					X
OEE (Overall Equipment Effectiveness)	2		X			
5S Workplace Organization	5					X
Visual Management	7					X
Process Activity Mapping	4			X		
Kepner-Tregoe© Incident Mapping	2			X		
Error Proofing	5					X
Line Balancing (TAKT)	4			X		
Service Blueprinting	2,4	X		X		
Maintenance Task Identification (MTI)	5				X	
Failure Analysis (CAMF)	4			X		
Why Tree Analysis and 5 Whys	4		X	X		
4 Fields Mapping	4			X		
Single Minute Exchange of Dies (SMED)	5				X	
7 Wastes Analysis	4			X		
RACI (Responsible, Accountable, Consulted, Informed)	5					X

Appendix 4: Hierarchy of Root Cause Analysis Effectiveness

Whenever a root cause analysis is conducted, we should ask about how confident we are that the root cause is indeed the reason why we see the effect described as the event that starts the analysis. Offhand and cursory analysis is a curse in most industries. Depending on the consequences of basing decisions on the root cause, we should consider the following tables and score both the root cause effectiveness and the countermeasure effectiveness. Feed these back into the FMEA scoring under the detection and prevention columns.

Table 22 Effectiveness scores for root cause analysis

	RCA effectiveness	*Score*
1	The cause of an event is established by means of a physical investigation and the exact failure mechanism (and its location) of failure is known and fully reproducible under all normal operating conditions. A suitable level of cause and effect has been reached to enable actionable countermeasures to be taken.	100
2	The cause of an event is established by means of a physical investigation and the mechanism (and its location) of failure is known through scientific principles. A suitable level of cause and effect has been reached to enable actionable countermeasures to be taken.	90
3	The cause of an event is established by means of an experiment (one factor or DOE) with a 95% confidence level. A suitable level of cause and effect has been reached to enable actionable countermeasures to be taken.	80
4	The cause of an event is established through logic (such as IS, IS-NOT) but cannot be verified physically or by experimentation. A suitable level of cause and effect has been reached to enable actionable countermeasures to be taken.	60
5	The cause of an event is established through the application of principles and process knowledge but is not verified by experimentation or observation.	40
6	The cause of an event is established through experience and local knowledge.	20

Appendix 5: Assessment of Control Mechanisms

Table 23 Assessment scores for countermeasures

Description of Problem from Event Map (*Subject + Deviation*).			
Description of Root Cause from Event Map (*Subject, Deviation + Mechanism*).			
Description of Countermeasure from Event Map (*Subject + Verb*).			
ID	**Description**	**Points**	**CM Score**
A	**Failsafe, Modification** (score 76–100) choose one of A1–A2		
A1	Modification to product or process eliminates the possibility of this deviation/defect mechanism.	100	
A2	A failsafe device (100% effective) is applied to prevent deviation and failsafe testing is a routine task (in SAP).	95	
B	**Automation, Redesign** (score 60–85) choose one of B1–B4		
B1	System (IT, Process Control modification) changes to eliminate deviations and changes logged.	85	
B2	Automated solution is applied to detect and divert 100% of deviations and alert operators.	75	
B3	Automated solution is applied to reduce human error in creating deviation.	65	
B4	Deviations are detected via inspection systems and release criterion is specified.	60	
C	**SPC, Trending** (score 30–50) choose one of C1–C5		
C1	OCAP is highly visual and/or rule breaches are automated and alerting to relevant people.	50	
C2	OCAP is based on sound statistical rules and actions have been verified through experimentation.	45	
C3	OCAP is based on sound statistical rules, and actions have been verified through data analysis.	40	

(*continued*)

Table 23 *(Continued)* Assessment scores for countermeasures

C4	Trend monitoring of relevant KPI in daily work meetings.	35	
C5	Red/Amber/Green status of relevant measure is reviewed in daily work meetings.	30	
D	**Standard Work** (score 1–25) choose D1–D8		
D1	Standard Work includes manual reconciliation of actions and/or products and parts to detect deviations.	25	
D2	Visual factory principles have been applied to Standard Work to reduce the chance of error or mistakes.	20	
D3	Frequency of confirmation is temporarily increased to cover all shifts quickly.	15	
D4	Relevant Standard Work is built into confirmation cycle.	12	
D5	New standard built into competence assessments.	9	
D6	New or modified standard explicitly defining purpose and actions to be taken.	6	
D7	Training or retraining by unit trainer/team leader on existing standards.	3	
D8	Informal discussion with relevant people on existing standards.	1	
NOTE: **Core Tool Review (FMEA and Control Plan)** is a prerequisite for attaining the score.			
What is required to get to the next level of control? What is stopping us getting to the next level of control?			

Appendix 6: Where to Start?: Key Questions I Need to Discuss with Leaders

The very first question must always be what is the problem I want to solve? Be completely honest with yourself. Is the problem clear enough, or do you need to start with a complete diagnostic? You will remember from Chapter 3 that this includes having quantified issues.

If the problem is clear enough, you can start discussing with leaders the key questions arising from Knoster's change model.

Important note: you will need to think first about your own answers before you engage leaders. But leaders need to discuss these questions, otherwise you will not get the right level of commitment from them. And this discussion with them will give you a good feel for how much additional work you will need to get them on your side.

- **Vision:**
  - What is the compelling vision for this transformation?
- **Skills and resources:**
  - Do we need a PMO or not?
  - Do we have enough internal resource (quantity and quality) or do we need to bring in more people (and if so with which skills)?
  - What training program do we need? Who is going to create it? Who is going to deliver it?
  - Beyond the training program, how are we going to be multipliers? I.e., how are we going to make people autonomous over time from a problem-solving point of view?
  - Do we already have problem-solving and DM standards? I.e., which tool does the organization use and are they enough? Or do we need to create templates and train on A3, DMAIC, FMEA, Control Plans, and so on?
- **Motivation:**
  - Who are the likely initial adopters and the likely blockers?
  - What is in it for our people?
  - Carrot and stick: How will we reward/recognize early adopters and put pressure on laggards? Do we need to modify the way we measure daily, monthly, and annual performance?
  - What role do we expect leaders to play in creating motivation?
  - Even if the problem is clear to us, should we carry out a formal diagnostic involving members of the organization to engage them?

- **Action Plan:**
  - Communication priorities: Who do we need to keep informed, involved, consulted, empowered? See stakeholder matrix in Chapter 9.
  - What is the minimum I want to deploy everywhere?
  - What would be the best pilot areas to start deployment? Pick an area where the local manager is interested in our approach and supportive.

Appendix 7: Speaking Like a Broken Record: Our Main Aphorisms

Members of the improvement community use many adages that are nuggets of wisdom. Living by these simple ground rules will help you avoid very common mistakes. Here are some of our most useful aphorisms. Keep on repeating them and demonstrating them until people around you use them as well.

Speak with data: without data you are just someone with an opinion
In God we trust – everyone else brings data.

If you cannot prove what you are saying, you might be wrong. Make sure that you are always on solid ground. Everything is only a hypothesis until it is proved by data.

Anyone must be able to understand it

If my mother, my friends, the person on the bus, etc., can understand your standard or your presentation, it is probably good enough. Simplicity is difficult to achieve but is a key condition for engaging and sustaining.

The way people behave reflects what you tolerate, not what you want them to do

Readers with children will recognize this one. Although engagement is paramount in improvement, standards must be enforced.

Do not create new rules if you can use existing ones

A lot of problems do not come from the absence of a standard but from poor deployment of standards. Do not copy politicians who adopt a "one event – one new law" approach rather than enforcing existing mechanisms.

Only the doer learns

Reading a book about how to fly a plane will not make me a good pilot.

Improving the work is the work

A successful day of firefighting might make you feel great. Unfortunately, it only means you have not achieved much, as the same problem will come back. We are all paid to improve what we do. Otherwise, we might as well be replaced by automatons.

Analysis is not improvement

Don't get stuck in "analysis paralysis." At some point, you need to take action. We need to make improvements in the real world, not on paper or the PC.

And we leave you with one of the most powerful questions you can ask: *"What is the problem we are trying to solve here?"*

Appendix 8: The 7 Quality Tools

The 7 Quality Tools are an accepted set of basic tools that can be applied with very little training to help diagnose and investigate quality issues. They can be used as part of the A3 Thinking, 8D, or DMAIC methodologies. Many of these are shown in Appendix 3 in relation to where they are used as part of the A3 and DMAIC methodologies.

These tools are particularly applicable when conducting shop floor improvement activities as most can be readily constructed with flip chart and pens and they make good visual displays for the communication of the problem-solving process. Again, we encourage you to familiarize yourselves with these 7 Quality Tools:

1. Check Sheets (Data Collection)
2. Pareto Diagram

3. Cause and Effect Diagram
4. Graphs and Charts (specifically Control Chart)
5. Stratification
6. Histogram
7. Scatter Diagram

References

Ando, Y., & Kumar, P. (2011). Daily Management the TQM Way. Madras: Productivity & Quality Publishing Pvt. Ltd.
Bicheno, J., & Holweg, M. (2023). The NewLean Toolbox. Sixth Edition. PicsieBooks: Buckingham, England.
Bhote, K. R. (1991). World Class Quality. New York: Amacom.
Collins, J. (2001). Good to Great. London: Random House.
Daniels, A. C. (2001). Other People's Habits. New York: McGraw-Hill.
Deming, W. E. (1982). Out of the Crisis. Cambridge MA: Massachusetts Institute of Technology.
Devine, F. (2010). Accelerated Improvement. Retrieved from http://www.acceleratedimprovement.co.uk
Duran, J. M. (2017). Juran's Quality Handbook: The complete guide tp performance excellence. New York: McGraw Hill.
Goldratt, E. M. (1984). The Goal. New York: Routledge.
Goldratt, E. M. (1997). Critical Chain. New York: Routledge.
Harari, Y. N. (2017). Homo Deus. New York: Harper Collins.
Jones, D. T., Womack, J. P., & Roos, D. (1990). The Machine that Changed the World. London: Simon & Schuster.
Kahnamen, D. (2012). Thinking Fast and Slow. London: Penguin.
Kepner, C. D., & Tregoe, B. D. (1981). The New Rational manager. Princeton Research Press.
Kohn, A. (1993). Punished by Rewards. New York: Harcourt Publishing Company.
Kuper, S., & Szymanski, S. (2009). Soccernomics. New York: Nation Books.
Leake, C., & Kendall, A. (2005). The Z to A of Coaching. London: Cognitive Leadership Ltd.
Lewin, K. (1951). Field Theory in Social Science'. New York: Harper and Row.
Liker, J. K., & Meier, D. (2006). The Toyota Way Fieldbook. New York: McGraw-Hill.
Nomura, S. (2021). The Toyota Way of Dantosu Radical Quality Improvement. Abingdon: Routledge.
Rother, M. (2010). Toyota Kata. New York: McGraw-Hill.
Rother, M., & Shook, J. (1999). Learning to See: Value Stream Mapping to Add Value and Eliminate Muda. Brookline MA: The Lean Enterprise Institute, Inc.

Scholtes, P. R. (1998). The Leader's Handbook. New York: McGraw-Hill.
Seddon, J. (2005). Freedom from Command and Control. New York: Productivity Press.
Shook, J. (2008). Managing to Learn. Cambridge, MA: Lean Enterprise Institute, Inc.
Taguchi, G. (1993). Taguchi Methods: Design of Experiments. Michigan: American Supplier Institute.
Taleb, N. N. (2013). Antifragile. London: Penguin.
Ulrich, D., Kerr, S., & Ashkenas, R. (2002). The GE Work-Out. New York: McGraw-Hill.
Wilkinson, F. (2016). Front Line Problem Solving. Llantwit Major: Shine the Light Publishing.
Womack, J. P., & Jones, D. T. (1996). Lean Thinking. London: Simon & Schuster.

Index

Printed in the United States
by Baker & Taylor Publisher Services